Aris and Phillips Classical Texts

MIMNERMUS

Elegies

Edited with an Introduction,
Translation and Commentary by

Dimitrios Kanellakis

LIVERPOOL UNIVERSITY PRESS

First published 2023 by
Liverpool University Press
4 Cambridge Street
Liverpool
L69 7ZU

www.liverpooluniversitypress.co.uk

This paperback edition published 2024

British Library Cataloguing-in-Publication data
A British Library CIP record is available

ISBN 978-183764-2-601 (hardback)
ISBN 978-1-83553-765-7 (paperback)
eISBN 978-183764-2-748

Typeset by Tara Montane

Cover image: *Melancholy* by Edvard Munch (1894–1896), oil on canvas, Bergen Kunstmuseum. Public Domain.

CONTENTS

How blissful is the vanity
of youth, which lacking sanity
ignores its flowers' rarity.

Old age comes, anxiety.
Unhandsome and unmighty,
a shame to the society,
who'll treat you with impiety.

So may I die – at ninety!

PREFACE

This year I will celebrate my thirtieth birthday. Realistically speaking, I am not old, but cannot claim to be young either. Medical check-ups are becoming increasingly frequent, my hair is waving … goodbye, and I am no longer eligible for the Louvre's free admission: οἴμοι! My initial sympathy for Mimnermus, whom I first read at high school, has now turned to empathy. Only that now I can distinguish the lyrical persona from the poet and tell how tricky the dynamics between the two can be.

What I learned: don't judge a book by its cover. And so I chose Munch's *Melancholy* as cover illustration, not to predispose readers towards *my* take on Mimnermus, but rather to bring them *vis-à-vis* with the long-established view on the poet, or else, with the horizon of hermeneutical expectations which I aspire to exceed. Unlike many commentaries which either implicitly or explicitly claim to be objective, mine is programmatically oriented towards this specific purpose: to introduce a new Mimnermus, whose melancholy is only a generic (i.e. pertinent to elegy) pretext. Behind that poetic façade lurks a very playful poet, not just verbally and metrically spirited, but also ironical and risqué on occasions, and experimenting with advanced narrative techniques. This commentary is, therefore, a literary one: figurative language, alternative meanings, authorial markers, implied audience, performative clues, program of composition, narrative structure, intertextuality, and reception are my main focus, while issues of textual criticism and metre are discussed only insofar as they affect interpretation. Thus I deemed it unnecessary to include a critical apparatus, for which a specialist should now use Andrea Emiliani's copious thesis at the University of Messina, 2021. Some grammatical points are clarified to aid advanced students, but also because our elegist pursues syntactical ambiguity on several occasions. The commentary is supplemented by analyses of Archaic artefacts that are relevant to Mimnermus' repertoire. The purpose is not to decorate the book, but to compare the poet's imagery – and thus gauge his originality – with contemporary pictorial representations of the themes he worked on; for artefacts constitute as rich and valid a testimony on poetic/metaphorical language as parallel texts.

Recent discoveries of lyric fragments have excited both classical scholars and the general public. Our generation has been lucky enough to welcome the 'new Simonides' (1992), 'new Archilochus' (2005), 'new' (2004) and 'the newest Sappho' (2014), and these poets have gained immense popularity which has been 'cashed out' in new translations, conferences, edited volumes, commentaries, and so on. But Mimnermus has not been as lucky. Not updated by any recent papyrological discoveries, his corpus remains slim; only one monograph published in our century reserves some space for him in its subtitle (Slings 2000), while the last full-scale scholarly commentary on his poems is now thirty years old (Allen 1993). Emiliani's above-mentioned thesis marks the much-awaited renewal of interest in "the most accomplished and the most musical" of the early elegists (Bowra 1938: 34). His commentary, which covers eight fragments, is particularly detailed and strong on technical aspects and with exhaustive bibliography – hence immensely helpful for my own work – but rather thin on the hermeneutical side, as of course is the author's right. The same applies to a lesser degree to Archibald Allen's *Fragments of Mimnermus*, Stuttgart 1993, which has been my first port of call for various problems. It should therefore go without saying that my commentary does not aim to 'replace' either of them, but to become their collocutor. My sole aim is to bring this unjustly under-studied elegist back to the forefront of research, and to advocate that, however exciting a papyrological discovery may be, one does not need new fragments to rediscover a classical author, insofar as, to quote Italo Calvino, *every rereading of a classic is as much a voyage of discovery as the first reading.*

ACKNOWLEDGEMENTS

My primary debt is to Ewen Bowie and Andrea Emiliani, who generously offered their time and expertise; their detailed and constructive comments saved me from several careless errors. A special thanks to Alan Sommerstein, not only for reviewing my draft and approving publication under Aris & Phillips, but also because his own commentaries on Aristophanes (which inaugurated the series) were my first exposure to British classical scholarship – an influential exposure indeed. Geoffrey Horrocks, Armand D'Angour, Fiona Macintosh, Ioannis Konstantakos, Dimitris Papanikolaou and Fabio Grasso helped me with points of detail. Clare Litt and Tara Montane of Liverpool University Press dealt with my manuscript with exemplary care, for which I am grateful. An Early Career Fellowship for 2022–2023 at the Centre for Hellenic Studies, Harvard University, enabled the timely completion of the book and afforded me a memorable trip to Washington, DC.

March 2023

ABBREVIATIONS AND CITATIONS

In citing lyric fragments, I follow the numbering of West 1989–1992 for elegy and iambus (= W), Lobel and Page 1963 for Sappho and Alcaeus (= L-P), Page 1962 for the other melic poets (= *PMG*), Snell and Maehler 1987–1989 for Pindar, and Maehler 2003 for Bacchylides, unless otherwise specified on occasion. On my text and translation of Mimnermus, see further note on p. 53. Names of ancient authors and their works are abbreviated according to the *Oxford Classical Dictionary*[4] and journals according to *L'Année Philologique*. Other abbreviations to be found in this book are:

BAtlas	Talbert, R. J. A. (ed.) (2000) *Barrington Atlas of the Greek and Roman World*, Princeton.
CGL	Diggle, J. (ed.) (2021) *The Cambridge Greek Lexicon*, 2 vols, Cambridge.
CIG	Boeckh, A. (ed.) (1828–1877) *Corpus Inscriptionum Graecarum*, 4 vols, Berlin.
EDG	Beekes, R. (2010) *Etymological Dictionary of Greek*, Leiden.
FGrH	Jacoby, F. (ed.) (1923–1958) *Die Fragmente der Griechischen Historiker*, 15 vols in 3 parts, Berlin/Leiden.
GEF	West, M. L. (2003) *Greek Epic Fragments (Loeb Classical Library)*, Cambridge, MA.
G-P	Gentili, B. and Prato, C. (1988)[2] *Poetarum elegiacorum testimonia et fragmenta*, Leipzig.
K-A	Kassel, R. and Austin, C. F. L. (eds) (1983–2001) *Poetae Comici Graeci*, 8 vols, Berlin/New York.
LSJ	Liddell, H. G., Scott, R. and Jones, H. S. (eds) (1996)[9] *A Greek–English Lexicon* (with rev. Suppl.), Oxford.
LW	Gusmani, R. (1964) *Lydisches Wörterbuch*, Heidelberg.
M-W	Merkelbach, R. and West, M. L. (1967) *Fragmenta Hesiodea*, Oxford.
TrGF	Snell, B., Kannicht, R. and Radt, S. (eds) (1971–2004) *Tragicorum Graecorum Fragmenta*, 6 vols, Göttingen.

CHRONOLOGY AND MAP

c. 1100 BC	Pylian settlers found Colophon.
c. 1000 BC	Aeolian settlers found Smyrna.
c. 800–688 BC	Civic strife in Colophon: Colophonians of Pylian origin are ousted and settle in Smyrna. By 688 the city is considered Ionian (cf. Paus. 5.8.9).
c. 680 BC	Gyges usurps the Lydian throne (Sardis) from Candaules. Archilochus is born.
c. 670 BC	Mimnermus is born. By now Gyges has started his attacks on Miletus, Smyrna and Colophon, but only captures the latter.[1]
652 or 644 BC	The Cimmerians attack Lydia and Gyges is killed.[2]
6 April 648 BC	Total solar eclipse (probably the one of fr. 20).[3]
c. 638 BC	Solon is born.[4]
632–629 BC	Mimnermus 'flourished' in the 37th Olympiad.[5]
c. 600 BC	Alyattes, Gyges' great-grandson, besieges Smyrna. Mimnermus is probably dead by now.

1 It has passed to reference books (e.g. Gerber 1997: 108; Allen 2019: 121; Bartol 2022: 227) that Gyges attacked Smyrna (battle of the Hermus) *in* the 660s. But Herodotus (1.14.4) tells us that Gyges attacked those Ionian cities immediately upon usurping the throne, i.e. in the 680s or 670s (thus Gerber 1970: 114). West 1974: 73 argues that those assaults can be put in the 660s *at the latest*. If we trust Herodotus' order of mentioning – first Miletus, second Smyrna, third Colophon – then the Hermus battle is better datable to the 670s.

2 On the alternative dates, see Spalinger 1978.

3 Likewise visible from Paros or Thasos, the same eclipse was also thematised by Archilochus in fr. 122 (cf. Swift 2019: 308–309). The next total eclipse, 28 May 585 BC, is probably too late for Mimnermus (West 1974: 73).

4 That makes Mimnermus ≈30 years older than Solon (or ≈10 years younger, for those who accept a late birthdate in *c*. 630 BC, e.g. Sanz Morales 2000).

5 The Greek verb (γέγονε) in the *Suda* sometimes denotes a person's birth, but more often the date he *floruit*, i.e. a date at which he was known to have been alive (Campbell 1982: xi, 5 n.2).

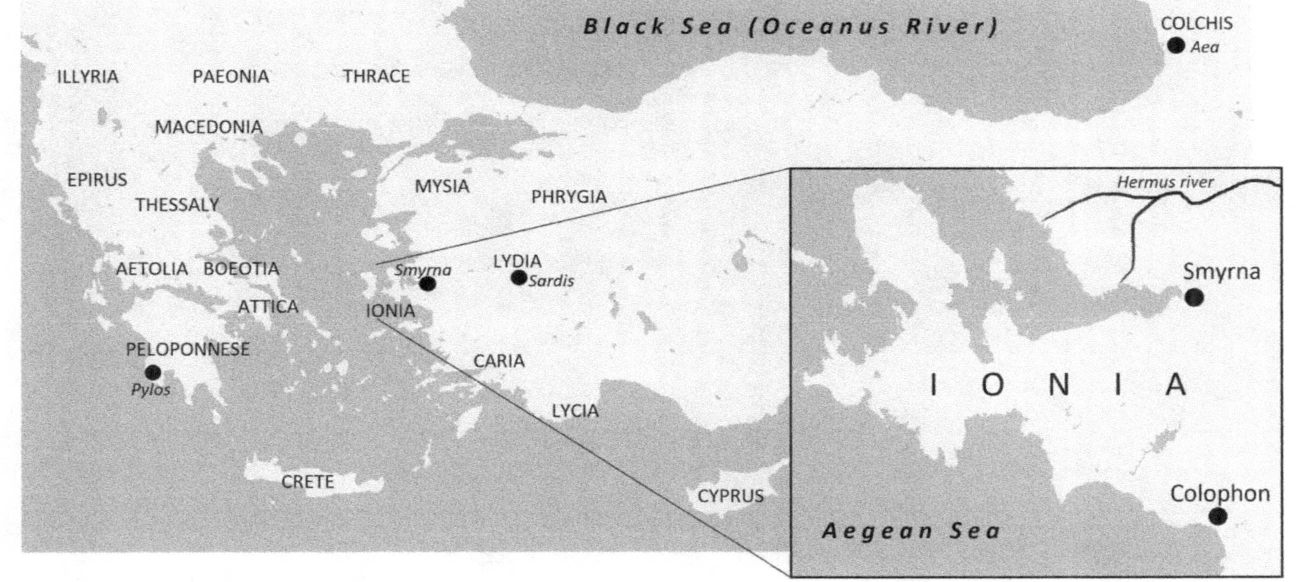
Black Sea (Oceanus River)
COLCHIS
Aea
ILLYRIA
PAEONIA
THRACE
MACEDONIA
EPIRUS
THESSALY
MYSIA
PHRYGIA
AETOLIA
BOEOTIA
Smyrna
LYDIA
Sardis
ATTICA
IONIA
PELOPONNESE
Pylos
CARIA
LYCIA
CRETE
CYPRUS
Hermus river
Smyrna
I O N I A
Colophon
Aegean Sea

INTRODUCTION*

What? – Elegy

Mimnermus composed elegy. In fact, the Hellenistic elegist Hermesianax from Colophon called him **the inventor** of the genre: Μίμνερμος δὲ, τὸν ἡδὺν ὃς εὕρετο πολλὸν ἀνατλὰς | ἦχον καὶ μαλακοῦ πνεῦμα τὸ πενταμέτρου ("And Mimnermus after much suffering discovered the sweet sound and breath given off by the soft pentameter"; fr. 7.35–6 Powell). But this is clearly Hermesianax trying to promote his old 'compatriot' to boost his own reputation, rather than making a researched claim, insofar as he totally ignores the other candidates mentioned by the Alexandrian scholar Didymus: εὑρετὴν δὲ τοῦ ἐλεγείου οἱ μὲν τὸν Ἀρχίλοχον, οἱ δὲ Μίμνερμον, οἱ δὲ Καλλῖνον παλαιότερον ("Some say Archilochus is the inventor of elegy, others say Mimnermus, and others say Callinus was earlier"; p. 387 Schmidt). Mimnermus' fr. 14 (*Nothing like that man's power...*), with its unusually and rather awkwardly dense use of epicisms, possibly mirrors the earliest (oral) stage of elegy: a new metric conception which was still too attached to the epic, thematically and verbally. But this is far from admitting Mimnermus as the genre's inventor – a title which, after all, did not necessarily belong to a single poet. Moreover, in the **prehistory of the genre** stand four auletes, Olympus of Phrygia, Clonas of Tegea, Sacadas of Argos, and Polymnestus of Colophon (who moved to Sparta), whose contribution to elegy as poetry is unknown. For example, how are we to understand the testimony that Sacadas was ποιητὴς μελῶν τε καὶ ἐλεγείων μεμελοποιημένων (Ps-Plut. *de mus*. 8.1134a)? What was his actual achievement: that he composed *elegies* set to music, or that he composed *music* for elegies? Searching for 'the inventor' is, therefore, futile. What matters is that Mimnermus anyway composed during the early years of the new genre and still managed to distinguish himself among the school of *aulos* music inaugurated by Olympus; see Nobili 2011: 30 and *passim*.

---

* Phrases set in **bold** are aimed at helping the reader navigate fast.

Elegy is sometimes classified under Greek **lyric poetry** (thus e.g. Campbell 1967, Gerber 1997, Swift 2022) and sometimes treated separately, but together with iambus (thus e.g. West 1974, Swift and Carrey 2016, Allan 2019). As a generic term, 'lyric' first appeared as late as in the 2nd century BC to describe the older poetry – from the 7th to the 5th century BC – which was composed for performance accompanied by the lyre (cf. *SIG* 660, ἐπιδείξεις ἐποήσαντο τῷ θεῷ διὰ τῶν λυρικῶν συστημάτων, "they gave many performances to the god with lyrical compositions"). Neither elegy nor iambus fitted that designation and so the Hellenistic scholars drew separate canons; see pp. 42–43 for the elegiac canon; Hadjimichael 2019 for the lyric and Rotstein 2010: 27–34 for the iambic ones. It is as recent as the late 18th/early 19th century that the term 'lyric' was expanded, with Goethe 1819 establishing three 'natural' forms of poetry: epic, lyric, and drama. These correspond to three representational modes, classified on a scale of objectivity subjectivity (Schlegel 1797), with lyric obviously being on the subjective end, expressing "a heart inwardly concentrated in depth of feeling" (Hegel 1835). In practice, lyric came to encompass anything that could not fit under epic or drama, in a taxonomy that is essentially a misreading and conflation of Plato and Aristotle; cf. Genette 1992: 38. With triadic canons having a long philological tradition, it is no wonder why Goethe's division survives to date (and why I follow it, e.g. in speaking of Mimnermus' *lyrical* subjects in my commentary).

But what is elegy? Starting from the term itself, three variants existed to name the genre: ὁ ἔλεγος, τὸ ἐλεγεῖον, and ἡ ἐλεγεία. The former appears for the first time in an inscription of 586 BC (ἀείδων μέλεα καὶ ἐλέγους, "singing songs and elegies"; Paus.10.7.6), while the latter two emerged in the Classical period (ἐλεγεῖον in Critias fr. 4.3 W and ἐλεγεία in Arist. [*Ath. Pol.*] 5). The possible **etymologies** put forward by the *Etymologicum Magnum* (326.48) are from ἒ ἔ λέγειν ('to cry woe, woe'), ἐλεεῖν ('to pity'), and εὖ λέγειν ('to eulogise'). At least the former two imply that elegy began as a mournful poem, and indeed elegiac couplets became the standard verse for epitaphs; cf. Simonides' most famous ὦ ξεῖν', ἀγγέλλειν Λακεδαιμονίοις ὅτι τῇδε | κείμεθα, τοῖς κείνων ῥήμασι πειθόμενοι ("Stranger, report to the Spartans that we lie here, obedient to their words"). It has even been proposed that elegy developed from a choral lament song (*thrênos*), after an intermediate genre of 'threnodic elegy'; the latter would be a monodic lead song (sung by a man) followed by a choral song (sung by a male or female chorus), which in time lost its choral element, under the influence of male-monodic performance at symposia; cf. Nagy 2010: 30–35. From the recorded elegies, however, we know that the thematic scope of the genre is much wider; "almost any topic apart from the scurrilous or obscene was deemed a suitable subject" (Gerber 1997: 91), and even *that* is relative.

The **main themes** of archaic elegy are indeed decent – war, love, life and death, politics, social relations, historical and mythological narrative and, of course, the symposium – but we do find on occasions some quite obvious *double entendres* (e.g. Archil. fr. 331 συκῆ πετραίη, a metaphor for 'old cunt') and, as I shall show, Mimnermus does not lag behind such games. Yet very few pieces are lamentatory (e.g. Simon. fr. 91, "Whenever I see the tomb of dead Megacles, I pity you, poor Callias, for your loss"). Therefore, we must assume that the close association of elegy to lament – hence the above-mentioned etymologies – is only a later invention owed to the popularity of epitaphs written in elegiac verse, and also to Euripides, who repeatedly used ἔλεγος for mournful songs in particular (e.g. *Tro*. 119, *Hel*. 185, *IT* 146; cf. Bowie 1986: 22–25). As a matter of fact, the archaic elegists themselves did not use ἔλεγος/ἐλεγεῖον/ἐλεγεία to name their own poems; in the few self-referential occasions, we find the word ἔπη (e.g. Thgn. 22, Solon fr. 1.2), which either means 'statements' in general, or points to the metrical affinity of elegy to epic. The **main functions** of elegy, which any theme may serve, are exhortation (e.g. Mimn. frr. 7, 8), celebration (frr. 9, 14), reflection (frr. 1, 2), and personal comment (fr. 6), and are by no means mutually exclusive; see West 1974: 14–18. [A partially overlapping but narrower taxonomy of functions is proposed by Aloni 2009: 182–85.] For example, fr. 8 is a personal plea leading to a general axiom. In terms of length, elegies varied from a single couplet to seven hundred lines (Panyassis test. 1 *GEF*).

Metre is, therefore, the sole defining element of (what was retrospectively labelled as) elegy: all poems composed in elegiac couplets belong to this genre. In any given elegy, the odd verses (1, 3, 5, 7…) are dactylic hexameters, i.e. the metre of the epic, while all even verses (2, 4, 6, 8…) are conventionally called dactylic pentameters and are typographically indented. It follows naturally that if a fragment begins with a pentameter (e.g. Mimn. fr. 15) or ends with a hexameter (fr. 11a), we must assume that one verse has been lost from the top or from the bottom, respectively. Some preliminary remarks on **Greek prosody** are necessary, before looking at hexameters and pentameters in more detail. Unlike English, or indeed Modern Greek, Ancient Greek had a quantitative (rather than dynamic) pronunciation. That means that the duration of pronouncing each syllable varied, according to its *quantity*. A syllable in Ancient Greek is:

1. *short*, if it contains the short vowels *ε* or *ο*, or any of the variable vowels *α*, *ι*, or *υ* when used as short (for example *ι* in the 3rd declension). A short syllable is marked with a *breve* on top ˘ and pronounced in half a beat. E.g. γε̆-νŏς is pronounced as */gé-nos/* (♪-♪).
2. *long*, if it contains the long vowels *η* or *ω*, or any of the variable vowels *α*, *ι*, or *υ* when used as long (for example *-ας* in the 1st declension), or any diphthong (*αι*, *ει*, *οι*, *υι*, *αυ*, *ευ*, *ηυ*, *ου*) except for final *-αι* and *-οι*. A long syllable is marked with a *macron* on top ¯ and pronounced in one beat. E.g. εῠ̄-νῆ̄ is pronounced as */eu-neé/* (♩-♩).
   - *Exception*: if a long vowel or diphthong at the end of a word is followed, at the beginning of the next word, by a vowel, then the former syllable usually becomes short (e.g. κᾰὶ εὐνή). This kind of shortening is called *epic shortening* and is not obligatory.
3. *long by position*, if it contains a short vowel *but* that vowel is followed, either in the same word or at the beginning of the next word, by a double consonant (*ζ*, *ξ*, *ψ*) or by two or more consonants (e.g. ε̄̓χθρός, θε̄ρμός). We treat such syllables the same as proper long syllables.

- *Exception*: if the two consonants following the short vowel are a mute consonant ($\pi, \beta, \varphi, \tau, \delta, \theta, \kappa, \gamma, \chi$) followed by a liquid or nasal consonant (λ, ρ, μ, ν) – and strictly in that order – then the syllable may remain short (e.g. τε̆θνάναι). This phenomenon, rare in Ionic verse, is called *Attic shortening*.

The occurrence of two vowels next to each other in two neighbouring syllables, with no consonant in between, is called *hiatus*. The Greeks tried to avoid hiatus by pronouncing the two vowels as one, in what is called *synizesis*. This usually happens in types liable to contraction (e.g. ἄνθεα=ἄνθη, ἐμέο=ἐμοῦ) and syllables with ε (e.g. θεῶν).

Back to the elegiac couplets. The **dactylic hexameter**, the metre in which the odd verses are composed, means 'a sequence of six dactyls' and a dactyl, in turn, means 'a finger'. Because the anatomy of a human finger, from palm to fingertip, is a long bone followed by two shorter ones, the dactyl describes three syllables with a metric value of – ᴗ ᴗ (or ♩ ♪ ♪), either covering a single word (e.g. ᾱ̆ν-θε̆-σῐν) or spreading over neighbouring words (e.g. οῡ̓-δε̆ τῐ́ς). Given that two short beats (or 'bones', to continue the anatomical metaphor) equal one long, a dactyl may be replaced by a spondee, whose metric value is – – (or ♩ ♩). Thus, for example, the words βε̄́λ-τῐ-ο̆ν (a dactyl) and ἡ̄-μεῖ̄ς (a spondee) are of the same total duration, but of different rhythmical pattern. Poets prefer to mix the two patterns to create variety, even though there exist some dactyls-only or spondees-only hexameters. The sixth/final unit of a hexameter is – ×, rather than a proper dactyl; the symbol × denotes a syllable of variable quantity (*anceps*), but in analysing a given line we have to specify whether that position is taken by a short or a long syllable. So the general pattern for a hexameter line (with commas separating the 'fingers', or, to use the technical term, the *metrical feet*) is: – ⏔,– ⏔,– ⏔,– ⏔,– ⏔, – ×

The poets used to take a short breath, we believe, at one or two points within each hexameter – not in the middle of a word, of course. If that pause falls *within* a dactyl or a spondee, 'breaking the bone' as it were, then it is called a *caesura* (marked with |), whereas when it falls *between* two adjacent dactyls/spondees, it is called a *diaeresis* (marked with ‖). The possible positions for those pauses are:

- Trihemimeral caesura: – ⏕,–|⏕,– ⏕,– ⏕,– ⏕, – ×
  e.g. Mimn. fr. 2.3 τοῖς ἴκελοι | πήχυιον ἐπὶ χρόνον ἄνθεσιν ἥβης
- Penthemimeral caesura: – ⏕,– ⏕,–|⏕,– ⏕,– ⏕, – ×
  e.g. Mimn. fr. 1.3 κρυπταδίη φιλότης | καὶ μείλιχα δῶρα καὶ εὐνή,
- ‘Feminine’ caesura: – ⏕,– ⏕,–⏑|⏑,– ⏕,– ⏕, – ×
  e.g. Mimn. fr. 1.9 ἀλλ’ ἐχθρὸς μὲν παισίν, | ἀτίμαστος δὲ γυναιξίν·
- Hepthemimeral caesura: – ⏕,– ⏕,– ⏕,–|⏕,– ⏕, – ×
  e.g. Mimn. fr. 2.9 αὐτὰρ ἐπὴν δὴ τοῦτο τέλος | παραμείψεται ὥρης,
- ‘Bucolic’ diaeresis: – ⏕,– ⏕,– ⏕,– ⏕, ‖– ⏕, – ×
  e.g. Mimn. fr. 2.11 πολλὰ γὰρ ἐν θυμῷ κακὰ γίνεται· ‖ ἄλλοτε οἶκος

Finding the right pause in a hexameter line is a matter of eliminating the least possible candidates. First, we preclude all potential pauses which do not coincide with word-ending. Thus, in the last quoted example, a hepthemimeral caesura is impossible, for it would fall on γί|νεται, and a ‘feminine’ caesura is also impossible, for it would fall on κα|κὰ. Secondly, we avoid pauses between syntactically inseparable words. Thus, in the same example, a trihemimeral caesura is improbable, for it would separate ἐν | θυμῷ. Of the remaining candidates we pick the one that best serves the meaning or is suggested by punctuation. Rarely, we may admit more than one pause on such grounds (e.g. Mimn. frr. 12.1; 12.7).

Moving to the **dactylic pentameter**, the metre in which the even verses are composed, it must be clarified that the term is used by convention but is actually inaccurate, for it does *not* describe ‘a sequence of five dactyls’, as one might expect. Instead, a pentameter is the sum of two *hêmiepê* (i.e. two hexameters from start up to where a penthemimeral caesura would fall), separated invariably by caesura. Only in the first *hêmiepes* are spondees allowed to replace dactyls. So the general pattern is: – ⏕,– ⏕,– | –⏑⏑,–⏑⏑,–

Overall, an elegy runs
– ⏕,– ⏕,– ⏕,– ⏕,– ⏕, – ×
– ⏕,– ⏕,– | –⏑⏑,–⏑⏑,–
– ⏕,– ⏕,– ⏕,– ⏕,– ⏕, – ×
– ⏕,– ⏕,– | –⏑⏑,– ⏑⏑,– and so on.

Even though this form is fixed, the variations allowed within it – between dactyls and spondees, between positions of pauses, between number of pauses, between the quantities of *anceps* – ensure that the rhythmical effect is not monotonous. Enjambment provides further flexibility, and Mimnermus employs that feature to the maximum, in a most elaborate manner, always to achieve meaningful emphases (e.g. fr. 1.5–6 ἐπέλθῃ | γῆρας) or to initiate a reappraisal of what comes before (e.g. fr. 2.4–5 οὔτε κακὸν | οὔτ᾽ ἀγαθόν, with note *ad loc.*), rather than to simply settle the 'left-overs' of previous lines. Moreover, his enjambments are 'violent': while in Homer one can barely find, for example, an attributive separated from its noun by enjambment (Parry 1929: 218), such arrangement is not alien to our poet; e.g. frr. 4 (κακὸν ἄφθιτον <ὁ Ζεὺς> | γῆρας); 5.5–6 (ἄμορφον | γῆρας); 14.10–11 (φυλόπιδος κρατερῆς | ἔργον). Reasonably, therefore, Bowra 1932: 17 asserted that "of the early elegists, he had the best ear. He manipulated his metre with great confidence". On a larger scale, we conclude that even the very defining element of elegy, its metre, proves very fluid.

Despite some attempts to argue for the opposite (Campbell 1964, Rosenmeyer 1968), it is widely accepted that Archaic elegy was sung to the accompaniment of the **double-pipes**, henceforth 'flute', as the frequent references to ἀείδειν and to αὐλός betray (cf. Solon frr. 1.2, 20.3; Thgn. 4, 242, 532–3, 824, 761, 938, 941, 943, 975, 1041, 1065). In fact, it has been proposed, and is now considered the most likely scenario, that elegy's actual etymology is Armenian *elegn*, 'reed' (Boisacq 1916: 240). That Aristotle (*Poet.* 1447b) mentions elegy as a kind of mimesis which employs words and metre *in opposition* to flute-playing which employs music – and similarly he contrasts epic to *kithara*-playing – must reflect the performance practices of his own day; or he simply wants to ontologically distinguish what is in practice inseparable: elegy from the flute, epic from the *kithara*. A contemporary of Aristotle, after all, the late-Classical biographer Chamaeleon of Pontus, testifies that the poems of Mimnermus were put to music (μελῳδηθῆναι), as were those of Homer, Hesiod, Archilochus, and Phocylides (Ath. 14.620c). Elegy and flute-playing were so intrinsically linked that artists of either genre were credited by later tradition as competent in the other genre too; some of them would reasonably have tried their powers in both arts, no doubt, but in principle we should be suspicious of possible confusion. For instance, Olympus of Phrygia, the inventor of flute-playing (Ps-Plut. *de mus.* 5.1132f; 7.1133d–f), who must have been slightly older than Mimnermus, is once called ποιητὴς μελῶν καὶ ἐλεγείων (*Suda*). That Tyrtaeus was ἐλεγειοποιὸς καὶ αὐλητής (*Suda*) is also unlikely, as far as the latter attribute is concerned; cf. Campbell 1964: 65, West 1974: 14.

In Mimnermus' case, however, our testimonies appear consistent in that he was both: αὐλητὴς ἅμα καὶ ποιητὴς ἐλεγείας, according to Strabo (14.1.28), he held revel "equipped with the lotus-pipe" (λωτῷ κνημωθεὶς κώμους εἶχε), according to Hermesianax (fr. 7.37–8 Powell), and he performed on the flute (Μίμνερμον αὐλῆσαι) an ancient melody called Cradias, according to Hipponax as claimed by the pseudo-Plutarchian *De musica* (8.1133f). The latter treatise continues thus: ἐν ἀρχῇ γὰρ ἐλεγεῖα μεμελοποιημένα οἱ αὐλῳδοὶ ᾖδον ("for in the beginning those who sang to the pipe sang elegies set to music"). Of course, because a single person cannot simultaneously sing and blow the flute, we must either admit (*a*) that an elegist sang his poems to the melody played by another person – a professional auletes or a flute-girl or a fellow-symposiast with basic skill, depending on availability – and if that elegist wanted to play the flute in turn, he would do so for another poet to sing; or (*b*) that an elegist recited or sang his poems *without* musical accompaniment but had intervals where he played the flute; or (*c*) some other form of 'in-betweenness' which allowed for both sung and recited delivery and was open to variability in accordance with the occasion (Budelmann and Power 2013). The reference to τὴν Μιμνέρμου αὐλητρίδα Ναννὼ (Ath. 13.597a) supports the first scenario – even though Nanno might just have been a Hellenistic invention – and so does a famous early-5th-century Athenian cup (Munich 2646), which depicts a piper accompanying a singing symposiast; beside the latter's mouth runs the inscription ΟΥΔΥΝΑΜΟΥ, which Hartwig 1893: 258 n.8 identified as Theognis 939–42 <u>οὐ δύναμ</u>αι φωνῇ λίγ' ἀειδέμεν … <u>οὐ</u>δὲ τὸν αὐλητὴν προφασίζομαι… ("I cannot sing sweetly … nor do I give the piper as an excuse").

The main context for performing elegy was indeed **the symposium**, where a group of male aristocrats gathered at a friend's house to drink together (< συν+πίνειν), have snacks, play games, tell jokes, flirt, sing, and discuss anything from current affairs and gossip to poetry and philosophy. The host invited his friends to his house and they occupied the *andrôn* ('for men only') area – citizen women were prohibited – where they reclined in pairs on cushioned couches arranged around a square, so that everyone could see each other. The party began once the meal (*deipnon*) had been cleared away, and only disserts and crackers would be offered now. At the centre of the hall stood a large bowl (*kratêr*) for mixing wine with water – it was considered a barbarian's trait to drink undiluted wine – while smaller cups (*kylikes*) circulated, passing hand to hand, to drink from. A related game was *kottabos*: flinging the sediment from a *kylix* at a target in the middle of the room, with the winner receiving a prize; it is no surprise, therefore, that sympotic scenes are so often depicted on *kylikes*. Not only Dionysus', but Aphrodite's gifts too were at the centre of those parties. High-class prostitutes, the *hetairai* (as opposed to common *pornai*), were invited to offer their services, which included – other than the obvious – playing music, dancing and performing acrobatics; some, being educated, also engaged in the sophisticated discussions. But **male bonding** was the priority at those by nature homoerotic parties, which offered a relaxed environment for *erastai* and *erômenoi* (older and younger males respectively), both existing and prospective couples, to spend time together, meet new people, and have sex or simply admire male beauty – e.g. the boy serving the wine (*oinochoos*) sometimes performed his duties naked. With our evidence ranging from scenes of flirting in Plato's and Xenophon's *Symposium* to group orgies represented on pottery, we cannot tell how much sex was actually involved, but as with modern parties, we must assume that the degree of (in)formality depended on occasion.

Male bonding aside, the symposia also offered **ideological bonding**, i.e. affirmation of the participants' elite status. Those gatherings were not only an opportunity for the host to show off his riches and acquaintances, but also for the guest to prove that he met the requirements for such an invitation, e.g. knowledge of 'savoir vivre' and literature, as well as a willingness to host in turn – otherwise he would be named a *parasite,* i.e.

that he joined the party for the free food! Once the symposium was over, the drunken revellers returned home disturbing the sleeping neighbours with their loud songs (*kômos*), harassing innocent citizens on the streets, and damaging public property, in a ritualised exhibition of their aristocratic privilege; cf. Murray 1990: 150. Of course, some aristocrats were more aristocratic than others in reality, but it was essential to establish perfect **equality** within the symposium, a provision expressed in the circular arrangement of the couches, in taking up the speech or song in rotation, and in selecting one guest to act as coordinator, *symposiarchos*, whose regulations (e.g. on mixing the wine) applied to everyone, including the host. The passing from Homeric feasting, where warriors were seated in the *megaron* of a *basileus* to receive their respective *geras* ('share of honour'), to the symposium of reclining and equality must date as early as the last quarter of the 8th century BC. For, even though our iconographical evidence begins a century later and our earliest poetic description of a symposium also comes from that period (Alcman fr. 19), the poetry of Archilochus (fr. 2) and Callinus (fr. 1.1) already hint at the practice of reclining at the dawn of the 7th century; cf. Murray 1994: 52–53. The new fashion of lazy-and-luxurious feasting was introduced from the near east and proved one of the most powerful legacies of the Orientalising Period; cf. Matthäus 1999. In fact, it would not be a hyperbole to say that many of the political developments of the Archaic (and the Classical) era – an era of constant coups and revolts within the *poleis* – were orchestrated by different clubs/lobbies (*hetaireiai*) at the symposia, as reflected in Alcaeus' poems; cf. Rösler 1980.

Elegy had a prominent role at the symposia (and the *kômos* that followed; cf. Thgn. 829, 940, 1046, 1065, 1207, 1351–2). Thanks to its wide thematic repertoire, elegy served various functions (cf. p. 3) and therefore fitted any kind of symposium: formal or informal, for close friends or for a wider company, organised upon a happy occasion or in troubled times. Tyrtaeus, for instance, "upon his arrival [to Sparta] sang his elegiac and anapaestic verses, both privately to those in office and to as many as he could gather together" (Paus. 4.15.6); his elegies were sung after a banquet in the king's tent (Bowie 1986: 15). However, not *any* elegy was appropriate for *all* symposia; when Archilochus visited Sparta he was expelled from the city for having composed the notorious *Fuck that shield!* (fr. 5), an elegy which presumably did not cause any fuss in its original performance, since the (anecdotal?) incident in Sparta is reported as something striking (Plut. *Instit. Lac.* 34.239b). No explicit references to a sympotic context occur in Mimnermus, as they do in the elegies by Theognis (e.g. 237–43), Xenophanes (fr. 1), Simonides (fr. 25), and Ion (fr. 27), but hints are plenty: enjoying oneself/ourselves (frr. 2.4, 7.1), staring at the young (fr. 5.2), sleeping on soft and luxurious beds (fr. 12.5–8) and, of course, the second person *singular* (frr. 7, 8). Furthermore, the fact that some of Mimnermus' lines slipped into the openly-sympotic *Theognidea* (795–6, 1017–22) and that many of his poems were included in a collection called *Nanno*, i.e. a typical name for a *hetaira*, illustrates how obvious the sympotic nature of his poetry was to the ancient reader. And as said earlier, Hellenistic tradition saw in Mimnermus an active *kômastês* who would revel with a certain Examyes, playing the flute (Hermesianax fr. 7.37–8). A piece which would fit the *kômos* is fr. 7 (*Enjoy yourself! Of the ruthless citizens | some will speak ill of you, some better*): here Mimnermus may be consoling, if cynically, the unsuspecting passers-by, who are harassed by his own 'ruthless' friends!

But the symposium was not the only occasion for singing elegies. In fact, it is an unlikely setting for some of them. Very long elegies would be both impractical to perform at the symposium, for a professional *aulêtês* with an analogous stamina would be required, and hard for the participants to follow, for their urge for wine would distract them – only shorter poems can win a tipsy man's attention. Besides, the convention of equal speaking among the symposiasts would be undermined, if a single person sang hundreds or thousands of verses. So Bowie 1986 made a strong case for performance at **public festivals** (and also rejected West's 1974: 12 proposal for "weekday recitation in the agora"), arguing that narrative elegies dealing with a city's mythological and/or recent past, such as Mimnermus' *Smyrneis*, Tyrtaeus' *Eunomia*, Simonides' *Salamis* (cf. test. 1), and Panyassis' *Ionica* (test. 1 *GEF*) were intended for such performance. Even more, there is evidence suggesting **competitive** performance of elegy at public festivals. I have already mentioned (cf. p. 8) pseudo-Plutarch's reference to elegies set to music (ἐλεγεῖα μεμελοποιημένα, *de mus.* 8.1133f), and it should now be added that he made that reference in connection to the music competition which Pericles introduced at the Panathenaea (Παναθηναίων … μουσικοῦ ἀγῶνος, 8.1134a; cf. Plut. *Vit. Per.* 13.11). A second but problematic testimony is offered by Pausanias (10.7.4–6), who says that until 586 BC the Pythian Games at Delphi featured competitions in singing to the flute and in flute-playing (αὐλῳδίας ἀγώνισμα καὶ αὐλῶν); but the singing competition in particular was abolished at the following games of 582 BC, because the organisers deemed that "the music was ill-omened to listen to; for the tunes of the flute were most dismal, and the words sung to the tunes were lamentations" (οὐκ εἶναι τὸ ἄκουσμα εὔφημον· ἡ γὰρ αὐλῳδία μέλη τε ἦν αὐλῶν τὰ σκυθρωπότατα καὶ ἐλεγεῖα {θρῆνοι} προσᾳδόμενα τοῖς αὐλοῖς). The last victor in *aulôdia*, Pausanias continues, was Echembrotus, who "sang tunes and lamentations" (ἀείδων μέλεα καὶ ἐλέγους). In these passages ἐλεγεῖον and ἔλεγος do not mean 'elegies' in general, but 'lamentatory elegies' (or just 'lamentations', as in Jones' translation from Loeb). The passages lack coherence – how can Echembrotus have won if his performance caused such distress? – and "the text is worthless as evidence for the nature of early elegy", as it only reflects the Hellenistic (mis)conception of elegy (Bowie 1986: 23). In fact, a copyist spotted the inaccuracy and felt the need to add {θρῆνοι} as a gloss on ἐλεγεῖα. So Pausanias' *aulôdia* may have nothing to do with elegy, or, if it does, it only describes the public performance of a certain (narrow) type of elegy.

Back to the textual aspect of the genre. One cannot exclude the possibility that some elegies began their life as spontaneous oral creations which the poets reworked and finalised on 'paper' at a later stage. Of course, this only applies to elegies of the sympotic sort, for those intended for public consumption could not have been left to improvisation. At any rate, Mimnermus' dense and elaborate metrical and verbal tricks (in the longest pieces, at least) leave no room to question a **written composition** *ab initio*. We should not assume that *that* was always the case. For example, the divergent wording in any pair of doublets in Theognis (e.g. 39–42 ≈ 1081–2) is possibly – if not an error in textual transmission – an index of oral workings; each version may represent a different stage in a poem's evolution (cf. Nagy 1985: 47–49). In Mimnermus, only frr. 15–16 could theoretically constitute an analogous case, but that is unlikely, for those two lines are quoted side-by-side in the same source, hence they must have been drawn together from a single edition. On the notoriously difficult question of, and the methodological flaws in, dating the introduction and spread of Greek alphabetic writing, see Astoreca 2021: 8–12, 18. Even in the lowest possible scenario, i.e. an introduction of Greek alphabet(s) just few decades before the recording of the Homeric epics, whose dating is also debatable (cf. p. 34), the spread appears (judging from the similarities of the local scripts) to have been rapid, i.e. completed well before Mimnermus' time. Yet, I doubt that such spread was a matter of "few weeks rather than months or years" (Wachter 2021: 23).

Moving from composition to consumption, the assumption is that "throughout the archaic period works and poets were achieving classic status within the circulating *oral* songbook [...] at symposia across the Greek world" (Carey 2011: 445, 448, my italics). Indeed, we have no testimony on a pre-Alexandrian edition for any elegist, but some evidence to the contrary exists. First, we know that the Peripatetics in Athens published monographs on lyric poets and such monographs presuppose that those poets would be available "in some readable form by the late fourth century" (Carey 2011: 453). Several elegies would have naturally slipped into those corpora, given that Simonides and Anacreon, for example, on whom Chamaeleon (*c.* 350–275 BC) wrote treatises, are 'lyric' *and* elegiac poets. Even Sappho, on whom Chamaeleon also wrote, is said to have composed elegies (cf. Rotstein 2010: 35). Secondly, Theognis' persistence in using Cyrnus' name as a means of putting his signature on his work, a literary device called *sphragis* ('seal'), betrays the elegist's anxiety to secure his authorship *not* only in view of future (oral) reperformance of his poems (cf. Bowie 1986: 14), but also in view of their written circulation; for in vv. 245–52 he envisions his work's immortality, its spread all over Greece, and its use "even by future generations [καὶ ἐσσομένοισιν] as long as earth and sun exist", an expectation which cannot rely on oral transmission alone. And it was perhaps Theognis himself who first published his collection, reserving those verses for the epilogue – a risky hypothesis, for it would give us "the oldest verifiable book edited by the author himself" (Reitzenstein 1893: 267), yet a reasonable one; cf. Selle 2008: 180–82, 319–20, 381–82, who rejects that scenario. Bowie 2012: 142 accepts it partially, proposing that the greater part of 'Book 1' of the *Theognidea* was compiled by the late-5th-century philosopher and poet Euenus of Paros for the education of his pupils, but probably that was done in the example of an earlier collection put together by Theognis himself late in the 6th century. We find no *sphragis* in Mimnermus to allow us make an analogous hypothesis for such early a publication, but a late-Classical-period edition *is* tenable. Already by Aristophanes' later period, **book circulation** was relatively wide (cf. *Ran.* 51–2) and in Euripides, a contemporary of Aristophanes, we find two echoes of Mimnermus' poetry (frr. 1.1; 11) and a potential third one (fr. 5). One of them entails a strikingly close engagement with the source-elegy (Eur. *Med.* 6–10 ≈ fr. 11), which presupposes either good memory or a book at hand. And conceivably, Euripides' frequent references to ἔλεγος (cf. p. 3) resulted from owning such a book.

On the Alexandrian editions of the elegies, the evidence is scarce. In the *Suda* we only read of Semonides of Amorgos' two collections of elegies (ἔγραψεν ἐλεγείαν ἐν βιβλίοις β΄); of Tyrtaeus' five collections (ἔγραψε … βιβλία ε΄) which included but were not limited to elegies; and of Mimnermus' "collections [?] which are plenty" (ἔγραψε βιβλία † ταῦτα πολλά). Unfortunately, the text is corrupt at the most critical point – a number would appear where the crux is. Luckily we have another source to provide us some rough guidance, but, ironically, that is also corrupt! Namely, the Latin grammarian Porphyrio testifies (*ad* Hor. *epist.* 2.2.101) *Mimnermus duos libros †luculentibus† scripsit* ("Mimnermus wrote two books of splend[id verses]". Even if we accept the text as emended (*luculent<is vers>ibus* : West), there is no ground to accept that those two book-rolls were *all* that was known from Mimnermus. The only safe conclusion is that *at least* two Alexandrian books existed and amounted to the poet's most popular works; see more on pp. 21–23.

Who? – Mimnermus

Our poet is the only 'Mimnermus' recorded. The name is of uncertain **etymology**. Pasquali 1923: 293–95 proposed that it comes from μιμνήσκω + Ἕρμος, meaning "the one who commemorates Hermus", which in turn would be a reference to the Smyrnaeans' victory at the battle of Hermus (cf. pp. 143–44). West 1974: 73 suggests that only a baby born shortly after the battle would receive such a name, and so we have an additional clue for dating our poet early. The hypothesis sounds most compelling only because we happen to have fr. 14, in which Mimnermus indeed commemorates that battle. But such a retrospective aetiology for 'speaking names' only works for fictional characters (e.g. Πενθεύς is the mythical king of Thebes who *ended up* being mourned) and for nicknames given to historical persons (e.g. the philosopher Aristocles *ended up* being called Πλάτων, according to biographical anecdotes, due to his πλατύ forehead or torso). 'Mimnermus' cannot have been a pseudonym for our poet, who would imaginably have received this nickname after fr. 14 becoming popular. If he had one, that would be 'Ligyastades', and even that is almost certainly an *ad hoc* invention by Solon (cf. p. 107). The plethora of -ερμος names used in Ionia and nearby Chios (e.g. Ἀγήσερμος, Ἀνάξερμος, Ἄρχερμος, Δίερμος, Κίκερμος, Κράτερμος, Μελήσερμος, Νικήσερμος, Πύθερμος) makes 'Mimnermus' not striking enough to have worked as a nickname. At the same time, it is unlikely that *all* these -ερμος names referred to Hermus river, as Allen 1993:14 reasonably notes. Another potential etymology, which I find the most persuasive, is from μίμνω (poetic form of μένω) + Ἑρμῆς, meaning "the one who awaits Hermes" (Szádeczky-Kardoss 1968: 937 after Sittig 1911: 113–14) and, metonymically, "the one who expects profit". As for the first compound, we find it in names such as Μιμναγόρας, Μιμνοκράτης, Μιμνόμαχος and Μιμνόπολις (cf. Bechtel 1917: 318–19); as for the second, it makes perfect sense that names evoking the god of trade would be so common in Ionia. It has been objected that such a meaning would require Ἑρμῆς to be the first compound (Meister 1921: 215 n.1), as in Ἑρμογένης or Ἑρμαγόρας, but there are counterexamples where a god's name comes second, as in Μενάρης ("the one who awaits Ares / who does not retreat before Ares / who persists in the war"; Emiliani 2021: 12 n.63). More recently, Masson 1990: 623 suggested that -ερμος is an auspicious toponym related to rivers, which adds no meaning to compound names but simply comes to positively emphasise the first compound; then Νικήσερμος, for example, would mean the idea of 'victory', Ἄρχερμος the idea of 'authority', and Μίμνερμος the idea of 'persistence'. [Cf. the English suffix -berry, which linguistically groups fruits and plants that are otherwise unrelated. Botanically speaking, strawberries, blackberries or raspberries are not 'berries', while bananas, cucumbers, and avocados are!]

More essential is the question of Mimnermus' **dating**. It was first believed that our poet was born in *c.* 630 BC (e.g. Wilamowitz 1913: 280; Lavagnini 1950: 2; Dihle 1962: 275) but then *c.* 670 BC became the prevailing theory (e.g. Szádeczky-Kardoss 1968: 938; West 1974: 72–74; Allen 1993: 12). More recently, Sanz Morales 2000 reinstated the former case and suggested that Mimnermus' poetic innovations fit better with a low chronology – a thesis which essentially undermines those innovations, if they cannot be imagined as having come 'prematurely' in the lyric tradition. Finally, Emiliani 2021: 9, after a very balanced presentation of the arguments from both sides, takes a neutral position, admitting the high chronology only as a working hypothesis. Not wishing to delve at similar detail here, I shall only summarise the key elements and confidently support the high chronology, starting from what is, to my opinion, a crucial (if often ignored) clue. The fact that Mimnermus is listed by Didymus as one of the likely inventors of elegy, together with Archilochus and Callinus (p. 1), suggests that *according to all evidence available to an Alexandrian scholar* – much more evidence than what we have today – all three poets were considered old enough to qualify as candidates. On the other hand, Solon's famous response (fr. 20) to Mimn. fr. 6 is unduly (if too often) brought up in the discussion, as it can fit any biographical scenario, whether Mimnermus was dead at the time of the Solonian composition or alive, and (if alive) whether he was older than Solon or younger (cf. pp. 106–107). So Solon aside, the rest of our evidence suggests the following:

- *terminus post quem* for birth: Mimnermus must have been born after 680 BC, for in fr. 14 he thematises Gyges' attack against Smyrna as something which he only knows via his elders' narratives, either because he himself was not yet born, or because he was too young to have any memories (let alone to have fought). Gyges launched his attacks immediately upon his usurpation of the Lydian throne in *c.* 680 BC, Herodotus says, but realistically speaking, given that Smyrna was Gyges' second target after Miletus and that such a grandiose military plan would require time to execute, the 670s appears the most likely decade for the attack on Smyrna. And if Mimnermus in 670 BC was alive but too young – the highest possible chronology – to have had a living memory of the war, he cannot have been born before 680 BC.
- *terminus ante quem* for birth: Mimnermus must have been born before 655 BC, because the solar eclipse he mentioned in his now-lost fr. 20 (in *Appendix II*) is most probably that of 6 April 648 BC (cf. Espenak 2022). We cannot deduce that "he was already writing verse in 648" (West 1974: 73–74) but, rather, that he was at least 6–7 years old – the lowest possible chronology – to have obtained a vivid memory of the eclipse. How much later in his life he decided to write about it, we cannot tell. But if he was born in *c.* 670 BC, as here sustained, then the eclipse occurred when he was about 22, an age at which an *ad hoc* composition of fr. 20 is likely – *pace* Sanz Morales 2000: 43–44, who finds that age too young (!) for composing poetry – yet not necessary. [Dihle placed Mimnermus' birth at *c.* 630 BC, because, by misreading Herodotus and by discarding Pausanias' testimony (5.8.9) that Smyrna was Ionian by as early as 688 BC, he assumed that the Colophonians settled Smyrna in the 660s and therefore Mimnermus ought to be a generation younger (Dihle 1962: 269–70; cf. Allen 1993: 11). Such a theory, of course, also required that the reference to the eclipse was 'buried' – and so it was.]
- *terminus post quem* for death: Mimnermus must have died after 632–629 BC, which is the date at which he 'flourished', i.e. was recorded to have been alive, according to the *Suda*. There is also a slim possibility that the above-mentioned eclipse of fr. 20 is

to be identified with that of 28 May 585 BC, in which case (in combination with the *terminus ante quem* for Mimnermus' birth) we would definitely conclude that our poet reached, and possibly surpassed, the age of 70. In fact, a death slightly after 585 BC does not even preclude the high chronology, for 670–585= 85 years old. But then, if Mimnermus outlived the siege of Smyrna by Alyattes *c.* 600 BC, it seems strange how 15 years of subsequent production (600–585) left no reference – inasmuch as we can trust his slim corpus – to that historic moment (cf. West 1974: 73).

- *terminus ante quem* for death: precisely because Mimnermus makes no traceable reference to Alyattes' sack of Smyrna, which would be the most traumatising experience for a Smyrnaean, especially one without experience of Gyges' attacks, our poet was very likely dead by *c.* 600 BC. [If scholars are right that in frr. 9 and 14 Mimnermus implicitly exhorts his contemporaries to be courageous in facing Alyattes (cf. pp. 118, 144), then Mimnermus must have been alive and poetically active soon before Smyrna was sacked. But this is all too hypothetical.]

Unlike his dating, there is now long established consensus on Mimnermus' **homeland**. According to the *Suda*, the poet was Κολοφώνιος ἢ Σμυρναῖος ἢ Ἀστυπαλαιεύς, and our other sources limit the candidate cities to the former two, also given that Ἀστυπάλαια is used in many places to simply mean the 'old site' of a city. Colophon is the candidate city mentioned more often, e.g. by Strabo 14.643 (ἄνδρες δ' ἐγένοντο Κολοφώνιοι τῶν μνημονευομένων Μίμνερμος, "Native Colophonians for whom we have record include Mimnermus…"); Procl. *Chr.* 24 Severyns (ἀριστεῦσαι τῷ μέτρῳ Καλλῖνόν τε τὸν Ἐφέσιον καὶ Μίμνερμον τὸν Κολοφώνιον, "Callinus the Ephesian and Mimnermus the Colophonian distinguished themselves in metre"). But then we have a 1st-century-AD funerary inscription from Smyrna, which mentions a gymnasium called Μιμνερμεῖον (*CIG* 3376), and that would be a poor trademark if Mimnermus was not a native. The decisive argument was put forward by Jacoby 1918: 268–70: a Colophonian poet addressing Colophonians would not have said of their recently left-behind homeland κεῖθεν ἀπορνύμενοι ("departing from that place", fr. 9.5). It is therefore clear that Hellenistic tradition confused the poet's homeland (Smyrna) with his ancestral home (Colophon) which, in turn, goes back to Pylos, Messenia (fr. 9.1). This confusion could be intentional: Hellenistic poets from Colophon (Hermesianax, Nicander, Phoenix) appropriated Mimnermus' legacy (as well as that of Antimachus) to advertise their local 'school', Patocchi 1983: 76 suggests ingeniously.

About Mimnermus' **family**, we only know that his father was probably named Λιγυρτυάδης (*Suda*), assuming that the nickname Λιγυᾳστάδης which Solon grants to our poet must have been modelled on his actual patronymic (cf. p. 107). In a similar manner, Aristophanes called the son of Lamachus (υἱὸς Λαμάχου) an ἀνδρὸς βουλομάχου καὶ κλαυσιμάχου τινὸς υἱός, "MacWannafight-MacGonnacry" (*Pax* 1290–2). Wilamowitz 1913: 276–85 thought that Mimnermus was "a plebian" from Colophon, who sided with the ordinary hoplites and attacked the local aristocrats, and consequently his father could only be a random commoner of unknown name. The idea was based – apart from accepting the low chronology and the wrong homeland – on the misconception that playing the flute is an index of lowborn **status**. Should one believe that Tyrtaeus, an ἐλεγειοποιὸς καὶ αὐλητής (*Suda*) was also a plebian? (Jacoby 1918: 283 n.1). The misconception arises from a tradition according to which Archilochus, another flute-related poet (frr. 58.12; 93a, 269; cf. Corrêa 2009), was the bastard son of a noble Parian with a slave woman, who left Paros and went to Thasos out of poverty (fr. 295; cf. Wilamowitz 1913: 276). But the story is evidently fake, for Archilochus' family took part in *colonising* Thasos, and Paros established a hero-cult for him; cf. Swift 2019: 5; Rotstein 2010: 305–308. By default, i.e. unless there is solid evidence for the contrary, one has to assume that a poet singing at symposia is an aristocrat. And a poet of *that* calibre and at such early stage of literary tradition cannot but be an aristocrat.

The **social network** of Mimnermus included Examyes, together with whom our poet used to play the flute during the *kômos* (cf. p. 8). Sometimes 'playing the flute' is a sexual metaphor for 'giving blowjobs' – as it still is in Modern Greek slang – and the particular setting here, the after-symposium revelling, only reinforces that possible interpretation. Cf. Archil. fr. 269, where he says that a male flute-player (αὐλητής) is effectively a horn-blower (κεραύλης), and fr. 247 confirms that the 'horn' (κέρας) was a euphemism for the penis. But the metaphor also works in heterosexual contexts, e.g. in Theoc. *Id*. 27.13–14 "enjoying the pipe" (σῦριγξ) evidently refers to a penis offered to, yet rejected by, a girl (cf. p. 112 – I assume a single-stem *sŷrinx*; cf. West 1992: 113). Passages from comedy suggest that flute-girls openly performed fellatio upon the men at symposia (Henderson 1991: 51, 167–68, 183 n.120; cf. Ar. *Vesp*. 1341–6) and it is probably that very context where such metaphors were generated. Back to Hermesianax's testimony (fr. 7.37–40 Powell): if the 'grey lotus-pipe' (πολιῷ … λωτῷ) which Mimnermus is said to have been playing is a metonymy for him being old, then Mimnermus is to be imagined as the *erastês* and Examyes as the *erômenos* in their duet (cf. Allen 1993: 18, *pace* Caspers 2006: 26). The passage goes on: "Mimnermus warred [?] with ever-cruel Hermobius, and loathed his enemy, Pherecles, for his jibes" (†ἠδ' ἤχθεε† δ' Ἑρμόβιον τὸν αἰεὶ βαρὺν ἠδὲ Φερεκλῆν ἐχθρὸν μισήσας οἷ' ἀνέπεμψεν ἔπη). The antagonistic relations described here are not clear, not least because of the textual problem. Were Hermobius and Pherecles two of Mimnermus' rival poets? Were they rival lovers for Nanno (or for Examyes)? Or were they a couple – *erômenos* and *erastês* respectively – whom Mimnermus did not succeed in breaking up, and then held a grudge against? At least one source is explicit about our poet's pederastic interests (cf. p. 72).

But, above all, Mimnermus was on fire for **Nanno** (καίετο μὲν Ναννοῦς), says Hermesianax, and he is seconded by Posidippus (Ναννοῦς … †φιλεράστου† Μιμνέρμου, *AP* 12.168.1–2). Nanno, according to Athenaeus (13.597a), was our poet's αὐλητρίς and, since that testimony comes amid a list of famous *hetairai*, we have to assume that she was his flute-player *and* 'flute-player'. Her name is probably Lydian (cf. *LW*), so "she may have been a slave, perhaps the daughter of a Lydian woman taken captive during the Smyrnaeans' war with Gyges"; Allen 1993: 18. But Nanno may simply have been a Hellenistic invention, a kinky muse to whose inspiration the erotic poetry of Mimnermus was credited in retrospect, so that contemporary poets could legitimise that practice *of theirs*; consider e.g. Meleager's *hetaira* Phanion ('Fanny', transl. Woodward 1924: 68; *AP* 7.207; 12.53, 82, 83), who indeed anticipates Catullus' Lesbia (cf. Thomas 1999: 60–62; Holzberg 2000: 31). I do agree, of course, that "Nanno cannot have been invented from nothing" (West 1974: 75), but the name itself, at least, seems too suspiciously stereotypical for a *hetaira* (cf. Ναννάριον Men. *Kolax* fr. 4 Sandbach; Νάννιον fr. 414 K-A).

Whether true or invented, Mimnermus' crush lent her name to one of our poet's **collections**; frr. 4, 5, 8, 9 and 12 are recorded as coming from *Nanno*, and given how wide the thematology of those poems is, Allen 1993: 20–21 suggests that the entire corpus of Mimnermus may have been published as, and so all extant fragments may belong to, *Nanno*. West 1974: 74 rejects that possibility, pointing out that none of our sources makes the specification ἐν α΄ or ἐν β΄ Ναννοῦς – we have already seen that Mimnermus was credited with at least two books (p. 14) – nor can we easily fit *Smyrneis* (Σμυρνηίς), under whose title fr. 13a is recorded, in *Nanno*. Allen (*op. cit.*) deems that *Smyrneis* "was almost certainly not long enough to deserve a separate book-roll", in which case we would have to admit that *Smyrneis* was part of, or even another name for, *Nanno* (Gerber 1970: 113), whereas for West (*op. cit.*), *Smyrneis* "may well count as a book". In fact, we know that other narrative elegies about a city's history and mythology *did* reach great lengths (p. 3), but on *Smyrneis*' length, in particular, the only certainty is that it was long enough to contain a genealogy of the Muses and the main narrative, i.e. the war between the Smyrnaeans and Gyges (fr. 13 in *Appendix II*). Allen 1993: 25–26 is right that all these could be covered in as few as 400–500 lines, but he admits that even such short a historical elegy "would have been unsuited to the symposium". So the decisive factor is whether *Nanno* included only sympotic poems. I strongly believe it did, for the title of the collection is a *hetaira*'s name, the fragments certainly belonging to *Nanno* have unmistakable sympotic hints, and our longest piece from *Nanno* (fr. 12) is just twelve verses. By contrast, the title *Smyrneis* resembles titles of epics (Θηβαΐς, Ἀλκμαιωνίς, Αἰθιοπίς), thus anticipating a lengthy poem, and refers to Smyrna, which was named, in turn, after the eponymous Amazon (p. 117). That a *virgin* warrioress (cf. Aesch. *PV* 416; Hdt. 4.117; Hippoc. *Aer.* 17) would lent her name to a substantial portion of *Nanno* is improbable.

Therefore, I agree with Colonna 1952 (as do West 1974: 74, Töchterle 1980, Gentili and Prato 1988: 42 and Bowie 1986: 28) that *Nanno* and *Smyrneis* are the two books by Mimnermus which Porphyrio has in mind (p. 14), and which **Callimachus** alludes to when he says (*Aetia* fr. 1.11–12 Pf.):

> τοῖν δὲ] δ̣υ̣οῖν Μίμνερμος ὅτι γλυκύς, α[ἱ κατὰ λεπτὸν]
> [ῥήσιες] ἡ μεγάλη δ' οὐκ ἐδίδαξε γυνή

> *Of his two (works), it was his slender* [*sayings*], *rather than the big lady, that taught us how sweet Mimnermus was.*

The gaps were first supplemented by Rostagni 1928, who drew on a notoriously corrupt scholium (*P. Lit. Lond.* 181, col. II, 11–13) which, according to his emendation, had glossed the passage thus: ἐδίδαξαν αἱ κατὰ λεπτ(όν) | οὐκ ἐδίδ(αξεν) ἡ μεγάλ(η) | λέγει ὅτι γλυκ(ὺς) ὁ Μίμ(νερμος). The London scholium was revisited by Bastianini 1996: 73–77, who in turn offered a different reconstruction of the Callimachean fragment:

> τοῖν δὲ δυοῖν Μίμνερμος ὅτι γλυκύς α[ἱ μετὰ τήνδε]
> [ἦτε μέν,] ἡ μεγάλη δ' οὐκ ἐδίδαξε γυνή

> *Between the two, it was surely those* [*ladies*] *following the big lady, rather than she herself, who taught us how sweet Mimnermus was.*

With either reconstruction, the correspondence which Callimachus attempts is clear. On the one hand, *Nanno* is Rostagni's "slim lady" (with a possible hint at νᾶνος, 'dwarf', suggests Bowie 1986: 28), i.e. a collection of *short* poems named after a petite *hetaira*, or Bastianini's "ladies following the big lady", i.e. *varied* poems which comprised the second book-roll of the Alexandrian set. On the other hand, *Smyrneis* is Rostagni's "big lady", i.e. a *long* elegy named after a bulky Amazon, or Bastianini's "big lady", i.e. a *single* elegy which constituted the first book-roll of the Alexandrian set. The reverse correspondence would be nonsensical: Hunt 1927: 52 thought that ἡ μεγάλη γυνή referred to *Nanno*, i.e. "the most celebrated" of Mimnermus' works, but that ignores Callimachus' intention (cf. similar attempts by Della Corte 1965: 375–76, Garzya 1965: 371–72, Torraca 1969: 46, and Wimmel 1960: 91). Callimachus' preference for Mimnermus' slim lady (or varied ladies), which must reflect the *opinio communis* of his day (unless ἐδίδαξε is a forced assumption), is programmatically placed at the prologue of his *Aetia*, to defend his own writing of small-scale poems (or of diverse poems). In fact, λεπτότης, 'refinement/slimness', and πολυείδεια, 'generic/stylistic variety', became trends in Hellenistic poetics precisely because of Callimachus. In response to those critics who 'bullied' him for not composing pure epic, Callimachus asserted that big books are bad books (τὸ μέγα βιβλίον ἴσον ἔλεγεν εἶναι τῷ μεγάλῳ κακῷ, Ath. 3.72a) and asked with indignation "Who said 'You, write pentameters; you, hexameters; and to you the gods have assigned tragedy'? No one, I think!" (*Ia*. 13, fr. 203.30–33 Pf.); cf. Cameron 1995: 308–14, 372–73 and Acosta-Hughes 2002: 60–103, esp. 72–73. [An alternative theory (cf. Puelma 1957, Matthews 1979: 134–37, Müller 1988: 209–11) is that Callimachus pursues an 'external' comparison, not between Mimnermus' two books, but between the Hellenistic poets Philitas of Cos and Antimachus of Colophon; supposedly he praises Philitas' short elegies for promoting Mimnermus' legacy, and rejects Antimachus' *Lyde*, the 'bulky lady'. This theory is multiply weak; cf. Allen 1993: 151–52. Lightfoot 2009: 20–23 leaves both Callimachus' fragment and the crucial part of the London scholium unsupplemented.]

Callimachus' testimony, like that of Porphyrio, does not mean that Mimnermus' books numbered only two, but that *Nanno* and *Smyrneis* were his two most noteworthy – recall the excruciatingly deficient reference in the *Suda*: ἔγραψε βιβλία † ταῦτα πολλά. Conceivably, any of the fragments not reported as coming from either *Nanno* or *Smyrneis* (i.e. frr. 1, 2, 3, 6, 7, 11+11a, 14, 15, 16, 17) could come from another collection. However, insofar as thematic affinity is a key criterion, a conservative **allocation** should be our working hypothesis:

frr. 1–3 and 6 (on old age) seem to belong to the same work as frr. 4–5 (*Nanno*), fr. 11+11a (on exploring new lands) to the same work as fr. 9 (*Nanno*), and fr. 14 (on the war against Gyges) to the same work as fr. 13a (*Smyrneis*). Frr. 7, 15 and 16 (on bad reputation) must be sympotic, and fr. 7 in particular may be *kômastic* (p. 11), hence they all fit *Nanno*, whereas – what is left – fr. 17 (on leading cavalry) better fits *Smyrneis*.

There is a slim possibility, almost a 'conspiracy theory', given how unreliable our evidence is, that Mimnermus also composed **iambic poetry**. West prints the following iambic passages under the poet's *dubia et spuria*:

F24 Source: Stob. 4.38.3 (περὶ ἰατρῶν καὶ ἰατρικῆς), specifying the fr. as κατὰ ἰατρῶν Μιμνέρμου *Ναννοῦς* [*νάννου* in manuscripts M and A]

× οἷα δὴ φιλοῦσιν ἰατροὶ λέγειν
τὰ φαῦλα μείζω καὶ τὰ δείν' ὑπὲρ φόβον,
πυργοῦντες αὑτούς. – ⏑ –, × – ⏑ –

Doctors love to say things such as "minor conditions are most dangerous, while major ones are nothing to fear", just to show off!

F25 Source: Stob. 4.57.11 (ὅτι οὐ χρὴ παροινεῖν εἰς τοὺς τετελευτηκότας), specifying the fr. as Μιμνέρμου ἐκ *Νεοπτολέμου*

δεινοὶ γὰρ ἀνδρὶ πάντες ἐσμὲν εὐκλεεῖ
ζῶντι φθονῆσαι, κατθανόντα δ' αἰνέσαι.

We are all prone to envy a famous man while he's alive,
but once he's dead we praise him!

F26 Source: *Epimerismi Homerici* γ25 Dyck, specifying the fr. as παρὰ Μιμνέρμῳ

ὦ Ζεῦ πολυτίμηθ', ὡς καλαὶ νῷν αἱ γυναί

Oh much-honoured Zeus, how beautiful are the wives of both of us!

One may also take the *sine versibus* fr. 21a (cf. p. 156) as testimony to an iambic fragment, since the proverb it preserves (*A cripple fucks the best!*) can fit into iambic trimeters thus (cf. Diehl 1949: 56):

× – ⏑ – , × – ⏑ – , × – ⏑ –
[ ]ἄριστα χωλὸς <ὤν>
× – ⏑ – , × – ⏑ – , × – ⏑ –
οἰφεῖ [ ]

But the proverb can also fit into elegiacs thus (cf. Crusius and Kugéas 1910: 77):

– ⏕, – ⏕, – ⏕, – ⏑ ⏑, – ⏑ ⏑, – –
[ ]ἄριστα <γὰρ> οἰφεῖ
– ⏑ ⏑, – ⏕, – | – ⏑ ⏑, – ⏑ ⏑, –
χωλός [ ]

…or thus (cf. Ercole 1929: 487 n.1):

– ⏕, – ⏕, – ⏕, – ⏑ ⏑, – ⏑ ⏑, – –
[ ] χωλὸς ἄριστα <γὰρ> οἰφεῖ
– ⏕, – ⏕, – | – ⏑ ⏑, – ⏑ ⏑, –
[ ]

…or thus (cf. Gentili 1965: 386):

– ⏕, – ⏕, – ⏕, – ⏑ ⏑, – ⏑ ⏑, – –
[ ]ἄριστα <δὲ> χωλὸς
– –, – ⏕, – | – ⏑ ⏑, – ⏑ ⏑, –
οἰφεῖ [ ]

A reasonable objection against an elegiac reconstruction of the lost fragment, or else an argument defending Mimnermus' iambic production, would be that such an openly obscene proverb is unthinkable in elegy. But fr. 21a only says that Mimnermus 'recalled' – not 'quoted' – the proverb (μέμνηται τῆς παροιμίας Μίμνερμος), and this may well have been done in a very allusive manner; cf. Kassel 1969: 97–98. Indeed, there is one elegiac fragment of the *Nanno* (fr. 9) where the poet does speak of an Amazon (Smyrna) in an allusively pornographic context (cf. pp. 119–20). As for the other three candidates for iambic composition:

- fr. 24 is written in Attic, so it cannot be Mimnermus'. In Stobaeus' citation (Μιμνέρμου *Ναννοῦς*) we should probably correct Μιμνέρμου to Μενάνδρου – the comedian may have composed a play called *Nanno* (p. 114) – if not the entire citation (Μενάνδρου *Φανίου*, suggests Meineke 1841: 217). A very appropriate home for this fragment would be the scene with the fake doctor in Menander's *Aspis* 305 ff., the most extensive surviving scene with a doctor in Greek comedy. At any rate, some author of Middle or New Comedy must be our working hypothesis: "doctors emerge increasingly as central characters in Middle and New Comedy; we know of at least four plays entitled *Iatros* (Philemon, Antiphanes, Aristophon, Theophilus) while in others medical specialists appeared frequently as stock characters"; Kazantzidis 2018: 31.
- fr. 25 is also written in Attic and it comes from a *Neoptolemus*, probably a tragedy, so we have to either postulate a tragedian called Mimnermus (cf. Nauck in fr. adesp. 6a *TrGF*) or, more reasonably, attribute *Neoptolemus* to a known tragedian whose name a copyist misspelled as 'Mimnermus'. I propose the 4th-century-BC tragedian Mamercus and emend Stobaeus' citation accordingly: Μαμέρκου ἐκ *Νεοπτολέμου*. Mamercus is said to have composed "an offensive elegy" (ἐλεγεῖον ὑβριστικὸν ἐπέγραψε, *TrGF* I 87), hence he is doubly suspicious: both his name and his involvement with elegy make him the perfect poet to confuse Mimnermus with.
- fr. 26 must be attributed to Menander, whose name is confused with Mimnermus' at least in one other occasion (p. 114) and whose fr. 249 K-A (ὦ Ζεῦ πολυτίμηθ') constitutes a striking parallel; cf. Fileni 1997.

The hypothesis that Mimnermus wrote iambic poetry should therefore be abandoned for good, unless, of course, ground-breaking evidence comes to light one day. However, what is important to keep in mind, and pertinent to my analysis, is that Mimnermus was *repeatedly and unreservedly* assumed to have composed iambs. Despite the relevant claims proving wrong, they are an index of the *heretical potential* of his elegiac poetry – a potential which misled early scholars into thinking that he wrote iambs.

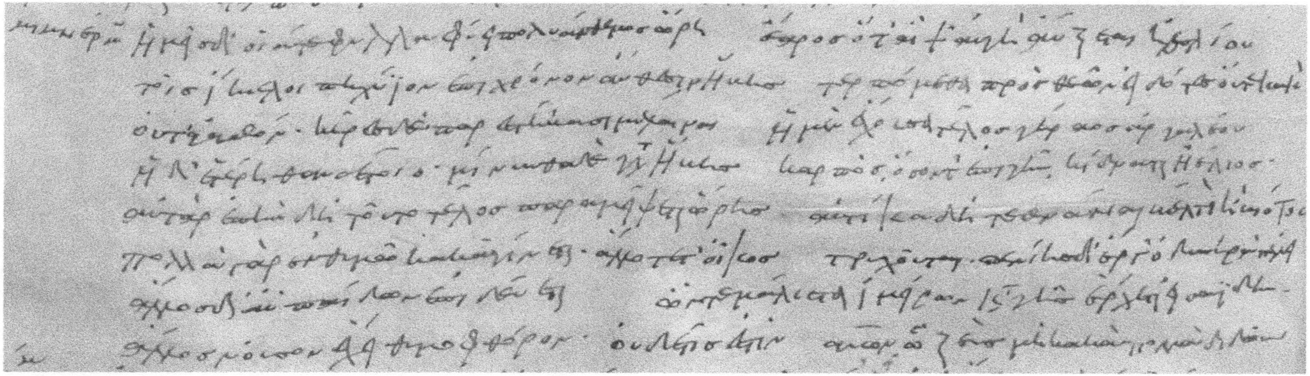

Mimnermus fr. 2, quoted in Stobaeus' Florilegium *in a late 10th-century manuscript (Vienna, Österreichische Nationalbibliothek, phil. gr. 67, 162v). Each elegiac couplet occupies a line – an arrangement which gives the impression of two columns, one for hexameters, one for pentameters. On the left margin: Μιμνέρμου.*

When? Where? – Archaic Smyrna

A historical overview of Archaic Smyrna would fall outside the scope of this literary commentary. However, it is necessary briefly to point out some key political and cultural developments of the 7th century BC which played a crucial role in the shaping of elegy, and whose impact has left a mark on Mimnermus' fragments.

The foremost historical development was the rise by 700 BC of poleis, i.e. of institutionally organised urban communities, which fortified a defensible 'acropolis' in a larger territory which they controlled from that point, and claimed to have divine legitimisation. Already the Homeric epics draw attention, above all, to the question of internal social hierarchies; Ulf 2009: 96. A genre as engaged with contemporary socio-political matters as elegy, whether intended for performance at public festivals or at the symposia of the elite, is unthinkable before and outside **the polis**. Smyrna, Mimnermus' homeland and (by extension) elegy's potential birthplace, is the best investigated early Greek city in Asia Minor and is often considered the archetypal archaic polis. Founded by Aeolian settlers *c.* 1000 BC, Smyrna is by far the earliest city in the post-Mycenaean Greek world to have been walled (*c.* 850 BC). After a disastrous earthquake *c.* 700 BC, the Ionians, who had meanwhile captured Smyrna, redesigned the city according to a rectilinear plan and erected a temple dedicated to Athena, adjacent to the north fortifications. In Mimnermus' day, the temple was renovated (630–610 BC) and now displayed Proto-Ionic features in its architecture, while the fortifications were rebuilt by the end of the century, with an unparalleled, for Greek standards, 15-metre-thick base. However, this was not enough to prevent the success of Alyattes' siege of Smyrna *c.* 600; cf. Cook and Nicholls 1998: xxviii, 85; Mazarakis Ainian and Leventi 2009: 225–26; Crielaard 2009: 351–52, 361, 365. These dramatic changes could not have left our poet uninvolved, and so he composed an entire book-long elegy entitled *Smyrneis* (cf. pp. 21–22). In today's extant corpus, Mimnermus refers to his fellow citizens (frr. 7, 14.2), to Smyrna's Aeolian past and Ionian capture (fr. 9), to the Lydian attacks (of Gyges' day) and to Athena's role as patron of the city (fr. 14).

The developments in monumental architecture are indissolubly linked to the rise of the poleis. A city's institutional (secular and sacred) functions, as well as the urge to display wealth and power in competition with other cities, led to new types of buildings (*stoa, telestêrion, hestiatorion*) and to the extension and standardisation of temples. It is during the 7th century that the Doric and Ionian orders in architecture were formed, the earliest traces coming from Corinth (e.g. the temple of Poseidon at Isthmia) and Naxos (e.g. the temple of Dionysus at Yria) respectively. The Doric Order stands out for its stocky and simple columns, the Ionian for its slender and ornamental ones – Vitruvius compared them to the male and the female body, respectively. However reasonable that gendered comparison might seem, it also reflects the long-standing stereotype of eastern effeminacy. The **Ionian order**, as its name betrays, dominated Ionia – and migrated west in the mid-5th century, hence the Parthenon in Athens combines elements of both orders. But Smyrna's temple of Athena (phase III, 610–600 BC) did not feature typical Ionian column-capitals but Aeolic ones, with two spiral scrolls *and* a palmette rising from between, i.e. an even more flowery version; and the working hypothesis is that those stone capitals had immediate wooden predecessors (phase II, 630–610 BC); cf. Cook and Nicholls 1998: 103; Mazarakis Ainian and Leventi 2009: 220, 228. "It seems likely that the Ionian Aeolic capitals reflect some Near Eastern influence, although a direct prototype cannot be identified" (*Perseus Digital Library* [n.d.], with further bibliography). Whatever their origin, those public decorations were located at the city's most sacred spot and would make a rare attraction in an otherwise humble, we assume based on archaeological evidence, early-archaic landscape. Mimnermus witnessed several such decorations come and go in the various renovations that took place in his apparently long life, so when he compares men to flowers (frr. 1.4, 2.1), he probably draws inspiration not only from Homeric tradition, but also, and perhaps foremost, from his contemporary, tangible, and thus – like men – perishable art.

Art had entered the **Orientalising period** in the late-8th century and now reached its heyday, as particularly seen in pottery. Eastern

Aeolic capital from the Temple of Athena in Old Smyrna, c. 570 BC. Izmir Archaeological Museum.

influences, mostly Hittite, Assyrian, and Egyptian, grafted onto the geometric style (e.g. in Sub-Geometric 'bird bowls' and 'rosette bowls') and eventually overshadowed it. Ornamental motifs, mostly floral (palmettes, lotus blossoms), wild animals (lions, panthers, wild boars, goats, deer, birds) and hybrids (sphinxes, sirens, griffins) progressively dominate and 'break free' from their geometric 'cage'; cf. Cook and Dupont 1998, esp. pp. 29, 51–52, 59–60, 96 on Smyrna. If we had to attribute one adjective to this style, that would be 'exotic'. In Mimnermus, except for the central role of flowers, oriental exoticism is also apparent in the travel narratives of frr. 11+11a and 12, which indeed involve animals and luxurious imagery: Jason travels east to Aea to bring the *golden fleece* back; Helios and his *horses* travel far east each night on a *golden* and *adorned* bed. Apart from floral and bestial elements, or in combination with them, orientalising pots depicted human silhouettes, usually in scenes of fighting, hunting, or participating in some form of ritual; the most famous example is the Proto-Corinthian 'Chigi Vase' (*c.* 640 BC) which offers the earliest representation of the hoplite phalanx formation. In fact, potters at Smyrna drew on Corinthian models (cf. Kerschner 2017: 105–106 and Anderson 1958) and there survive 7th-century pottery fragments from Smyrna with warriors and riders; cf. Cook and Dupont 1998: 29, 31; Paspalas 2017: 114, 119–20. The impressionistic poetic portrayal by Mimnermus of a Smyrnaean warrior (fr. 14) and of Helios' chariot (fr. 12) chime with that iconographic trend; cf. pp. 139–41.

Mimnermus' interest in adventure, exoticism, and ethnic past is above all rooted to the legacy of the so-called **Ionian Migration** (during the 'Dark Age') and its contemporary 'sequel', the so-called Second Greek Colonisation (8th–6th century), the first of which determined, after all, the aforementioned developments in art, through the contact with eastern cultures. But the two migration-waves were fundamentally different, in that the former cannot actually be called a project managed by mother-cities (*metropoleis*), as it comprised independent costal settlements by various (Ionian *and* non-Ionian) ethnic groups, who *fled* their original cities. The mythicisation of those movements as a mass Ionian Migration initiated by Athens is an early-5th-century fabrication (cf. Thuc. 1.12; Paus. 7.2.1–4; Mac Sweeney 2017). The episodic and opportunistic quality of those movements is salient in Mimnermus: Colophon was captured by Pylian emigrants led by a certain Andraemon (fr. 10), and Smyrna by Aeolians and then, at the dawn of the Archaic era, by the Colophonians of Pylian origin (fr. 9). As for the **Second Greek Colonisation**, the most enterprising Ionian city in the 7th century was Miletus, which nearly-monopolised the colonisation of the Propontis and the Black Sea, becoming *metropolis* of Abydos, Olbia, Apollonia Pontica, Histria, Berezan, and many more – see the full table in Tsetskhladze 2006: lxvii–lxxiii. Smyrna did not found any colonies, presumably because the size and productiveness of its territory were sufficient, but ceramic findings suggest that people from Smyrna (and also from Samos, Chios, and Ephesus) did participate in the Milesian colonisation of Histria (657–630 BC) and Berezan (647–630 BC); cf. Tsetskhladze 1998: 36. A hypothesis not put forward so far: fragments 9 and 11+11a may have been composed on the occasion of those departures of Smyrnaeans, to wish them 'Godspeed' (just like Jason and the Pylian-Colophonians received divine aid in their journeys) and warn them to avoid *hubris*.

A natural consequence of the archaic colonisations is that a remarkable number of elegiac, iambic, and melic fragments suggest composition/first performance for an audience other than the poets' homeland – a 'natural consequence' insofar as poets belonged to the elite, i.e. the class who led such enterprises. Among the **wandering poets** Archilochus of Paros stands out: he composed some poems from a Thasian perspective, having settled on Thasos at a young age, and the perspective of a Parian emigré in particular. But Mimnermus is a different story, for he refers to his *ancestors* who migrated from Pylos to Colophon and then to Smyrna (fr. 9), but never to himself leaving home; cf. Bowie 2009: 105–108, 113–14. Of course, all poets travelled on occasion, to participate in festivals and as guests/ symposiasts of their elite friends. It has been proposed, for example, that Solon visited Mimnermus and it was on that occasion that the former sang his fr. 20 in response to the latter's fr. 6 (cf. pp. 106–107). This hypothetical encounter aside, it should be taken for granted that Mimnermus participated (at least) in some Ionian festivals held in, or organised by, other cities.

Already by Homer's day, twelve Ionian city-states (Miletus, Myus, Priene, Ephesus, Colophon, Lebedus, Teos, Clazomenae, Phocaea, Erythrae, Chios and Samos) had formed a religious confederation, the so-called Ionian League, which evolved into a military alliance in the late 6th century. Early in the 7th century, they established on Mt Mycale (opposite Samos) a common sanctuary dedicated to Poseidon Helikonios, the Panionion, where they celebrated the **Panionia festival**. We do not know the frequency of the gathering (cf. Frame 2009: 576) nor the rituals included, but the sacrifice of bulls, the performance of choral songs, and the recounting of each city's founding legends – stories such as that told by Mimnermus in fr. 9 – seem to have been essential elements; cf. Cross 2020, esp. 8, 11. But Smyrna in particular, and Mimnermus by extension, is a curious case. For Herodotus tells us that "the twelve cities [...] agreed among them to allow no other Ionians to use the Panionion, nor did any ask to be admitted, except the Smyrnaeans" (1.143.3). The inference is that Smyrna, an Aeolian settlement in origin, was denied access to the league for some unknown reason – conceivably because the Colophonians had vetoed it. But Smyrna was eventually admitted in the league 'in later times', as Strabo (14.1.4 χρόνῳ δὲ ὕστερον) and Pausanias (7.5.1 χρόνοις ὕστερον) let us know, without providing a specific date. That could be as early as *before* 688 BC, when our first reference to Smyrna as an Ionian city dates (Paus. 5.8.7), or as late as *c.* 300 BC; cf. Frame 2009: 515, 524–28, 541–42. Mimnermus does not refer to Smyrna's entry into the league, but this is far from proving that the entry happened much later. Especially if the aforementioned participation of Smyrnaeans in colonising Histria and Berezan together with Milesians, Samians, Chiots and Ephesians – all Ionian peoples – holds true, it is hard to imagine that Smyrna (in Mimnermus' day) was not already an 'approved' religious ally. We may reasonably imagine fr. 11+11a (Jason's adventure) being addressed to a Panionian audience at a festival for Poseidon, taking into consideration that the Oceanus river (mentioned twice in those few lines) is named after the Titan whom Poseidon came to replace; to put it simply, Mimnermus may be envisioning Jason as a proto-coloniser just as Oceanus is a proto-Poseidon.

As for the annual **Apaturia**, celebrated at nearly all Ionian cities and at Athens (cf. Hdt. 1.147.2), we know for certain that they included contests of boys reciting poetry, at least in the Athens of Solon's day (cf. Pl. *Tim.* 21b). A number of pottery fragments from 6th-century Smyrna depicting dancers, satyrs, maenads, and perhaps a Dionysus (cf. Beazley vases nos 306502, 306503, 306559, 306691) might be evidence of Smyrna celebrating the Apaturia – a festival which had a Dionysiac character by that time, if not a festival especially for Dionysus; cf. Lambert 1993: 146. Well documented is the Smyrnaeans' cult of Dionysus in Roman times, when he was worshiped as Dionysus 'Briseus', but the Lesbian connection of that epithet makes one suspect that the cult dates from Smyrna's Aeolic, prehistoric past; Hasluck 1912–1913: 90. That extreme (i.e. chronologically improbable) possibility aside, it is hard to imagine the Colophonian settlers of Archaic Smyrna *not* celebrating the god who, according to Herodotus, speeded their seizure of the city (cf. pp. 116–17). Be that as it may, Mimnermus does not provide evidence for such celebrations in Smyrna. We may at least suppose that, if Solon's poems were as popular at the *Athenian* Apaturia as Plato claims, then Mimnermus' fr. 6 would probably have been recited on the same occasion as Solon's fr. 20 (cf. pp. 106–107) – yet not by Mimnermus himself, for (even if he was still alive) there is no evidence of competitions open to adult men or to *xenoi*; cf. Bowie 2018b: 40–41.

We thus move on to, and conclude with, the most crucial historical factor in the making of a poet, i.e. his **literary context**. In Mimnermus' case, the key elements of that context were the epic tradition – the Homeric epics were written down perhaps as early as 730 BC (Wilson 2009: 549, 559) or as late as 680 BC (West 2011: 15–19) – and the contemporary poetic developments. The former factor is omnipresent in our poet's work: Homeric loans (phases, themes, and symbols) appear in dense succession, too dense sometimes; cf. p. 144. Conceivably, this is not merely a consequence of Mimnermus being an early poet, i.e. of not having many other predecessors to draw from, but also a consequence of local identity. Of the ancient cities competing for the right to be called Homer's homeland, Smyrna, Colophon, and Chios were already in antiquity considered the strongest candidates, and Mimnermus may be already fighting for Smyrna's candidacy, whether he is defending Homer's true homeland or trying to steal his legacy from another city. Even so, Mimnermus' intention to be original, even anti-Homeric, comes first, as evidenced by his pessimistic appropriation of the leaves simile (cf. pp. 76–77) or the repeated wish to die (cf. fr. 1 n.2). For that reason, hunting 'epicisms' without exploring their reframing is misleading; Suárez de la Torre 1985: 10. On a technical level, the deviation from Homer is dictated by metre; to put it simply, elegiac verse – the pentameter in particular – is conductive to the formal/expressive shrinking, and eventually the semantic undermining, of the epic. The catalyst, however, was the intellectual ferment among the contemporary lyric poets, which Bruno Snell 1953: 44 described thus in his landmark work *The Discovery of the Mind*: "Perhaps the most striking difference between the two genres, as regards the men behind the works, is the emergence of the poets as individuals. As compared with the grave problem of identity which the name of Homer continues to pose, the lyrists announce their own names; they speak about themselves and become recognisable as personalities. The era of lyric poetry is the first to introduce upon the stage of European history a number of highly individual actors, with a great variety of roles; […] their purpose is to make the present significant over and above the *hic et nunc*, to lend an air of permanence to the joy of the moment". It is precisely that joy which I hope to put forward in my reading of Mimnermus, against the longstanding critical negativity – see next section. Of the three poets who "show[ed] the new way of basing personality on the individual existence" (Fränkel 1973: 211), Mimnermus stands closer to Sappho thematically, at least as far as the melancholy of *erôs* and ageing is concerned, but his expressive powers and witty games, let alone his open call *Enjoy yourself!* (fr. 7), align him with Archilochus.

Why? – Reception

Why does Mimnermus merit our attention? And why in our times has "the greatest poet among the elegists" (Murray 1897: 81) failed – to be brutally honest – to receive a prominent place in the (modern) canon, despite his value being theoretically acknowledged by everyone? For example, while an Augustan elegist would wish to become a new Mimnermus more than a new Callimachus (Hor. *Epist*. 2.2.99), the comparative fame of these two poets has evidently been reversed today, if we are to judge from scholarly production, university syllabi, translations on the market, online presence, and so on – as I am writing these lines, Google returns *c*. 86.900 results for 'Mimnermus', ten times fewer than those for 'Callimachus'! How likely is that an undergraduate will be taught more than one or two, if any, Mimnermian fragments? How many people from the educated general public have heard of Mimnermus at all, or have heard more of him than of Sappho or Pindar? These questions are, of course, rhetorical. Part of the explanation for our poet's limited popularity lies in how slim his corpus is; it has not been added to since 1937

(Vogliano papyrus = fr. 13a). But the main reason, I wish to argue, is the long established – if unjust – fixation on a monolithic view of the poet, which makes one instinctively assume that his poetry is not challenging.

'Pessimism' and 'Asianic hedonism' have been deeply anchored in Mimnermus' reception, effectively monopolising his aesthetic evaluation (cf. Jacoby 1918: 283; Pasquali 1923: 297; Bowra 1938: 17, 24; Martinazzoli 1946: 191–14; Snell 1953: 176–77; Garzya 1965: 373; Kirk 1973: 141; de Romilly 1985: 30; Allen 1993: 15 n.25; Theunissen 2000: 158; Perotti 2013: 138 – to only cite one scholarly work per decade since the last century). But this image results from a very narrow reading of a very narrow selection from his very few surviving fragments – a triply biased premise which has become a common assumption. There is no lack of scholars who have pointed out how misleading that image is; "he was more than a languid Ionian singing only of the pleasures of youth and the horrors of old age", warns Campbell 1967: 222, and Miralles 1988: 37 exposes in detail the fallacy of "those who have spoken of hedonism in Mimnermus as if it were the most significant feature of his poetry and, at the same time, a kind of weakness to be excused and certainly alien to classical-Greek taste" (my transl.). The latter scholar also criticised (p. 35) the failure of Mimnermian scholarship of his day – not much has changed since – to catch up with the progress made in the study of other poets. Whereas, for example, the interpretation of Archilochus has been immensely benefitted by Modernist approaches (on the ironical use of lyrical personas, the fluidity of genres, the conception of lyric poems as works-in-progress, and so on), Mimnermus' reception has been stuck, for most part, in a Romantic perspective. This fixation owes much to Bowra's seminal work on the *Early Greek Elegists*, which became the foundation stone for scholarship on the genre until West 1974. Many astute evaluations aside, Bowra's belief that Mimnermus' philosophy "appeals more to the imagination than to the intellect" (1938: 24), let alone the very premise that there is a 'philosophy' behind his poems, constitutes a romantic stance which tells us more about Bowra himself and his time, rather than Mimnermus: "Maurice had discovered in the trenches of the Great War that poetry could literally save a personality from disintegration. It gave clues to a beauty of living, a spirituality, that dignified everyday events. It suggested that life might have a purpose after all"; Mitchell 2009: 93. Of course, it was not Bowra who invented the romantic Mimnermus. By later Antiquity the poet was treated as almost exclusively a love poet obsessed with the fleetingness of youth (Adkins 1985: 94) – a view which was prepared, or rather systematised, by Hellenistic poets, and whose roots may be traced back to Euripides. Here follow the milestones in the history of our poet's reception.

The intertextual links with Mimnermus' oeuvre during the **Archaic and early Classical** era demonstrate his popularity. Despite not being impressively many, those links show that the Smyrnaean elegist was already considered an authority. Semonides (or Simonides) points to Mimnermus – if implicitly – when he says that the Homeric 'men-as-leaves' simile should *not* be used as a motto for quitting life after youth has passed, but rather as a reminder to enjoy life until its very end (cf. pp. 76–77); and Solon openly cites and corrects Mimnermus' views on the ideal age to die (cf. pp. 106–107). Were Mimnermus' poems unpopular or trite, no serious poet would have bothered to counter them. On the contrary, to have fired such critical peer-reviewing, they must have been circulating widely at symposia. At the same time, they offered those peers an opportunity to increase *their own* popularity – in YouTube terms, a 'reaction video' about a 'viral video' has more chances to 'go viral' itself than any other 'reaction video'. There are also some striking thematic and phrasal similarities – too striking to admit as mere analogues – with other poets, e.g. with Tyrtaeus regarding the expression "fenced behind hollow shields" (cf. p. 143), but it is impossible to establish which direction the influence flowed. That is possible only when the poets' (tentative) dates are distant enough: it is obviously Mimnermus who inspires Pindar, rather than vice versa, regarding the 'life-as-dream' metaphor, if we are to assume a direct relationship (cf. p. 102).

The ***Theognidea***, a collection of divergent elegiac fragments attributed to Theognis of Megara, incorporated both authentic Mimnermian verses (795–6 = Mimn. fr. 7; 1017–22 = Mimn. fr. 5.1–6) and pieces which 'responded' to Mimnermus (e.g. 797–8, cf. pp. 112–13) or imitated his style (cf. *Appendix III*). While we do not know at which stage of the development of the collection each of those passages slipped in, i.e. whether it was Theognis himself or a nearly contemporary poet or a much later anthologist who deemed those verses appropriate for inclusion, I wish to argue that Mimnermus was already employed by 'Theognis' at an early stage. First, the existence of verbal variations between the Theognidean and the other versions of frr. 5.4–6 (in Stobaeus) and 7 (in the *Palatine Anthology*) suggest that orality, i.e. sympotic reuse, was still at play in the transmission of those poems, although those variations are not so great as to exclude their partial emergence in the course of written transmission. Whereas symposia never ceased to take place in Classical Athens, as the continuing production of sympotic pottery and literary evidence demonstrate, the decline of the symposium "may be symbolised in the death of the last great sympotic poet, Pindar, around 446 BC [...] There was a brief revival in the late 5th century with the rise of 'laconism' (the cult of Sparta) as a cultural fashion among the elite and the development of *hetaireiai* as oligarchic terrorist groups [... but] by the mid-Hellenistic period even the rituals of the symposium were largely forgotten"; Murray 2009: 522. Of course, this historical frame only provides a very general guide for hypothesising that frr. 5.1–6 and 7 passed into the *Theognidea* before Hellenistic times, and Emiliani 2021: 119–20 is right to warn us that oral reworkings may well have affected the Stobaean transmission too. For safer and more chronologically-specific evidence, we should shift focus onto the old core of the *Theognidea*, i.e. the passages addressing Cyrnus, which are conventionally considered to be Theognis' original corpus. Indeed, there we find traces of Mimnermian influence: verses 60 (οὔτε κακῶν γνώμας εἰδότες οὔτ' ἀγαθῶν, "knowing neither the opinion of the base nor of the noble"), 1114 (οὔτ' ἀγαθῶν μνήμην εἰδότες οὔτε κακῶν, same meaning), 135–6...141 (οὐδέ τις ἀνθρώπων ἐργάζεται ἐν φρεσὶν εἰδὼς | ἐς τέλος εἴτ' ἀγαθὸν γίνεται εἴτε κακόν | ...εἰδότες οὐδέν, "Nobody knows deep inside his heart whether his toil will end up well or badly ... for we know nothing"), 320 (τολμᾷ δ' ἔν τε κακοῖς κείμενος ἔν τ' ἀγαθοῖς, "he endures whether his situation is bad or good") betray a fixation to the 'either good or bad' motif, which is characteristically – and uniquely, when combined with εἰδότες – Mimnermian; cf. Mimn. fr. 2.4–5 εἰδότες οὔτε κακὸν οὔτ' ἀγαθόν. Moreover, the only surviving parallel/precedent for Theognis' ὑβριστήν…ἡγεμόνα ("impudent leader" vv. 1080–1) is Mimnermus' ὕβριος ἡγεμόνες ("leaders of impudence" fr. 9.4). [There is also Solon fr. 4.7–8 ἡγεμόνων…ὕβριος, but the two terms are not syntactically related there.] Apparently, Theognis himself started including his Smyrnaean colleague in his repertoire, and thus he gave the 'green light' to subsequent poets and editors of the *Theognidea* to do the same. It must be noted that none of the above-mentioned Mimnermian-esque lines by Theognis is used in an erotic context, but in discussing socio-political, financial, and philosophical/theological matters.

The crucial shift is first noticed in **Euripides**, who uses Mimnermus in a way that already betrays a narrowing-down of the elegist's reputation to that of an erotic poet concerned with the miseries of old age. A general comment in *Bacchae* about the gifts of Aphrodite being conditional (cf. p. 65), another comment in *Hercules* about old age hanging over our heads (cf. pp. 97–98), and a retelling in *Medea* of Jason's expedition to Colchis from the perspective of the enamoured heroine (cf. p. 124) are all that survive to testify the tragedian's debt to Mimnermus – few references indeed, but suspiciously consistent with the image which our elegist ended up having! This is not to say that Euripides consciously and methodically took the interpretation of the Smyrnaean poet in a certain direction which he liked – nor can we preclude this possibility either, given the tragedian's fixation with ἔλεγος (cf. p. 3) – but that *what survived* of Euripides and reached the Hellenistic poets was consistent enough to help/inspire them to rebrand Mimnermus towards that direction.

The **Hellenistic** era was the heyday of our poet's distorted fame. It has been hypothesised (De Marco 1939–1940: 336; West 1974: 75; Cameron 1995: 312; Sbardella 2018) that the pre-Alexandrian elegist Antimachus of Colophon (fl. *c.* 400 BC) was the person who compiled *Nanno* in an attempt to prepare/legitimise his own *Lyde*, an elegy filled with sad stories of ill-fated heroines in memory of his Lydian mistress or wife; cf. Hermesianax fr. 7.40–6 Powell; Matthews 1995: 26–39. Having proudly claimed that Homer was from Colophon (fr. 166 Matthews), Antimachus would not have hesitated also to present Mimnermus as a compatriot and a poetic precursor. An epigram by Posidippus of Pella (*AP* 12.168.1–2) proves that the enterprise had met with success already by the 3rd century BC: Νανvοῦς καὶ Λύδης…†φιλεράστου† Μιμνέρμου καὶ τοῦ σώφρονος Ἀντιμάχου ("Nanno and Lyde…of passionate Mimnermus and of chaste Antimachus [respectively]"). Hermesianax went a step further than Antimachus, his interest being no less personal; he claimed Mimnermus as the inventor of elegy altogether (p. 7), for he needed not only an archaic precedent for his three-book *Leontion*, named after his girlfriend (Ath. 13.597a), but also a lure to advertise his 'school' of Colophonian elegy (p. 19; cf. Spanoudakis 2001: 225–30). Theocritus too demonstrated his confident and self-referential engagement with the archaic poet. He introduced in a single *Idyll* two Mimnermian echoes: one 'faithful' imitation concerning the fleetingness of youth (*Id.* 27.8), which functions as a pointer to the archaic source; and then, a few verses later, a pornographic appropriation of the exhortation 'enjoy yourself' (*Id.* 27.13–14), to mark the passing from elegy, which is allusively sexual at best, to bucolic poetry – but still, the underlying assumption is that Mimnermus was an erotic poet (cf. pp. 102, 112–13). On Callimachus' programmatic appreciation of *Nanno*, see p. 23.

Thanks to Callimachus' contribution and Catullus' mediation – the latter probably owes the motif 'eternal sun *vs* ephemeral man' to the archaic elegist (p. 132) – Mimnermus' fame grew even greater during the **Imperial era**. "How much of Mimnermus' poetry was readily available at Rome is not easy to guess […but] no extensive knowledge of Mimnermus' poetry is necessarily assumed […in what survives.] He is a great (and perhaps shadowy) figure, made well known by (a single passage of) Callimachus, and of whom (perhaps) a few famous passages were familiar"; Hunter 2013a: 342. Ironically, Callimachus' agenda backfired on him on occasions; Propertius, despite proclaiming himself "the Roman Callimachus" in trying to link his own aetiological/antiquarian elegy to the successful model of Callimachus' *Aetia* (4.1.64), totally ignores his Greek alter-ego when he pronounces "when it comes to love, Mimnermus' verses outdo those of Homer, for calm Love requires gentle songs" (*plus in amore valet Mimnermi versus Homero:| carmina mansuetus lenia quaerit Amor*, 1.9.11–12). Some 5–10 years later, Horace seems to be mocking Propertius' opportunistic invoking of Greek precursors, and reveals that Callimachus actually came second to Mimnermus in the Augustan elegist's preference. Envisaging a contest between himself and Propertius, Horace says: "For him I am an Alcaeus [i.e. a lyric poet]. Then who is he for me? What else but a Callimachus! If he aspires to more, he becomes a Mimnermus and earns a greater surname" (*discedo Alcaeus puncto illius; ille meo quis? | quis nisi Callimachus? si plus adposcere visus, | fit Mimnermus et optivo cognomine crescit*. *Epist*. 2.2.99–101). If Horace appears ironical, he is so against Propertius, not against Mimnermus; and the fact that in *Ars Poetica* (73–82) he avoids naming a specific Greek author as master of the genre (whereas for epic and iambus he picks out Homer and Archilochus respectively) is not a sign of disdain for the Smyrnaean poet, but a sincere declaration of neutrality in a debate which was still open: "yet who first put forth humble elegiacs, scholars dispute, and the case is still before the court" (77–8 *quis tamen exiguos elegos emiserit auctor, | grammatici certant et adhuc sub iudice lis est*). After all, Horace himself resorts to Mimnermus (cf. p. 63) no less than Propertius, who in drawing the above-mentioned comparison with Homer may be thinking of Mimn. fr. 1.1, suggests Hunter 2013a: 343. Regardless of which genre or style each Roman poet promoted, they all saw in Mimnermus a precursor of hedonism. A century later, Plutarch says that Mimn. fr. 1.1–2 had become a motto of the dissolute people (ἀκολάστων φωναί) in defence of their lifestyle (*De virt. mor*. 455f); such mottos were indeed voiced by Horace (*Epist*. 1.6.65) and by Propertius, who had programmatically declared himself a victim of *Amor improbus* (1.1.4–6). It is unlikely, of course, that Plutarch has any Roman poet in mind on this occasion, but if he does, Horace is the only Roman poet the biographer ever cites in his works (Wet 1988: 22). As for Ovid, "the complete absence of explicit reference to archaic elegists [...] in a poet as conscious of literary history" is striking, while "it is not difficult to see what an Ovid would make" of Mimnermus' 'secret lovemaking' (fr. 1.2); Hunter 2013a: 341, 344. But Ovid's silence is far from inexplicable: aspiring to more serious themes than erotic elegy (Wilkinson 1956: 233) and assuming that *all* past poetry was essentially about love (cf. *Tr*. 2.361–408), he had to avoid the erotic elegist *par excellence*. Instead, he fashioned himself as a Callimachus who is ready to refute his critics and become world-famous (*Am*. 1.15.7–18); Hunter 2012: 162–63. [I have already mentioned the 1st-century-AD inscription which records a gymnasium in Smyrna called Μιμνερμεῖον (p. 18) and the Roman grammarian Porphyrio who spoke of Mimnermus' two most circulated books (p. 14).]

Unlike the canon of the nine lyric poets – 'lyric' in the narrow sense, i.e. those who composed songs (either monodic or choral) for performance accompanied by the lyre – no established **canon of elegists**, i.e. a standard list, existed in the Hellenistic and early Imperial period. Farrell 2012: 14–15 speaks of a 'proto-canon' introduced by Hermesianax, who brought together three lovestruck elegists (Mimnermus, Antimachus, and Philitas: fr. 7.35–7, 41–6, 75–7 Powell), thus offering a capsule-history of Greek love elegy and consigning all other forms of early elegy to oblivion; but Hermesianax was more interested in advertising a local tradition, rather than advocating a philological canon (p. 19). Similarly, Didymus' aforementioned testimony on the possible inventor of the genre (p. 1) does not presuppose *or* introduce a canon. Finally, when Quintilian says that "in elegy ... Callimachus is regarded as the best, the second place being occupied by Philitas according to the verdict of most critics" (*Inst*. 10.1.58–9: *elegiam ... cuius princeps habetur Callimachus, secundas confessione plurimorum Philetas occupavit*), he simply wants to clarify who is the most prominent, not to give a full catalogue of representatives or to pursue *damnatio memoriae* for Archaic elegists altogether (10.1.57–8: *Nec ignoro igitur quos transeo nec utique damno*, "and, certainly, I neither ignore nor condemn them"). Then what is our earliest sign of a canon for Greek elegy?

The Bobbio Scholiast, in the 7th century AD, records that "Callinus seems to have been the first to write an elegiac poem. Aristotle adds besides as poets of this kind Antimachus of Colophon, Archilochus of Paros, Mimnermus of Colophon, to whom Solon is also added, the distinguished Athenian lawgiver" (*Primus autem videtur elegiacum carmen scripsisse Callinus. Adiicit Aristoteles praeterea hoc genus poetas Antimachum Colophonium, Archilochum Parium, Mimnermum Colophonium, quorum numero additur etiam Solon Atheniensium legum scriptor nobilissimus*, Arist. fr. 937 Bekker-Gigon). Janko 1987: 65 includes this testimony "only by conjecture" (xxiii) in his reconstruction of Aristotle's early dialogue *On Poets*, but it is almost certain that the Bobbio Scholiast referred to a much later, pseudo-Aristotelian treatise, for no testimonia on Aristotle's own *On Poets* survive later than the 4th century AD; cf. Bekker and Gigon 1987: 263–67.

So the 'patent' of the elegiac canon has to be awarded to our next source, i.e. Proclus' *Chrestomathy* (5th century AD) as summarised in Photius' *Library* (9th century AD): "And Proclus says that Callinus the Ephesian and Mimnermus the Colophonian, but also Philitas of Cos, son of Telephus, and Callimachus, son of Battus, distinguished themselves in metre" (λέγει δὲ [*sc*. Πρόκλος] καὶ ἀριστεῦσαι τῷ μέτρῳ Καλλῖνόν τε τὸν Ἐφέσιον καὶ Μίμνερμον τὸν Κολοφώνιον, ἀλλὰ καὶ τὸν τοῦ Τηλέφου Φιλίταν τὸν Κῷον καὶ Καλλίμαχον τὸν Βάττου, Procl. *Chr.* 24 Severyns). Proclus' list anticipated the Byzantine canon, which is multiply attested in the condensed form ἐλεγείων ποιηταί· Καλλῖνος, Μίμνερμος, Φιλητᾶς, Καλλίμαχος (cf. Krohnert 1897:6, 13, 30). Johannes Tzetzes, 12th century AD, only listed Καλλίμαχος, Μίμνερμος, Φιλητᾶς (*Schol. ad Lycoph. Alex*. intr. 75), but rather ironically this may be our sole accurate record of the original canon, for a tripartite list is more likely than a quadripartite, and also 'Callinus' sounds suspicious; his name could have slipped in by pure luck, as it resembles 'Callimachus' and thus allows a memorable ring-composition. Conceivably, it was the ongoing debate on Callinus' potential inventorship of elegy (cf. Didymus in p. 1 and the Bobbio Scholiast above) that made Photius, or his sources, assume that Proclus too must have had Callinus in his account. At any rate, Mimnermus always features in the canon and "the fact that Mimnermus and Philitas are placed side by side […] may be due to the influence of Callimachus"; Spanoudakis 2002: 45.

Nearly half of Mimnermus' extant fragments survived thanks to **Joannes Stobaeus** of Macedonia, fl. 5th C AD, who compiled and arranged in thematic categories gnomological extracts from more than 500 Greek poets and prose-writers (from Homer to the 4th-century-AD philosopher and rhetorician Themistius), in creating a moral and practical guidebook for his son. To that anthology, initially published in two halves (*Eclogues* and *Florilegium*), we owe thousands of otherwise unknown fragments and, not surprisingly for a book of maxims, Euripides and Menander take the lion's share, with over 500 and 200 quotations respectively. Of the lyric (in the wider sense) poets, those quoted more often are Theognis, Pindar, Bacchylides and Archilochus; cf. Bowie 2010b: Appendix; Campbell 1984: 51–52. Judging from the varied length of his quotations, Stobaeus must have had both complete texts and earlier anthologies of maxims at hand. In Mimnermus' case, because three of his quoted fragments are specified as coming from *Nanno* (frr. 4, 5, 8) while the rest are generically labeled "by Mimnermus", it may be hypothesised that Stobaeus started with consulting an existing collection which named authors *but not works* and then, when he realised the value of Mimnermus, he resorted to a more detailed edition which had pieces explicitly taken from *Nanno*; Bowie 2010b: 588, 597. Mimnermus appears in Stobaeus' following themes/chapters: 'On Aphrodite' (fr. 1), 'On life' (fr. 2), 'Censure for old age' (frr. 3, 4, 5), 'On truth' (fr. 8) and 'On valour' (fr. 14) – the numbers themselves suggest a 'classic' status for this poet on the subject of old age; Hunter 2008: 339.

The first Mimnermian piece to appear in print upon the **invention of typography** was fr. 7 (= *AP* 9.50) in the *editio princeps* of the *Planudean Anthology* (Lascaris 1494). The following year came the *editio princeps* of Theognis, under whose name Mimn. fr. 7 (=Thgn. 795–6) and fr. 5.1–6 (=Thgn. 1017–22) were published (Aldine ed. 1495). Then were published the *editiones principes* of the *Etymologicum Magnum* which preserves frr. 15+16 (Musurus 1499), of Athenaeus who preserves fr. 12 (Musurus 1514), of Strabo who preserves frr. 9 and 11+11a (Aldine ed. 1516), of Diogenes Laertius who preserves fr. 6 (Froben ed. 1533), while our richest source for Mimnermus, i.e. Stobaeus who preserves frr. 1–5, 8 and 14, was published last (Trincavelius 1536). Up to then, Mimnermus' lines were published scattered in the corpora of other authors. The first book to compile (some of) his fragments, thus creating the first corpus under his name, was Turnebus 1553: 14–15 (= frr. 2, 5, and 3), followed by Hertel 1561: 186–91 (= frr. 1–5, 14, and some misattributed pieces). But the first **individual edition** of Mimnermus, which contained all known fragments, came as late as 1826, by German philologist Nicolaus Bach. He dedicated his book *in salutem Graecorum pro patria pugnantium* ("to the salvation of the Greeks fighting for their country" [at the Greek War of Independence, 1821–1830]). The reasoning, however, was not that he saw in Mimnermus a heroic poet capable of inspiring the revolting Greeks (which he could have done in view of fr. 14 [= fr. 13 in his numbering]), but that the archaic elegist was *uno ex antiquissimis Graecorum poetis* ("one of the most ancient Greek poets"), hence an appropriate gift to the Greek soul, which once fought at Marathon, Thermopylae, and Salamis (Bach 1826: vii). Mimnermus, therefore, offered a symbol of national continuity – not of fighting *per se*. Indeed, Bach concludes his dedication by quoting Tyrtaeus' fr. 10.13–6 (θυμῷ γῆς περὶ τῆσδε μαχώμεθα… "let's defend this land with our soul…"), as if Mimnermus had not composed any patriotic lines. Of course, in doing so, Bach only perpetuates the centuries-old prejudice that Mimnermus was essentially an erotic poet – a romantic poet who now needed 'a crutch' in order to serve the Romantic Nationalism of the day.

Yet a study of the **Romantics' reception** of Mimnermus is notably, and rather surprisingly, missing. It will suffice, however, for our general scope here to only mention two illustrative cases – the two most striking, i.e. those that most openly engage with Mimnermus. The English author and republican activist Walter Savage Landor (1775–1864) wrote the epistolary novel *Pericles and Aspasia*, "his mighty masterpiece" according to Swinburne in the *Encyclopaedia Britannica.* In one of the imaginary letters included there, the fictional Aspasia tells her friend Cleone that she finds Mimnermus *the least tender* – keep this adjective in mind – of the amatory poets, whose verses are graceless and can, at best, make the reader either smile awkwardly or look grave. Cleone agrees; she responds that effrontery characterises most of Mimnermus' poems and that "he is among the many poets who never make us laugh or weep. […] The earth swarms with these; they live their season, and others similar come into life the next. I have been reading works widely different from theirs; the Odes of the lovely Lesbian." Yet Aspasia takes the opportunity to quote one 'Mimnermian' poem which she deems to be – and Cleone agrees on that – just acceptable. Only this poem is a purely Landorian invention, drawing on actual Mimnermus very loosely and only in its closing lines (Landor 1836: 85–87):

In the first hour of ripeness fall
the tender creatures, one and all.
To take what falls with even mind
Jove [=Zeus] *wills, and we must be resign'd.*

The question how to read this exchange between Aspasia and Cleone seems quite perplexing: is the purpose to truly criticise Mimnermus, or to pretentiously undermine him so that Landor's pseudo-Mimnermian poem (i.e. a fictional discovery) stands out? Or, perhaps, to simply bring forward the Sapphic/Lesbian preference of his heroines? The answer, I believe, is to be sought in the main theorist of early Romanticism and advocator of Republican politics Friedrich Schlegel, who had posed the rhetorical question "Who does not see the rage of Archilochus, the *tenderness* [Zärtlichkeit] of Mimnermus, the ardour of Sappho and the love-frenzy of Ibycus?" (Schlegel 1798: 224). By denying the very quality which Schlegel had singled out in Mimnermus, Landor invites his well read readers to perceive his ironic stance towards his heroines' statements. After all, when Cleone asserts that poets like Mimnermus "live their season, and others similar come into life the next", she has essentially surrendered to the classical influence of the poet whom she disdains!

The second most striking case of our poet's influence in the Victorian era is the poem 'Mimnermus in Church' (1858) by the English educator and poet William Johnson Cory (1823–1892). Cory was an Eton College master, indeed "the most brilliant Eton tutor of his day" according to historian G. W. Prothero 1888: 130, but was forced to resign in 1872 because "he was dangerously fond of a number of boys" (Card 2004). He published two collections of homoerotic verse called *Ionica* (1858) and *Ionica II* (1877), later collated in a single edition (1891). Cory has less verve and energy than Landor, whom he resembles, but his 'Mimnermus in Church' (from the first *Ionica*) stands out for treating an essentially modern subject in the classical style (Walker 1910: 598). The poem reads:

You promise heavens free from strife,
Pure truth, and perfect change of will;
But sweet, sweet is this human life,
So sweet, I fain would breathe it still;
Your chilly stars I can forgo,
This warm kind world is all I know.

You say there is no substance here,
One great reality above:
Back from that void I shrink in fear,
And child-like hide myself in love:
Show me what angels feel. Till then
I cling, a mere weak man, to men.

You bid me lift my mean desires
From faltering lips and fitful veins
To sexless souls, ideal quires,
Unwearied voices, wordless strains:
My mind with fonder welcome owns
One dear dead friend's remember'd tones.

Forsooth the present we must give
To that which cannot pass away;
All beauteous things for which we live
By laws of time and space decay.
But O, the very reason why
I clasp them, is because they die.

Cory's poem is "agnostic about an afterlife" (Vance 1985: 187), in that "we have here a picture of a young man, a young English scholar, listening in Church to Christian teaching, but answering that teaching with the thought of the old Greeks" (Hearn 1917: 354). As the "odd title" betrays, Cory "seems to bring the old Greek fatalist to modern England and to conduct him to church upon a Sunday morning. But Mimnermus is impenitent. He confesses that the preacher is right when he says that all earthly pleasures are fugitive [...and] it was *because* they were fugitive that he clung to them"; Gosse 1891: 314–15. As for the exclusively homoerotic use of Mimnermus in the poem, I suspect that Cory reflects, other than his personal interests, the philological zeal of his day to retrieve Mimnermus out of Theognis (cf. p. 158).

As far as the **Modern Greek** reception of Mimnermus is concerned, I shall only offer a single notable case here and promise a detailed study in the near future. The most distinguished Greek poet, who was nevertheless more familiar with English poetry than with Greek, Constantine Cavafy (1863–1933) echoes Mimnermus – "no doubt unwittingly" according to Ricks 1989: 87 – in his repudiated poem of *c*. 1884 'Ελεγεία των λουλουδιών' ('Elegy of the flowers'). The initial title was Οἵαπερ φύλλων Γενεὴ, which is a misspelled borrowing from Homer (*Il*. 6.146 οἵη περ φύλλων γενεή, 'Similar to the generations of the leaves') – i.e. the very Homeric passage which Mimnermus subverts in fr. 2. Like Mimnermus, and unlike Homer, Cavafy sees a pessimistic symbol in the leaves. I only quote the first two stanzas:

Όσα λουλούδια υπάρχουν, το καλοκαίρι ανθίζουν
Κι' απ' όλα τα λουλούδια του κάμπου φαίνεται
η νεότης πιο ωραία. Αλλά μαραίνεται
γρήγορα, και σαν πάει δεν ξαναγένεται·
η πασχαλι[αίς] με της δροσιάς τα δάκρυα την ραντίζουν.

Όσα λουλούδια υπάρχουν, το καλοκαίρι ανθίζουν.
Αλλά τα ίδια μάτια δεν τα κυττάζουνε.
Και άλλα χέρια σ' άλλα στήθεια τα βάζουνε.
Έρχοντ' οι ίδιοι μήνες, πλην ξένοι μοιάζουνε·
τα πρόσωπα αλλάξαν και δεν τ' αναγνωρίζουν.

The loveliest flowers blossom in the spring.
And youth seems lovelier than all the flowers
of the field. But it withers early
and once it goes, it does not come again;
jasmine sprinkles it with the tears of dew.

The loveliest flowers blossom in the summer.
But the same eyes do not look at them.
And other hands place them on other breasts.
The same months come, but they look different;
the faces have changed and they do not recognise them.

(transl. R. Dalven)

Unlike Cory, Cavafy has not yet 'come out of the closet': his openly homoerotic poems date after 1915. However, while he has been anxiously hiding throughout his 'first period', even there can we trace the discourse of repression and silence, which *ipso facto* brings forth a 'semi-hidden' gay poet; cf. Papanikolaou 2005. Erotic failure *is* present in Cavafy's poem: the 'other' eyes, hands, and breasts which enjoy the 'flowers of youth' in the second stanza clearly mark a sexual anatomy; they belong to the successful lover whom the poet envies and craves for. But is that description specifically *homo*-erotic at all? I believe it is, because, Cavafy's influence from English Aestheticism's fixation on flowers aside (cf. Jeffreys 2015: 74), the very following line (Έρχοντ' οι ίδιοι μήνες, πλην ξένοι μοιάζουνε) may be read as "The same months come, but they look different" (transl. Dalven) but also "Similar months come, but they look *distant*". Cavafy could have used a female noun such as εποχές, 'seasons', εβδομάδες, 'weeks', ημέρες, 'days', or χρονιές, 'years', but opts for the masculine noun μήνες – the months are indeed males by name, and their names are indeed similar (Ιανουάριος, Φεβρουάριος etc.); they are all men who come and go, in a similar pattern of rejection. In support of this gendered reading of μήνες, note that some of Cavafy's openly homosexual 'Days'-titled poems rework earlier ('closeted') versions which were titled as months (e.g. the 1917 poem 'Μέρες του 1903' reworks the 1909 draft 'Μάρτιος του 1907'; cf. Papanikolaou 2014: 223–28).

Other notable Modern Greek receptions of Mimnermus in the area of literature are Odysseas Elytis' 1943 critical text 'Ποιητική νοημοσύνη' (cf. Dallas 2011: 171, 176), George Geralis' 1957 poem 'Δειλινό στο λόφο' (cf. Frouzakis 2011: 49, 124), and Nikos Gabriel Pentzikis' short story 'Θεσσαλονίκη και ζωή' from *Μητέρα Θεσσαλονίκη* 1970: 63 (cf. Paspalakis 2018: 24, 99–102).

A major event in the modern reception of Mimnermus has been his first **setting to music** in the contemporary world. Fragments 1 and 2 have been wonderfully scored for soprano and piano by Italian pianist and composer Fabio Grasso in his 2005 piece 'Due Liriche di Mimnermo' (available at www.rosenfinger.com/cvs01.htm#mimn). Grasso, who has studied both music and classical philology, is currently preparing an album with all his compositions drawing on Greek poets (Mimnermus, Sappho, Alcman, Callimachus and others), with the vocal pieces using the original text.

To conclude, Bowra's image of Mimnermus, the dominant image to date with which I began my review, is only a natural follow-up in this 'chain' of receptions. A heady cocktail of appreciation but also misrepresentation and/or under-representation (even when the recipient has a positive stance towards the archaic poet) has narrowed, if not lowered, our horizon of expectations. Fragments 2 and 1 – in this order – have essentially monopolised the attention of all generations since the Classical era, as if the survival of only 17 fragments is not sufficiently unfortunate. Mimnermus' heroic content was already ignored from a very early stage, and therefore was lost almost entirely. His amatory content has been seen as exclusively focussed on women and rarely (and somewhat embarrassingly) as addressed to boys, and strictly perceived in romantic terms. A poet who was once believed to have composed iambs and to have revelled in *kômoi*, Mimnermus ended up being a synonym of depression, an opposite pole to Archilochus – a dichotomy already apparent in Hellenistic times; cf. Hunter 2008: 556. My commentary aims at unveiling that very Archilochean spirit and technique of Mimnermian poetry: a poetry much wittier, sexier, more experimental, and more self-conscious than our iconolatry towards the 'scattering leaves' and the 'gifts of Aphrodite' allows us to see. Even these thematically pessimistic moments are manifestos of ambitious and playful poetics.

MIMNERMUS

ELEGIES

TEXT AND TRANSLATION

Note on the text

Only the surviving elegiac fragments are included here, while the *sine versibus* testimonia (frr. 10, 13, 18–23) are reserved for *Appendix II*, and the dubious iambic fragments (frr. 24–26) are discussed in the *Introduction*. I follow Martin West's numbering and text (*Iambi et elegi graeci*, Oxford 1992^{2}), with *iota subscript* instead of *adscript* and with the following deviations:

fr.	West prints	I print
4.2	< >	<ὁ Ζεὺς> (Gesner)
9.1	Αἰπὺ < >	αἰπεῖάν (Hiller)
9.5	†διαστήεντος	δ' Ἀλήεντος (Brunck)
12.6	ἐληλαμένη,	ἐληλαμένη

Note on the translation

Given that no translation can perfectly render a literary work, especially poetry, a translator's task is essentially one of establishing priorities. Here, considering the series' scope and intended audience, I have tried to stay as close as possible to the grammar and syntax of the original text, where this is possible in English (a language much less flexible than Greek in word order), and, secondarily, to cater for some striking stylistic and rhythmical features, such as enjambments and internal pauses. Readers are advised also to consult more poetic translations, e.g. the rhyming gems collected by Bowra 1938: 18, 20, 26 (= fr. 1 by G. Lowes Dickinson; fr. 2 by J. A. Pott; fr. 12 by G. Murray). It should also go without saying – yet an undergraduate may not fully appreciate – that translations are the product of, and a means for *interpreting* a poem, rather than an impartial take on the original text. In the commentary, the translations of passages of other authors are either mine or taken from the Loeb series, unless otherwise indicated.

F1 Source: Stob. 4.20.16 (περὶ Ἀφροδίτης)

τίς δὲ βίος, τί δὲ τερπνὸν ἄτερ χρυσῆς Ἀφροδίτης;
  τεθναίην, ὅτε μοι μηκέτι ταῦτα μέλοι,
κρυπταδίη φιλότης καὶ μείλιχα δῶρα καὶ εὐνή,
  οἷ' ἥβης ἄνθεα γίνεται ἁρπαλέα
ἀνδράσιν ἠδὲ γυναιξίν· ἐπεὶ δ' ὀδυνηρὸν ἐπέλθῃ
  γῆρας, ὅ τ' αἰσχρὸν ὁμῶς καὶ κακὸν ἄνδρα τιθεῖ,
αἰεί μιν φρένας ἀμφὶ κακαὶ τείρουσι μέριμναι,
  οὐδ' αὐγὰς προσορῶν τέρπεται ἠελίου,
ἀλλ' ἐχθρὸς μὲν παισίν, ἀτίμαστος δὲ γυναιξίν·
  οὕτως ἀργαλέον γῆρας ἔθηκε θεός.

F2 Source: Stob. 4.34.12 (περὶ τοῦ βίου)

ἡμεῖς δ', οἷά τε φύλλα φύει πολυάνθεμος ὥρη
  ἔαρος, ὅτ' αἶψ' αὐγῇς αὔξεται ἠελίου,
τοῖς ἴκελοι πήχυιον ἐπὶ χρόνον ἄνθεσιν ἥβης
  τερπόμεθα, πρὸς θεῶν εἰδότες οὔτε κακὸν
οὔτ' ἀγαθόν· Κῆρες δὲ παρεστήκασι μέλαιναι,
  ἡ μὲν ἔχουσα τέλος γήραος ἀργαλέου,
ἡ δ' ἑτέρη θανάτοιο· μίνυνθα δὲ γίνεται ἥβης
  καρπός, ὅσον τ' ἐπὶ γῆν κίδναται ἠέλιος.
αὐτὰρ ἐπὴν δὴ τοῦτο τέλος παραμείψεται ὥρης,
  αὐτίκα δὴ τεθνάναι βέλτιον ἢ βίοτος·
πολλὰ γὰρ ἐν θυμῷ κακὰ γίνεται· ἄλλοτε οἶκος
  τρυχοῦται, πενίης δ' ἔργ' ὀδυνηρὰ πέλει·
ἄλλος δ' αὖ παίδων ἐπιδεύεται, ὧν τε μάλιστα
  ἱμείρων κατὰ γῆς ἔρχεται εἰς Ἀΐδην·
ἄλλος νοῦσον ἔχει θυμοφθόρον· οὐδέ τίς ἐστιν
  ἀνθρώπων ᾧ Ζεὺς μὴ κακὰ πολλὰ διδοῖ.

F3 Source: Stob. 4.50.32 (ψόγος γήρως)

τὸ πρὶν ἐὼν κάλλιστος, ἐπὴν παραμείψεται ὥρη,
  οὐδὲ πατὴρ παισὶν τίμιος οὔτε φίλος.

F1 From Stobaeus' *Florilegium* (on Aphrodite)

So what life, what enjoyment exists without golden Aphrodite?
I wish to die when I will no longer mind these things:
secret lovemaking and kind gifts and the bed –
things which are youth's charmful flowers
for both men and women. But whenever painful old age
is about to attack, making a man miserable and ugly,
then ugly concerns always beset his mind:
he doesn't even enjoy watching the sunlight
but is hated by boys and depreciated by women.
So harmful did god make old age!

F2 From Stobaeus' *Florilegium* (on life)

For we, like the leaves which the much-blossoming season
of spring produces and which grow quickly beneath the sunlight –
similar to them, for only a brief span do we enjoy ourselves
with the flowers of youth, knowing neither evil nor good
from the gods. But the Fates stand beside in black,
one bearing the destiny of painful old age
and the other, of death. Youth's fruit is short-lived,
as short as it takes for the sun to pass over the earth.
Once the effect of this season has passed by,
straightway to die is better than living.
For many miseries ensue in the heart: sometimes one's
household is ruined and the lamentable results of poverty appear;
another in turn has no children and, still yearning
for them so much, he passes under the earth to Hades;
another has a mind-wasting disease. There is no one
among men to whom Zeus does not give multiple troubles.

F3 From Stobaeus' *Florilegium* (censure for old age)

After one's prime passes, no matter how gorgeous he was before,
he's neither respected nor loved – not even a father
by his own children!

F4 Source: Stob. 4.50.68 (ψόγος γήρως), specifying the fr. as *Ναννοῦς*

Τιθωνῷ μὲν ἔδωκεν ἔχειν κακὸν ἄφθιτον <ὁ Ζεὺς>
   γῆρας, ὃ καὶ θανάτου ῥίγιον ἀργαλέου.

F5 Source: vv.4–8: Stob. 4.50.69 (ψόγος γήρως), specifying the fr. as *Ναννοῦς*. vv.1–6: Thgn. 1017–22

αὐτίκα μοι κατὰ μὲν χροιὴν ῥέει ἄσπετος ἱδρώς,
   πτοιῶμαι δ' ἐσορῶν ἄνθος ὁμηλικίης
τερπνὸν ὁμῶς καὶ καλόν· ἐπὶ πλέον ὤφελεν εἶναι·
   ἀλλ' ὀλιγοχρόνιον γίνεται ὥσπερ ὄναρ
ἥβη τιμήεσσα· τὸ δ' ἀργαλέον καὶ ἄμορφον
   γῆρας ὑπὲρ κεφαλῆς αὐτίχ' ὑπερκρέμαται,
ἐχθρὸν ὁμῶς καὶ ἄτιμον, ὅ τ' ἄγνωστον τιθεῖ ἄνδρα,
   βλάπτει δ' ὀφθαλμοὺς καὶ νόον ἀμφιχυθέν.

F6 Source: Diog. Laert. 1.60, specifying the fr. as intertext for Solon fr. 20

αἲ γὰρ ἄτερ νούσων τε καὶ ἀργαλέων μελεδωνέων
   ἑξηκονταέτη μοῖρα κίχοι θανάτου,

F7 Source: *AP* 9.50 (παραίνεσις εἰς τὸ ἀνέτως ζῆν: Cod. Pal. graec. 23)=Thgn. 795–6

σὴν αὐτοῦ φρένα τέρπε· δυσηλεγέων δὲ πολιτέων
   ἄλλός τίς σε κακῶς, ἄλλος ἄμεινον ἐρεῖ.

F8 Source: Stob. 3.11.12 (Περὶ ἀληθείας), specifying the fr. as Μενάνδρου *Ναννοῦς* and Gaisford corrects to Μιμνέρμου *Ναννοῦς*

[– ⏖ , – ⏖ , – ⏑] ἀληθείη δὲ παρέστω
   σοὶ καὶ ἐμοί, πάντων χρῆμα δικαιότατον.

F4 From Stobaeus' *Florilegium* (censure for old age)

Zeus gave to Tithonus the attribute of awful, immortal
old age, which is more horrible than even painful death.

F5 From Stobaeus' *Florilegium* (censure for old age) and Theognis

Suddenly, endless sweat flows down my skin
and I tremble looking back on the flower of our generation:
delightful and beautiful – it ought to have lasted longer!
But short-lasting like a dream
is precious youth. Harsh and deformed
old age now hangs over our heads;
loathsome and shameful, it makes a man unrecognisable
and afflicts his eyes and his mind, once it's spread all around.

F6 From Diogenes Laertius' *Lives and Opinions of Eminent Philosophers*

Without diseases or painful sorrows,
may the fate of death reach me at the age of sixty!

F7 From the *Palatine Anthology* (exhortation to live in a relaxed manner) / Theognis

Enjoy yourself! Of the ruthless citizens
some will speak ill of you, some better.

F8 From Stobaeus' *Florilegium* (on truth)

...Let there be truth
between you and me, that is the most righteous thing of all.

F9 Source: Strabo 14.1.4, specifying the fr. as ἐν τῇ *Ναννοῖ*

αἰπεῖάν τε Πύλον Νηλήϊον ἄστυ λιπόντες
ἱμερτὴν Ἀσίην νηυσὶν ἀφικόμεθα,
ἐς δ' ἐρατὴν Κολοφῶνα βίην ὑπέροπλον ἔχοντες
ἑζόμεθ', ἀργαλέης ὕβριος ἡγεμόνες·
κεῖθεν δ' Ἀλήεντος ἀπορνύμενοι ποταμοῖο
θεῶν βουλῇ Σμύρνην εἵλομεν Αἰολίδα.

F11+11a Source: Strabo 1.2.40, noting καὶ ὑποβάς ('And then he says') between the frr.

οὐδέ κοτ' ἂν μέγα κῶας ἀνήγαγεν αὐτὸς Ἰήσων
ἐξ Αἴης τελέσας ἀλγινόεσσαν ὁδόν,
ὑβριστῇ Πελίῃ τελέων χαλεπῆρες ἄεθλον,
οὐδ' ἂν ἐπ' Ὠκεανοῦ καλὸν ἵκοντο ῥόον.
< >
Αἰήταο πόλιν, τόθι τ' ὠκέος Ἠελίοιο
ἀκτῖνες χρυσέῳ κείαται ἐν θαλάμῳ
Ὠκεανοῦ παρὰ χεῖλος, ἵν' ᾤχετο θεῖος Ἰήσων.

F12 Source: Ath.11.470a, specifying the fr. as *Ναννοῖ*

Ἠέλιος μὲν γὰρ ἔλαχεν πόνον ἤματα πάντα,
οὐδέ ποτ' ἄμπαυσις γίνεται οὐδεμία
ἵπποισίν τε καὶ αὐτῷ, ἐπὴν ῥοδοδάκτυλος Ἠὼς
Ὠκεανὸν προλιποῦσ' οὐρανὸν εἰσαναβῇ.
τὸν μὲν γὰρ διὰ κῦμα φέρει πολυήρατος εὐνή,
ποικίλη, Ἡφαίστου χερσὶν ἐληλαμένη
χρυσοῦ τιμήεντος, ὑπόπτερος, ἄκρον ἐφ' ὕδωρ
εὕδονθ' ἁρπαλέως χώρου ἀφ' Ἑσπερίδων
γαῖαν ἐς Αἰθιόπων, ἵνα δὴ θοὸν ἅρμα καὶ ἵπποι
ἑστᾶσ', ὄφρ' Ἠὼς ἠριγένεια μόλῃ·
ἔνθ' ἐπέβη ἑτέρων ὀχέων Ὑπερίονος υἱός.

F9 From Strabo's *Geography*

Leaving behind us steep Pylos, the city of Neleus,
we arrived on ships to longed-for Asia,
and with our overwhelming force in lovely Colophon
we settled – we instigators of painful hubris.
From there, setting out from the Ales river,
we captured Smyrna the Aeolian city, by the gods' will.

F11+11a From Strabo's *Geography*

Jason himself would never have brought back the great fleece
from Aea accomplishing a painful journey,
thus fulfilling a difficult labour for shameless Pelias;
nor would they (Argonauts) have reached the fair
stream of Oceanus.
…
To Aeëtes' city (Aea), where the swift Sun's
rays rest in a golden chamber
at the edge of Oceanus – there did glorious Jason go.

F12 From Athenaeus' *Learned Banqueters*

The Sun has been assigned daily pain indeed
and no rest is ever possible at all
for him and his horses, as soon as rosy-fingered Dawn
abandons Oceanus and mounts the sky!
Indeed, a lovely bed carries him over the waves,
an adorned (forged by Hephaestus' hands
of precious gold) and winged bed, while he's sleeping delightfully
on the surface of the waters, taking him from the
place of Hesperides
to the land of the Ethiopians, where his swift chariot and horses
rest until early-born Dawn arrives.
Thereafter, he 'son of Hyperion' mounts his other vehicle.

F13a Source: Comm. in Antim. F105 Matthews, specifying the fr. as ἐν τῇ *Σμυρνηΐδι*

ὣς οἳ πὰρ βασιλῆος, ἐπε[ί ῥ'] ἐ[ν]εδέξατο μῦθο̣ν̣,
ἤ[ϊξ]α̣ν κοίλῃ̣[ς ἀ]σπίσι φραξάμενοι.

F14 Source: Stob. 3.7.11 (Περὶ ἀνδρείας)

οὐ μὲν δὴ κείνου γε μένος καὶ ἀγήνορα θυμὸν
τοῖον ἐμέο προτέρων πεύθομαι, οἵ μιν ἴδον
Λυδῶν ἱππομάχων πυκινὰς κλονέοντα φάλαγγας
Ἕρμιον ἂμ πεδίον, φῶτα φερεμμελίην·
τοῦ μὲν ἄρ' οὔ ποτε πάμπαν ἐμέμψατο Παλλὰς Ἀθήνη
δριμὺ μένος κραδίης, εὖθ' ὅ γ' ἀνὰ προμάχους
σεύαιθ' αἱματόεν<τος ἐν> ὑσμίνῃ πολέμοιο,
πικρὰ βιαζόμενος δυσμενέων βέλεα·
οὐ γάρ τις κείνου δηίων ἔτ' ἀμεινότερος φὼς
ἔσκεν ἐποίχεσθαι φυλόπιδος κρατερῆς
ἔργον, ὅτ' αὐγῇσιν φέρετ' ὠκέος ἠελίοιο

F15+16 Source: *Etymologicum Genuinum* = *Etymologicum Magnum*, *s.v.* βάξις

καί μιν ἐπ' ἀνθρώπους βάξις ἔχει χαλεπή.
< >
ἀργαλέης αἰεὶ βάξιος ἱέμενοι.

F17 Source: *Schol.* T *ad* Hom. *Il.* 16.287

Παίονας ἄνδρας ἄγων, ἵνα τε κλειτὸν γένος ἵππων.

F13a From a 2nd-century-AD *Commentary on Antimachus*

... so did the commander's men rush into the battle
upon his order, fenced behind hollow shields.

F14 From Stobaeus' *Florilegium* (on valour)

"Nothing like that man's power and noble spirit",
I learn from my elders who saw him
routing the dense ranks of the Lydian cavalry
at the plain of Hermus. He was Spearman!
Never at all did Pallas Athena question his
heart's fierce power, whenever he hasted
into the battle of bloody war among the fore-fighters,
repelling the enemies' bitter darts.
And none of his enemies was more eminent
in going about the task of mighty fighting,
since he was borne by the rays of the swift sun.

F15+16 From Byzantine lexical encyclopaedias

Bad reputation follows him among men.
...
They're always eager for harsh judgement.

F17 From scholia on the *Iliad*

He leads men from Paeonia, land of a famous breed of horses.

COMMENTARY

FRAGMENT 1

The theme of the poem is the absence of *erôs* from the lives of the elderly. The question raised is: what is the point of living any longer without love? And the answer given: no point – better die. The Homeric heroes and gods were certainly not insensitive to the lure of love, but none of them would ever have made it the very reason for living (Neri 2011: 151). It is ironic, of course, to see Mimnermus express such un-Homeric thoughts in language which is almost entirely Homer's (Campbell 1967: 223–24). In Homer, old age may be described with negative adjectives such as 'baneful', 'difficult', 'destructive' and 'hated' (λυγρός, χαλεπός, ὀλοός, στυγερός), but is also associated with wisdom (e.g. *Il.* 4.322–3), civil duty (*Il.* 3.105), and a happy family life (*Od.* 19.367–8), all of which are missing from Mimnermus (Galhac 2006: 64). The benefits of growing old are totally ignored – contrast Solon fr. 27, where a man is said to be at his best, in terms of wisdom and speech, in his fifties. However, the pessimistic conclusion perhaps implies a positive message: "The paraenesis is now *carpe diem*: enjoy life, and the gifts of Aphrodite in particular, while you are young" (Henderson 1995: 98–99). This interpretation was already put forward by Horace, in a parody of Mimnermus' poem: "If, as Mimnermus believes, there is no joy without love and jests, you better… live amid love and jests!" (*si, Mimnermus uti censet, sine amore iocisque | nil est iucundum, vivas in amore iocisque. Epist.* 1.6.65); Horace puts 'better live' *para prosdokian* for 'better die'.

The structure is clear and symmetrical: an opening question (v.1), two opposing main sections (vv.2–5a and 5b–9), and the moral at the conclusion (v.10). The poem is thematically, logically, and aesthetically complete, as all recent scholars agree (cf. Faraone 2008: 19 n.10; Faraone himself hypothesises that a standard archaic elegy had ten-line stanzas, with Mimn. fr. 1 being an exemplary case, but he also acknowledges that fr. 14 challenges that hypothesis, for it has eleven lines; 2008: 157–58). The lyrical subject is a man, as is revealed progressively (vv.5, 6, 9), and expresses the male view on the subject matter; he is not an old man yet (vv.2, 5) but probably not an adolescent either, as we gather from his profound anxiety. A very youthful speaker (admitted by Adkins 1985: 96 and Allan 2019: 122) would normally not even consider the prospect of growing old (Simon. fr. 20.7–8). The personal perspective (vv.2, 5) seems to overshadow the gnomic tone, to the extent that the poem sounds like a self-addressed monologue. The tone is melancholic, in line with the original purpose of elegy as mournful song. [An exaggerated hypothesis, Nagy 2010: 41 argues that elegy evolved from the genre of *thrênos*, a choral song with a female lead-singer who laments for the death of a dear one, and he spots remains of *thrênos* in this poem, such as the alliterations of -οι (v.2) and -αι (v.7), which resemble the formulaic cries *oimoi* and *aiai*.]

The expression is poetically rich, with pairs of opposites (βίος/τεθναίην, 'life/to die', ἥβης/γῆρας, 'youth/old age'), repetitions (τερπνὸν/τέρπεται, 'enjoyment/enjoy', κακὸν/κακαὶ, 'ugly [man]/ugly [concerns]'), puns (μέλοι/μείλιχα, 'mind/kind', ἁρπαλέα/ἀργαλέον, 'charmful/harmful'), witty alliterations (τίς δὲ…Ἀφροδίτης, τερπνὸν ἄτερ, 'what enjoyment…without Aphrodite'), euphemisms (μείλιχα δῶρα, 'kind gifts'), ambiguities (ἁρπαλέα, 'charming/consuming') and so on. It has been pointed out that young age is mostly rendered by metaphors, old age by realistic and objective descriptions (Henderson 1995: 99), which strengthens the case that the protagonist is not yet old – otherwise he would have a more subjective impression of old age (Sapere 2016: 454–56). Adverbs and conjunctions of time are naturally abundant in a poem about the passing of time (ὅτε, 'when', μηκέτι, 'no longer', ἐπεὶ, 'whenever', αἰεί, 'always'); what is striking is their distribution along the poem, moving from density to sparsity (vv.2, 2, 5, 7). This may be seen as a neat slowing-down effect which reflects the ageing of the protagonist: "as we approach the horrors of old age, the verse becomes slower, the sentences shorter, the stops more emphatic, until the poet closes with a short, damning line of summary" (Bowra 1938: 19). Thus "the absence of any attempt to match a slower rhythm to age and woe" (Adkins 1985: 96) is a wrong observation; even if 'rhythm' is understood strictly in metrical terms, we still notice the slowing-down effect: contrast the enjambments of vv.5–6 and 6–7 with the metrically autonomous pentameter of v.10.

1. So: δέ does not require a (now missing) preceding μέν-section, as older scholars assumed, e.g. Skiadas 1979: 134, but is probably a marker of the performative nature of the poem, for example in the context of a symposium, where poems were sung in succession; cf. the 'sympotic chain' of Thgn. 939–44 with Vetta 1984. In v.5 there is another δέ without a μέν. "Why live if…?" is a common expression of pathos, especially in tragedy (e.g. Aesch. *PV* 747; Soph. *Ant*. 548, 566, *Aj*. 393; Eur. *Alc*. 960, *Andr*. 113, 404, *Hec*. 349, *Hel*. 56, *HF* 1301, *Med*. 146, 798, *Or*. 1072). **what life … exists:** the poem opens with this question which, despite being rhetorical, receives a detailed answer below. The next question, **what enjoyment exists**, which is explicitly answered to in v.8 (οὐδ'…τέρπεται, "he doesn't … enjoy"), comes to narrow down the first question, to clarify that the speaker worries about the quality of his life, rather than living *per se*. In other words, the first question should be understood as ποῖος δὲ βίος ("what quality of life"). **golden Aphrodite:** she is the goddess of, and thus a metonym for love. Her description as golden is formulaic (e.g. *Il*. 3.64; Hes. *Theog*. 822; *Hymn. Hom. Ven*. 93; Thgn. 1293) but chosen wisely, among other formulaic epithets, to resonate with the sunlight imagery of v.8 (Adkins 1985: 99). Simonides' fr. 584 imitates this specific line (τίς γὰρ ἁδονᾶς ἄτερ θνατῶν βίος ποθεινὸς…; "What human life is desirable without pleasure…?"; cf. Allen 1993: 33, Sider 1996: 274). An echo is also found in Euripides' *Bacch*. 773–74 (οἴνου δὲ μηκέτ' ὄντος οὐκ ἔστιν Κύπρις | οὐδ' ἄλλο τερπνὸν οὐδὲν ἀνθρώποις ἔτι, "If there is no wine, there is no Aphrodite or any other pleasure for mortals"; Halleran 1988).

2. This is the only line in the poem where the protagonist openly speaks of himself. **I wish to die (τεθναίην):** the very first word answers the preceding question, leaving no room for self-consolation. Perotti 2013 draws attention to the perfect tense of the verb: Mimnermus does not actually wish to die (θνήσκοιμι or θάνοιμι) but 'to lie dead' or 'to have died already'; in other words, he wishes for the peaceful state of being dead rather than the fearful moment of dying. The argument is attractive but τέθνηκα is more like οἶδα and δέδοικα, which are essentially present in sense ('I die', 'I know', 'I fear'). Wishing death for oneself is common in lyric poetry (e.g. Mimn. frr. 2.10, 6.2, Sappho fr. 95.11, Anac. fr. 411, Thgn. 343) and erotic poetry in particular (e.g. Sappho fr. 94.1, on losing a dear one). Whether this is merely a rhetorical topos, as Page 1955: 83 maintains for the Sapphic case, or the poet's honest intention is a trivial question, because lyrical personas have no intentions in themselves and because the extra-dramatic Mimnermus – if he is to be identified with his lyrical protagonist – may well have preferred a common phrase in expressing an otherwise personal thought. A milder alternative to 'better die' is 'better to never have been born' in Thgn. 425–8 and Soph. *OC* 1224–38. **when I will no longer mind:** the conditional-time clause is unusual, having both its protasis and its apodosis in bare optative, i.e. a mixture of future less vivid ("when I shall no longer mind") and future more vivid ("may I die"): Smyth §2404. The protasis in particular (ὅτε μέλοι), in place of a more expected subjunctive (ὅταν μέλῃ), may be seen as a mitigation of the categorical apodosis, or else, as a slim beam of hope for the speaker: it is not the *absence* of love that will make him die, as one assumes from v.1, but his *indifference* to love – and he is not yet indifferent to it, if he has bothered to compose a love-poem. **ταῦτα μέλοι:** *singular* verb with neutral *plural* subject is found in all Greek dialects (e.g. Homer uses it 75% of the time) but sometimes referred to as 'Attic figure' in older scholarship (e.g. Farrar 1870: 65); cf. frr. 1.4; 2.1–2; 2.11; 2.12; Smyth § 958–9.

3. the … and … and the: this line specifies the preceding ταῦτα ("these things"). Dawson 1966: 48–49 and Gerber 2003 have suggested that the tricolon here describes three successive stages in an erotic encounter: intimacy (a stolen kiss or embrace), sending gifts, and finally consummation. But the 'first step', φιλότης, is an unreservedly sexual term in epic and Archilochus, so all three items, joined in polysyndeton for emphasis, must refer to sexual desire and/or intercourse (a *hendiatris*): the first is a literal mention, the second a euphemism, and the third a metonymy. **secret lovemaking:** our poet's φιλότης is κρυπταδίη, an adjective which confirms the sexual meaning – it refers to "the clandestine love-affairs of the young" (Allan 2019: 122) rather than to adultery, as it does in Homer (*Il.* 6.161 κρυπταδίῃ φιλότητι μιγήμεναι, "[the wife of Proetus desired] to lie with him [i.e. Bellerophon] in secret love"). It crystallises the idea that erotic passion is a force under the surface, i.e. unconscious (cf. Archil. fr. 191 φιλότητος ἔρως ὑπὸ καρδίην ἐλυσθεὶς). Whereas Homer in his objective fashion called the intercourse of the sexes 'a natural thing (θέμις) for men and women' (*Il.* 9.134 with Sommerstein 2010: 98–99), Mimnermus added "fragrance and colour" (Fränkel 1973: 209). **and kind gifts:** *sc.* of Aphrodite; cf. *Hymn. Hom. Ven.* 2. The adjective μείλιχα ('gentle', here 'kind'), connected by folk etymology with μέλι ('honey'; *EDG*), may be intended as a word-play with μέλοι ('mind') of v.2. If so, *erôs* is conceived as a paradox: rough but smooth, upsetting but soothing. **and the bed:** it comes at the end to remove any doubt about the preceding phrases; rather than love or affection in general, they signify sex-drive in particular (cf. *Il.* 6.25 μίγη φιλότητι καὶ εὐνῇ, "he lay in (her) bed and got laid").

4. οἷ[α] … γίνεται: cf. n.2 on ταῦτα μέλοι. **youth's charmful flowers:** ἥβης is both an attributive genitive ('genitive of quality') to ἄνθεα (= youthful flowers) and a genitive of time (= youth-time flowers, i.e. which blossom when one is young). The metaphor is formulaic (cf. *Il.* 13.483; *Hymn Merc.* 375; Hes. *Theog.* 988; Thgn. 1070; Tyrt. fr. 10.27; Simon. fr. 8.6; Pind. *Pyth.* 4.187) and repeated in Mimn. frr. 2.3 and 5.2. A legal term in Classical Athens, ἥβη was the age of sixteen for boys, 'the time before manhood' and a threshold celebrated at the Apaturia festival; two years later, the adolescents (ἔφηβοι) were enrolled in their deme's register; see Winkler 1990: 24–25. But here the word is used in its wider sense, 'youth', including women (v.5). Syntactically, ἥβης ἄνθεα is either a predicate ("things which are charmful flowers of youth…") or an appositive to οἷ[α] ("things, flowers of youth, which are charmful…"). Apart from 'charmful', ἁρπαλέος also means 'consuming', 'devouring' and perhaps it is this negative sense (*pace* Allen 1993: 36) that Mimnermus wants to put forward: "things, flowers of youth, which become consuming…"; cf.

next note. The ambiguity is probably deliberate, as it is in Thgn. 1352 πικρὸς καὶ γλυκύς ἐστι [*sc*. ὁ ἔρως] καὶ ἁρπαλέος καὶ ἀπηνής, "love is bitter and sweet, kind and harsh".

5. for both men and women: ἀνδράσιν and γυναιξίν are datives of advantage/disadvantage, depending on how we translate ἁρπαλέος (see above), or dative of possession if γίνεται is not copulative but used absolutely ("…things, charming flowers of youth, which men and women have"). At this point the speaker makes no distinction between genders, and one may even imagine that the lyrical subject is a woman, especially if mourning by referring to Aphrodite is a feminine trait (cf. Margulies 2021); but this impression will soon collapse. Moreover, the reference to 'men and women' rather than to 'boys and girls' strengthens the hypothesis that **ἁρπαλέος** is meant in its negative sense: by time, the flowers of youth are proven devouring – a proleptic predicate. A strong grammatical and metrical pause follows and splits the poem in two almost equal halves; their distinction is not just thematic (Aphrodite's gifts *vs* the misery of old age) but also narrative (gender-neutral perspective *vs* male perspective; see next note). Faraone 2008: 20 speaks of shift of mood, but as I have suggested so far, it is inaccurate to say that the first half is "a fairly upbeat description of joyful youth"; the positive semantics of individual words are always undermined in context, e.g. the word 'enjoyment' by being placed in a rhetorical question (v.1), 'golden Aphrodite' by the preposition 'without' (v.1), and 'flowers' by being described as ἁρπαλέα (v.4). **painful old age:** for old age as something ὀδυνηρὸν, cf. Pind. fr. 52a.1 πρὶν ὀδυνηρὰ γήραος σ̣[χεδὸν μ]ο̣λεῖν ("Just before the pains of old age arrive"). **is about to attack:** the verb ἐπέλθῃ must be understood in its military sense – τείρουσι, 'oppress', and ἐχθρὸς, 'enemy', below also carry such nuances. It is placed in the anticipatory subjunctive ("when old age is about to attack"; cf. Smyth §1810) rather than in the indicative ("when old age attacks"), not because the future it describes is something uncertain, but to highlight the present emotional condition of the lyrical subject, who speaks from the perspective of someone who is not *yet* old (v.2). A similar verb is used by Sappho fr. 58.3–4 γῆρας ἤδη ἐπέλλαβε ("old age has overcome me"). Normally we would expect ἐπήν (ἐπεί+ἄν) with the subjunctive, but ἐπεί with the subjunctive is acceptable in gnomic phrases; Monro §296.

6. old age: the enjambment is very much a conscious choice here; not only is γῆρας the main concern of the protagonist, hence it deserves a prominent place at the very middle of the poem, but it also comes as an unexpected subject to ἐπέλθῃ, hence it benefits from the pause. Before Mimnermus, the verb was used metaphorically for the coming of sleep (*Od.* 4.793), destiny (*Od.* 10.175), or disease (*Od.* 11.200); here it is old age that attacks – almost an oxymoron, given that γῆρας entails physical weakness. This surprising combination was repeated by two poets in the *Theognidea* and Solon: κακὸν γῆρας ἐπερχόμενον (Solon fr. 24.10 = Thgn. 728); ἀργαλέον γῆρας ἐπερχόμενον (Thgn. 1132); γήραος…ἐπερχομένου (Thgn. 527–28); the influence of Mimnermus is certain, as the adjectives κακὸν and ἀργαλέον betray. **miserable and ugly:** manuscripts M and A deliver the reading ὁμῶς καὶ καλὸν, which would produce the convenient meaning "[old age makes] *even a handsome* man ugly", if we corrected ὁμῶς to ὅμως (Verdenius 1953, followed by Allen 1993). Instead, I prefer to retain ὁμῶς and correct καλὸν to κακὸν (Hermann 1822, followed by West 1992), which produces the equally convenient meaning "[old age makes a man] miserable and ugly *alike*"). The latter option is not only perfectly Mimnermian in style (cf. fr. 5.3, 7) but also entails a fine allusion: the combination αἰσχρὸν…καὶ κακὸν seems to be a reversal of the καλὸς κἀγαθός ideal for young men; that ideal is considered a trademark of Classical Athens, first attested as a set phrase in Hdt. 1.30.4, but actually dates (albeit describing a man's actions, not a man himself) to Tyrt. fr. 12.13–14 ἥδ' ἀρετή, τόδ' ἄεθλον ἐν ἀνθρώποισιν ἄριστον | κάλλιστόν τε φέρειν γίνεται ἀνδρὶ νέῳ ("This is excellence, this the best human prize and the fairest for a young man to win"); cf. Perysinakis 2012: 192 with reference to Tyrt. fr. 10. The reversal by Mimnermus of this military ideal should be read in connection to ἐπέλθῃ (v.5): when old age attacks, men cannot fight back. **a man:** the word ἄνδρα, like 'man' in English, may be used for 'mankind' or, more accurately in our context, for the mankind as opposed to the gods (cf. Slater 1969, 2b). But also ἄνδρα is a first sign that the focalisation is shifting towards a male perspective; and for those who recognise the reversed καλὸς κἀγαθός description, the sign becomes a proof. According to Solon, an ugly man does not necessarily have awareness of his bad looks and may even consider himself handsome (fr. 13.40 [δοκεῖ ἔμμεναι ἀνήρ] καλὸς μορφὴν οὐ χαρίεσσαν ἔχων, "[another man considers that] he's handsome, though his form is without charm"). Such delusions do not exist in Mimnermus, whose line of thought is closer to Tyrtaeus' provoking statement that even the nude corpse of a young man is beautiful (καλὸς) to stare at, whereas an old man in the same condition would make a shameful sight (fr. 10.21–30; cf. Föllinger 2005: 33–35). **τιθεῖ** = τίθησι.

7. always: the generalisation αἰεί in practice means 'from now on', 'until death', and seems to ignore the youthful past of the elderly, as if old age came to erase it. **ugly concerns:** they refer to erotic rejection, the sadness of loneliness, and eventually the fear of death. That these concerns are described as κακαὶ, i.e. with the same adjective as the elderly themselves (v.6), creates a pessimistic effect, insofar as 'ugly' people can only experience 'ugly' emotions. For Nagy 2010: 41, μέριμναι refracts the sound of 'Mimnermus', giving the impression that the poet is mourning for himself. **beset:** the verb ἀμφιτείρω suggests that these feelings fall upon the elderly as an outer force, rather than generating from inside. In other words, the ageing men appear totally victimised, without any involvement in defining their emotions. The 'tmesis' of the preposition (cf. LSJ, citing Quint. Smyrn. 9.368) allows its emphatic placement early in the sentence, thus underlying the inescapability from those ugly concerns. If we had to ascribe a literal referent to ἀμφὶ, 'from both sides', that could possibly be the two sources of erotic rejection: boys and women (v.9). For the choice of the verb, cf. *Il.* 4.315 (σε γῆρας τείρει, "but evil old age presses hard on you") and *Il.* 15.61 (αἳ [ὀδύναι] νῦν μιν τείρουσι κατὰ φρένας, "the pains which now distress his heart"). **his mind:** I render φρένας as 'mind' rather than 'heart', because μέριμναι here and μέλοι in v.2 introduce a cognitive vocabulary (cf. 2.15 for a similar treatment of θυμός).

8. [not] even: I take οὐδ[έ] as an adverb intensifying τέρπεται ("he doesn't even enjoy"; cf. LSJ, B.I) rather than a connective to the preceding clause ("and he does not enjoy"), for this line introduces an extreme example of, rather than an additional element to, the above-mentioned 'pains'. **watching the sunlight:** the uncontracted form ἠελίου is Homeric. Seeing the sunlight is a metonymy for being alive (cf. *Od.* 15.349), so not enjoying the sunlight means not enjoying life altogether (cf. *Il.* 8.480–81; Soph. *OT* 1334–35 τί γὰρ ἔδει μ' ὁρᾶν, | ὅτῳ γ' ὁρῶντι μηδὲν ἦν ἰδεῖν γλυκύ; "For why did I have to see, when there was nothing I could see with pleasure?"). The meaning is also literal: there is nothing beautiful to the eye of the ageing beholder. This line answers to the otherwise rhetorical question of v.1. (τί δὲ τερπνὸν, "what enjoyment exists"), so we can reasonably connect the sunlight to the 'golden-shining Aphrodite': the elderly cannot even enjoy the former, let alone the latter, according to the poet. To the pessimistic message of this particular fragment Pindar *Pyth.* 8.95–97 offers a response, according to Segal 1976 (cf. Theunissen 2000: 151–53). Whereas for the elegist old age entails eternal darkness, which indeed hinders the individual from even enjoying the physical light of the sun, Pindar claims that a Zeus-given gleam, a spiritual light, leads men to great accomplishments on several occasions in their lives, i.e. regardless of age: ἀλλ' ὅταν αἴγλα διόσδοτος ἔλθῃ | λαμπρὸν φέγγος ἔπεστιν ἀνδρῶν καὶ μείλιχος αἰών ("But whenever Zeus-given brightness comes, a shining light rests upon men, and a gentle life"). The sun is a recurring motif in Mimnermus: frr. 2.2, 2.8, 11a, 12, 14.11, 20, 23.

9. by boys and ... by women: this line confirms the male identity and perspective of the speaker. He articulates the negative consequence of Tyrtaeus' positive observation that *young* men are ἀνδράσι μὲν θηητὸς ἰδεῖν, ἐρατὸς δὲ γυναιξί ("a marvel for men to admire, and for women to desire", fr. 10.29). For Percy 1996: 153, even though Mimnermus' poem does not express amorous feelings for male adolescents, it is instructive and "entirely consonant with a pederast's concern", which suggests that the poet's homeland was a "world of institutionalised pederasty". While I agree with the latter statement, the scholar absurdly ignores the lyrical subject's evident pederastic taste (perhaps not to present the poet himself as a pederast, as if the poem must be biographical or as if Mimnermus only fell in love with Nanno; Adkins 1985: 97 also assumes a heterosexual intention). Mimnermus' own sexuality aside, the order in which the speaker states his erotic target-groups, boys first, women second, perhaps reflects his (i.e. the speaker's) order of preference. Indeed, the Hellenistic poet Alexander of Aetolia associates Mimnermus' poetry with παιδομανεῖ ἔρωτι (Ath. 15.699c), and we should also recall the testimony on Mimnermus' ambiguous interaction with Examyes (cf. pp. 19–20). Pederasty was highly esteemed in Archaic Greece in principle, unlike in Classical Athens when it was often problematised; see Lear 2014: 104–15. **depreciated:** the adjective ἀτίμαστος is a *hapax*. The wording resembles fr. 3 (οὐδὲ…παισὶν τίμιος οὔτε φίλος) but there it refers to the relationship between old fathers and their children. Pindar, speaking of homoerotic relationships in particular, says that "one must pluck loves, my heart, in due season and at the proper age" (fr. 123), meaning that one can *feel* such love at any age, but "it is right to *practise* it at only one age, conventionally the years before marriage" (Hubbard 2002: 259). This is a piece of moral advice, whereas for Mimnermus ageing imposes a practical restriction, that is ugliness, on both homo- and heterosexual pursuits. Other poets did not see maturity as 'the kiss of death' for sex, at least not as categorically as Mimnermus did. Archilochus praises young women whose extraordinary breasts "could even turn an old man to a lover" (fr. 48.6) – a statement which, of course, underlines how rare such a 'warm response' would normally be. In *Anacreonteum* 1.6–7, the male poetic persona praises Anacreon for being καλὸς δὲ καὶ φίλευνος ("an old man but handsome, handsome and amorous") – even though in his own poems Anacreon presents himself as rejected; for example, he laments how Eros summons him to play with a girl "but she finds fault with my hair because it is white" (fr. 358; see Kantzios 2010: 581–82).

10. So: οὕτως is syntactically ambiguous and the meaning rests upon enunciation: either an intensifier of ἀργαλέον ("So harmful…") or a conclusion marker appropriate to the moral of the story ("Therefore, harmful…"). Perhaps ἀργαλέον, also used in frr. 2.6, 4.2, 5.5, 6.1, 9.4

and 16, is intended as a pun to ἁρπαλέα, 'charmful' (v.4), just like μείλιχα to μέλοι (see n.3). If so, we have to acknowledge Mimnermus' elaborate wit, since both puns capture the positive *and* negative side of love: gentle yet bothering, charming yet painful. In a sort of ring composition, the poem began with Aphrodite and concludes with the anonymous god who made old age painful. This could be Zeus, who would make a shared 'end-marker' here and in fr. 2 (D'Ippolito 1993: 290), or Old Age as a deity itself (cf. Hes. *Theog.* 225 Γῆρας οὐλόμενον, "devastating Old Age"), or a synecdoche for all gods. For the wording, cf. *Od.* 11.101 τὸν δέ [*sc.* νόστον] τοι ἀργαλέον θήσει θεός [*sc.* Ποσειδῶν] ("but the god will make your return hard").

Looking at artefacts

Not only a poetic metaphor, the flower of youth is also a pattern in visual arts. The exceptionally preserved Phrasikleia Kore, a late archaic funerary statue by Ariston of Paros, movingly captures how short-living that flower can be. Dedicated to an aristocratic girl who possibly belonged to the Alcmeonidae family (which later produced Pericles), the memorial has the following epigram on its base: σε̄μα Φρασικλείας· κо̄ρε̄ κεκλε̄́σομαι αἰεί, ἀντὶ γάμο̄ παρὰ θεο̄ν τοῦτο λαχο̄σ' ὄνομα ("Tomb of Phrasikleia: I shall be called a Maiden evermore, for instead of marriage I was allotted this name by the gods"). The lady died unmarried, hence the lotus she holds, an Egyptian funeral symbol adopted by the Greeks, is unopened: "Like the girl herself, the choicest [bud] has been plucked before it could bloom" (Stieber 2004: 173). On her crown, lotus buds and opening flowers alternate, for she "died on the verge of the full maturity represented by marriage, but without attaining it" (Livingstone and Nisbet 2010: 30; see further Svenbro 1993: 8–25; Sourvinou-Inwood 1995: 249–50). Mimnermus and Ariston use the flower motif almost in opposite directions: the former to lament the short duration of youth, the latter to remind us of those who did not even have the privilege of enjoying theirs. "So harmful did god make old age" sings the elegist, "very painful did god make young age" shows the sculptor – the gods are to blame in either case. If Mimnermus implicitly wishes for the immobilisation of time so that youth and beauty could last forever, Phrasikleia has been tragically trapped in such eternal youth: physically intact for centuries, she never got the opportunity to know “secret lovemaking and kind gifts and the bed” as a woman.

Phrasikleia Kore by Ariston of Paros, c. 550–540 BC. Parian marble statue found at Merenda, Attica. ©National Archaeological Museum of Athens.

FRAGMENT 2

The theme of the poem is the short duration of youth and the troubles of old age. While the affinity with fr. 1 is obvious, here there is no mention or implication of *erôs*. Here the anxiety of growing old involves issues of family, property, and health. The two fragments may have been parts (stanzas) of a single composition which addressed the effects of old age from different angles, hence there would be no reason to repeat the erotic concerns here; or Mimnermus may have composed the second poem at a later stage ("in his old age": Schmiel 1974: 288–29), as a response to, supplement, or even renunciation of his earlier poem, offering a more inclusive account this time. Compared to sexual retirement and the decline of physical looks (fr. 1), the concerns about bloodline, the well-being of the *oikos*, and one's mental state (fr. 2) reveal a more profound, existential reflection – an observation which fits both hypotheses, either climactic construction or later composition. In the latter hypothesis, it is again not clear whether fr. 2 constitutes a complete poem, but if not, the surviving part was conceivably ('probably' for Fränkel 1973: 209) preceded by a description of the gods' eternal life (Griffith 1975: 84–85). The male perspective is more subtle than that of fr. 1, given that worrying about the prosperity of the *oikos* was no less a female anxiety, as the Sapphic 'Brothers Song' attests to.

The structure resembles that of fr. 1, with two opposing sections (vv.1–5a youth / 9–15a old age) and a similar conclusion (15a–16 blame the gods), but here there is a more progressive transition (5b–8 expectation of the lurking Fates). Thus the structure corresponds to a past→present→future division, with the lyrical subject placed in the middle, i.e. he is an "older individual taking a retrospective look at his younger years" (Galhac 2006: 72–73) as well as worrying about the future. That v.9 is the turning point is also suggested by the ring composition which is formed by the chiastic repetition of the endings in vv.1–3 and 7–9: ὥρη, 'season' (1) → ἠελίου, 'of the sun' (2) → ἥβης, 'of youth' (3) ≈ ἥβης, 'of youth' (7) ← ἠέλιος, 'sun' (8) ← ὥρης, 'of the season' (9); Gerber 1970: 108.

The expression is rich in literary tropes: the 'growing leaves' simile (vv.1–2 αὔξεται), the personification of the Fates who are on standby

(5–7 παρεστήκασι), the comparison of life to the course of the sun (8 κίδναται) and the traditional metaphor for dying (14 ἔρχεται εἰς Ἀΐδην) are kinetic images which crystallise the passing of time – a fast passing indeed (2 αἶψ', 'quickly'; 7 μίνυνθα, 'short'; 10 αὐτίκα, 'straightway'). Scholars have especially focussed on the leaves simile, debating whether it is a conscious adaptation of/response to *Il.* 6.146–9 (Bowra 1938: 19; Griffith 1975: 75–78; Adkins 1985: 99; Garner 1990: 3–8; Sider 1996: 265, 273–76; Galhac 2006; Bowie 2010a: 60 n.10) or mere poetic commonplace (Fowler 1987: 32–33; Lardinois 1995: 235–36; Burgess 2001: 117–25; Kelly 2015: 23–24; Allan 2019: 124). The Homeric passage reads:

> *Just as are the generations of leaves* [οἵη περ φύλλων γενεή], *such are those also of men. As for the leaves, the wind scatters some on the earth, but the luxuriant forest sprouts* [φύει] *others when the season of spring has come* [ἔαρος δ' ἐπιγίγνεται ὥρη]; *so of men one generation springs up and another passes away.*
> (transl. Murray and Wyatt)

Allen 1993: 41 summarises the semantic differences: "Homer mentions the wind which brings leaves to the ground, while Mimnermus speaks of the sun which makes them grow; Homer sees the dead leaves of one season followed by the fresh leaves of the next, Mimnermus the leaves of only one brief season." I too see no conscious engagement with the specific passage, for two other Homeric passages are verbally closer to Mimnermus' wording, yet irrelevant to the theme of old age: *Il.* 2.468 (ὅσσα τε φύλλα καὶ ἄνθεα γίγνεται ὥρῃ (said of the mass arrival of the Achaeans on the plain of Sacamnder); *Od.* 7.105–6, 9.51 ὅσα φύλλα καὶ ἄνθεα γίγνεται ὥρῃ (said of the mass attack of the Cicones against Odysseus' men).

A widely accepted intertextual relationship, on the other hand, is the reception of Mimnermus' fragment by Simonides frr. 19–20 W = Semonides fr. 29 D (see West 1993: 9–10 and West 1974: 179–80 in favour of a Simonidean authorship, Hubbard 2001: 226–31 and Babut 1971 for a Semonidean one; for the history of the debate, see Merisio 2021):

> *The man from Chios* [*sc.* Homer] *said one thing best: "As is the generation of leaves, so is the generation of men"* [= *Il.* 6.146]. *Few men hearing this take it to heart, for in each man there is a hope which grows in his heart when he is young. As long as a mortal has the lovely bloom of youth, with a light spirit he plans many deeds that will go unfulfilled. For he does not expect to grow old or die; nor when healthy does he think about illness. Fools are they whose thoughts are thus! Nor do they know that the time of youth and life is short for mortals. But you* [ἀλλὰ σὺ], *learning this at the end of your life, endure, delighting in good things in your soul.*
>
> (transl. Sider)

The poem, clearly quoting Homer (for "the man of Chios", see Burgess 2001: 122–23 and Burton 2011: 66–67), is a polemic response to Mimnermus. Simonides/Semonides is correcting Mimnermus' pessimistic presentation of ageing, arguing that the elderly too have some good things to indulge themselves with (Hubbard 1994: 191–93). Mimnermus misappropriated the Homeric simile, Simonides/Semonides implies; "where [Homer] describes the passing away of one generation to make room for the next, Mimnermus rather gloomily focuses on the withering and death half of the simile" (Sider 1996: 274). The addressee of Simonides/Semonides' poem (ἀλλὰ σὺ, 'But you') may be its very author – a formulaic self-address in second person singular – an unspecified fellow symposiast, a generalised Everyman, or even Mimnermus himself (Sider 1996: 279 and 2020: 299). However unlikely, the latter hypothesis should not be hastily rejected on the argument that Mimnermus was not alive by Simonides' time (Obbink 2001: 83–84), first because Semonides of Amorgos, who is traditionally considered to have flourished in the 7th century BC, might have been the author; secondly, because Simonides/Semonides might be addressing the mature lyrical subject of Mimnermus' elegy, not the real (now dead) poet. The lyrical subject *is* alive every time the poem is read, and conceivably, Simonides/Semonides gave his response-poem after a fellow symposiast had recited Mimn. fr. 2.

1. For we: whereas in Homer the 'deictic part' of the leaves simile, i.e. the mankind, is rendered from the perspective of a distanced speaker ("...so is the generation of men"), Mimnermus prefers the subjective ἡμεῖς ("...so are we"). Here the gnomic tone gives place to personal confession, and contrary to epic, the lyrical narrator is emotionally involved as equal among others. At the same time, the placing of ἡμεῖς at the beginning of the fragment also allows Mimnermus to greet his specific addressees, his fellow symposiasts. For inceptive δέ, see fr. 1 n.1. **the leaves ... produces:** the alliteration arising from the *figura etymologica* φύλλα φύει conveys a sense of repetition – a point missed by those scholars (e.g. Sider and Allen, quoted above) who say that Mimnermus, in contrast to Homer, ignores the new generations coming to replace the older ones. By writing φύλλα φύει ('produces flowers'), Mimnermus essentially means φῦλα φύει ('produces people'), in a witty game of homophones. For a short anthology of Greek and Latin passages using this simile, see Sider 1996 and Garner 1990: v–vi. **much-blossoming:** the adjective πολυάνθεμος/πολυανθής is typical for ὥρη, 'season' (Pind. *Ol.* 13.17) and ἔαρ, 'spring' (*Hymn. Hom. Pan.* 17). On the textual issue, see next n.

2. of spring: like with γῆρας, 'old age', in fr. 1.6, here ἔαρος (genitive of explanation to ὥρη, 'season': Smyth §1322) is the poem's key word, emphasised by enjambment. Despite the pause in between, ὥρη ἔαρος would be a noticeable alliteration to the ear. In combination with the assonance αἶψ' αὐγῇς αὔξεται it makes a most musical line, pertinent to the joy of youth. At the same time, however, this line brilliantly captures the shortness of youth: with a synizesis in ἔαρος and an epic shortening in αὔξεται ἠελίου, the metre exemplifies the limits of that season (cf. fr. 1.4). **which grow quickly:** the subject of αὔξεται is φύλλα, 'the leaves' (cf. fr. 1 n.2 on ταῦτα μέλοι) from the previous line, where it serves as object to φύει, 'produces', whose subject is ὥρη, 'the season'. Allen 1993: 42 considers this "an uncomfortable change of subject" and prefers Bergk's 1853 change of πολυάνθεμος ὥρη to πολυανθέος ὥρῃ (i.e. an adjective qualifying ἔαρος + a dative of time = "leaves which come forth in the season of much-blossoming spring"). But this reading not only ignores the manuscripts' agreement on ὥρῃ, it also corrects a witty syntactical choice: where others would have slipped into an anacoluthon, Mimnermus shows off that φύλλα can perfectly be a subject *and* an object at the same time, the nominative and the accusative of neuters being identical. **the sunlight:** the uncontracted form ἠελίου is Homeric, repeated in v.8. Cf. Timotheus 804 *PMG* ὅτ' αὔξεται ἡλίου αὐγαῖς, "when she grows with the sunrays".

3. similar to them: τοῖς is a Homeric demonstrative pronoun (= τούτοις), here dative objective to ἴκελοι. **for only:** the preposition ἐπὶ interrupts the noun-phrase to add emphasis on πήχυιον, 'a brief span'. For the same purpose, a trihemimeral caesura comes after ἴκελοι. **with the flowers of youth:** ἄνθεσιν is instrumental dative to τερπόμεθα, 'we enjoy ourselves'. For the 'flowers of youth', see fr. 1 n.4. **a brief span:** as a measure of length, already used in Homer, πῆχυς ('cubit', lit. 'arm') is the distance from the elbow to the tip of the middle finger (Pollux 2.158); cf. *Il.* 8.494 ἔγχος ἐνδεκάπηχυ ("a spear of eleven cubits"), *Il.* 24.270 ζυγόδεσμον ἐννεάπηχυ, ("a yoke-band of nine cubits"). For the poetic license of applying such physical units to count time, cf. Alcaeus fr. 346 δάκτυλος ἀμέρα ("the day is a finger's breadth"). Given that one πῆχυς equals twenty-four δάκτυλοι, perhaps Mimnermus uses πήχυιον χρόνον to implicitly identify the 24th year of age as the limit of youth.

4. we enjoy ourselves: the plural governs the first section of the poem (ἡμεῖς δ', οἷά τε φύλλα…, τοῖς ἴκελοι…τερπόμεθα, "we, like the leaves…, similar to them … we enjoy"). An equivalent construction would be the generalised singular (e.g. πᾶς ἀνὴρ, οἷόν τε φύλλον…, τῷ ἴκελος…τέρπεται, "Everyman, like the leaf…, similar to it…he enjoys") but the poet purposedly avoids it, reserving the singular for the second half of the poem (13-15 ἄλλος ἐπιδεύεται… ἄλλος ἔχει…οὐδέ τίς ἐστιν, "one has no … another has … there is no one"). He thus achieves an antithesis between the sociable youth and the isolated elderly; the former have each other to enjoy their flowers with – the latter endure their miseries in solitude. On an extradiegetic and performative level, τερπόμεθα might refer to the context of the symposium, as if Mimnermus were saying: "Dear fellow symposiasts, this is an exceptionally pleasant occasion, which makes us feel young again". **knowing neither evil nor good:** the rest of the period has generated extensive scholarly debate; characteristically, the journal *Otia* requested its readers to comment on the passage and published five responses in three successive volumes (1967–1969; review in Gerber 1975: 263–65). Here I shall be as schematic as necessary. While "knowing no evil from the gods" *prima facie* means "experiencing no troubles sent from the gods" (*CGL s.v.* οἶδα 5), the following "knowing no good either" makes us reconsider. If youth is a desirable condition for Mimnermus, then he cannot mean that the young "experience no pleasures either". Therefore, we must read εἰδότες in its cognitive sense: the young have *no awareness* of either evil or good (Griffith 1975: 78). But what do 'evil' and 'good' mean in this case? For some scholars, these two are understood as abstract concepts/moral categories which the young are incapable of perceiving and distinguishing between (Josserand 1967; Broccia 1969; Schmiel 1974: 286; Gerber 1975: 265–68). But this is unlikely to be Mimnermus' intention, for the poem is not about making decisions or addressing ethical dilemmas. Others, with whom I agree, interpret thus: the young have neither awareness of the imminent pains of old age, nor of their privilege of still being young (Crahay 1968; Pironet 1968; Giannini 1977: 23–25; Anhalt 1993: 45; Slings 2000: 19–20; Gentili and Catenacci 2007: 46). Allen 1993: 45 objects that "if εἰδότες οὔτε κακὸν is to mean 'knowing neither the evil' (*sc.* 'which awaits us'), οὔτ' ἀγαθόν must mean '…nor the good' (*sc.* 'which awaits us'), for κακὸν and ἀγαθόν are parallel objects of εἰδότες". And he continues: "the clause is built upon a so-called polar expression. Mimnennus says, in effect, that in our youth, by the gods' favour, we are as unaware of imminent evil as we are of imminent good […] But it is obviously only the evil (old age more than death) which concerns him […]. Thus in the antithesis κακὸν…ἀγαθόν, the ἀγαθόν is simply rhetorical." My reservation against this solution is that οὔτ' ἀγαθόν is too highlighted (by the enjambment and the trihemimeral caesura) to be irrelevant to the narrative of the poem and to merely serve as a formulaic supplement of οὔτε κακὸν. Admittedly, such polar expressions (cf. 'for better or for worse', 'whether you like it or not') usually mean the latter part alone (i.e. 'for worse', 'despite you don't like it'), while the former part ('for better', 'if you like it') is added just for the sake of balance and politeness. However, if special emphasis is placed upon the former part, as Mimnermus does with οὔτ' ἀγαθόν, then it may denote a realistic possibility. The poet seems to want to *avoid* using a polar expression in a trite manner. **from the gods:** the ignorance of 'evil' and 'good' is blamed on the gods. In other words, it would be for the gods to instil into the young an awareness of the two. Thus πρὸς θεῶν modifies εἰδότες, not κακὸν and ἀγαθόν (which would be the case if εἰδότες meant 'experiencing'; cf. Gerber 1975: 266 n.8). But would such an awareness – whatever 'evil' and 'good' may mean – be desirable in the first place or not? For Crahay 1968 the ignorance of good and evil is an unfortunate condition and Stégen 1969 points out that Aristotle distinguishes infantile innocence from true happiness. However, the logic of the poem is clear on this matter: the young are blissed precisely because they are ignorant; had they known what follows, they would not be able to enjoy their flowers; they would still be young, of course, from a biological point of view, but not carefree (cf. Martinazzoli 1946: 194–95; Broccia 1969; Gerber 1975: 268).

5. the Fates stand beside in black: Κήρ is the goddess of death or doom, appearing either alone (e.g. *Il*. 18.535, 23.79; *Od*. 11.171) or as a group of two or more Κῆρες (e.g. *Il*. 2.834, 9.411, 12.326). In plural, they are sometimes identified with the Erinyes (Aesch. *Sept*. 1060) but this cannot be the case here, as there is no reference to punishable actions. They are akin to the Moirai – in Hesiod they are virtually indistinguishable – but the Moirai are standardly three and bring both happiness and sorrows (*Theog*. 217–22). Lachesis, in particular, is the Moira who by lot (<λαγχάνω) assigns to each man his destiny, which thus may be good or bad. Κήρ/Κῆρες, on the contrary, is/are equivalent to Atropos alone (the 'irreversible' Moira, i.e. death). The most characteristic example is Achilles having to choose between two κῆρας θανάτοιο: either a heroic life with an early death, if he joins the war, or an unheroic life with a late death, if he returns home

(*Il.* 9.411–16). Mimnermus' Κῆρες are (dressed in) black, as always in Homer, in contrast to the bright sun (v.2) which is associated with youth (Griffith 1975: 78; Allan 2019). They stand right beside us, or better, they are *already* standing near the young, who merely ignore their presence (Schmiel 1974: 284, Theunissen 2000: 143, Möller 2014: 35–36). For the verb, cf. *Il.* 16.853 = 24.132 ἄγχι παρέστηκεν θάνατος καὶ μοῖρα κραταιὴ ("death and resistless fate stand hard by you"), *Hymn. Hom. Ven.* 269 ὅτε κεν δὴ μοῖρα παρεστήκῃ θανάτοιο ("but when their fated death is at hand").

6. one bearing … and the other…: Mimnermus may have modelled his two Κῆρες on the specific Iliadic passage (Bowra 1938: 21) but there are considerable differences: the elegiac ageing individual does not really have the opportunity, as Achilles does, to decide between the two destinies; and the alternative to a late, miserable old age is not a heroic death – an option available to Achilles – but an ordinary, if premature, one. The latter kind is considered preferable, we infer, by the poet. Strictly speaking, i.e. judging by the standards of the Homeric intertext, here θανάτοιο, '[destiny] of death', would make a *para prosdokian* for κλέος ἐσθλόν, 'great honour' (Griffith 1975: 78–79). However, identifying old age and death as two homologous Κῆρες is not surprising at all; cf. Thgn. 767–68 τηλοῦ δὲ κακὰς ἀπὸ κῆρας ἀμῦναι | γῆράς τ' οὐλόμενον καὶ θανάτοιο τέλος ("Better […] keep far away those evil Spirits, baleful Eld and the end that is Death"). In other words, ἡ μὲν…ἡ δ' ἑτέρη does not necessarily mean two alternative destinies, but two successive ones (cf. Bowra 1938: 21). **of painful old age … of death:** γήραος and θανάτοιο are genitives of explanation to τέλος ("the destiny of old age/of death"). Here too (cf. fr. 1.10) the adjective ἀργαλέος, a favourite of Mimnermus', possibly entails an implicit pun. Despite deriving from ἄλγος ('pain'), here the adjective may have been chosen for its phonetic resemblance to ἀργός: a neat way to say that youth moves (αὔξεται, κίδναται) fast (αἶψ[α], πήχυιον ἐπὶ χρόνον, μίνυνθα), whereas old age is idle/inactive/unproductive and, as such, painful.

7. Youth's fruit is short-lived: the Homeric adverb μίνυνθα, 'for a short time' (<μινύθω = 'to diminish'), is found only here among the archaic lyric poets. For its combination with the absolute γίνεται, i.e. not followed by predicate, cf. *Il*. 4.466 μίνυνθα δέ οἱ γένεθ' ὁρμή ("his effort lasted for a short time"). At first sight ἥβης | καρπός seems a trite choice given ἄνθεσιν ἥβης (v.3), but as noted above, Mimnermus purposedly repeats ἥβης at the end of both lines to achieve his tripartite ring composition (vv.1–3 and 7–9). Moreover, ἄνθεσιν and καρπός have different nuances: the 'flowers' render the ongoing happiness of being young, while the 'fruit' is the end of that process, i.e. a retrospective appreciation of youth (Skiadas 1964: 32 n.3).

8. for the sun to pass over the earth: the verb κίδναμαι is the poetic equivalent of σκεδάννυμαι, 'to be spread over', used by Homer for the dawn: *Il*. 7.451, 8.1, 23.227. The duration indicated here is the daytime, rather than the dawn alone (*pace* Campbell 1967: 227) or the few minutes it takes for the sunrays to reach the earth (perhaps *pace* Neri 2011: 154, who is vague). In the two latter cases, the sunlight is *not* followed by darkness but by further light, which would be incompatible with Mimnermus' conception of old age. The use of ἐπὶ γῆν, instead of περὶ γῆν, is not due to the presumed flatness of the earth – besides, the idea of a spherical earth, traditionally credited to Pythagoras or Parmenides, possibly dates as far back as Hesiod (Diog. Laert. 8.48). Here περὶ γῆν would anyway be unsuitable, for Mimnermus is not concerned with the route of the sun, as he is in fr. 12, but with how individuals enjoy the sunlight from their fixed positions on earth. The ancient Greeks did not count their day from midnight to the next midnight and divide into 24 equal parts, as we do today; instead, they counted 12 seasonal hours (i.e. of unfixed duration, depending on season) from sunrise to sunset, and another 12 seasonal hours from sunset to the following sunrise; Evans 1998: 95. This is why Mimnermus considers *the sunrise* as the starting point of human life – in contrast, for example, to the birth of Jesus at midnight in Christian tradition.

9. has passed by: παραμείβομαι = 'to leave on one side', 'to pass by', 'to flow past'. The preposition suggests that we should read this image in connection with παρεστήκασι (v.5): the season of youth 'passes by' only for the Κῆρες 'standing by' to take over. Thus the passing of time is rendered in terms of spatial antagonism. **the effect of this season:** in τοῦτο τέλος…ὥρης (lit. "when *this* effect/perfection of season [*sc.* of youth] passes by") the demonstrative refers to the entire description of youth so far, i.e. to its flowery, carefree, and bright happiness. Alternatively, and so I translate, we may take τοῦτο τέλος…ὥρης as a *hypallage* for τέλος…ταύτης ὥρης ("when the effect/perfection of *this* season passes by"). Cf. fr. 3.1: ἐπὴν παραμείψεται ὥρη. However tempting, here τέλος cannot mean 'the end' of the season of youth, because of παραμείψεται: an end 'comes', not 'passes by'.

10. straightway to die: for the 'better die' motif, cf. fr. 1.2 (with n.) and 4.2. In all three cases, old age is considered a worse alternative to immediate death. The combination of αὐτίκα, 'straightway', and τεθνάναι, strictly speaking 'to have died', possibly underline the paradoxicality of such a wish: death cannot be forced to come too soon (Griffith 1975: 79), unless one commits suicide, which is nowhere implied in the poem. But as noted earlier, the grammatical tense of τέθνηκα cannot be taken too seriously in interpretation (fr. 1.2), hence I translate with present infinitive. **better than living:** the imposing alliteration βέλτιον ἢ βίοτος and the absence of ἐστί (both missed in my translation) intensify the gnomic/philosophic character of the line. Of all comparatives of ἀγαθός, Mimnermus picks the one better serving his own purpose: to prefer death is neither a matter of excellency or bravery (ἄμεινον), nor of strength (κρείττον), nor of desire (λῷον), but of moral virtue (βέλτιον). Contrast Hdt. 1.31.3, for example, where the premature death of the prize-winning athletes Cleobis and Bito leads to the conclusion ἄμεινον εἴη ἀνθρώπῳ τεθνάναι μᾶλλον ἢ ζώειν ("it was better for a man to die than to live"). In their case, early death is an indication of *excellence* (ἀριστῶν γενομένων), hence the comparative chosen is ἄμεινον. But in Mimnermus' poem, the struggle of the ageing individual to maintain his dignity is internal, not a competition in masculinity for public entertainment.

11. many miseries ensue: lines 11–15 enumerate the reasons why sudden death is preferable, or else, a specification of γήραος ἀργαλέου (v.6): poverty, childlessness, and illness are (without precluding other reasons) what make old age painful. These do not appear in order of grievousness but are considered equally devastating (ἄλλοτε… ἄλλος… ἄλλος, cf. Solon fr. 13). All three involve deprivation: the financial ruin of the *oikos* signifies a cut from the past, i.e. loss of the property that one's ancestors have fought to maintain and grow; childlessness means exclusion from the future, i.e. cut of the bloodline; and mental illness entails alienation from the present. κακὰ γίνεται: cf. fr. 1 n.2 on ταῦτα μέλοι. **in the heart:** here θυμῷ must refer to the heart rather than the mind (but see n.15 below), because the miseries described are hard to *emotionally* endure (cf. ὀδυνηρὰ, ἱμείρων), not just hard to think about (*pace* Allan 2019: 125); and also by analogy to youth, which also affects the heart (τερπόμεθα, 'we enjoy ourselves'). The heart is the location (cf. Darcus Sullivan 1981: 148) whose territory the spatial antagonism between youth and the Fates is about (cf. n.9).

12. sometimes one's household is ruined: for the use of verbs in the singular in this section of the poem, see n.4. The verb τρυχόω (but τρύχω in Homer) literary means 'to waste', 'to consume'. Whereas in Homer it is explicitly the suitors who τρύχουσι δὲ οἶκον of Odysseus (*Od.* 1.248 = 16.125 = 19.123, perhaps a euphemism for τρώγουσι, 'they gnaw'), here the passive voice shifts the focus from the violator onto the victim. It does not really matter how, or by whom, the *oikos* is wasted; it could be due to war, due to an overspending family, due to many hairs claiming their share (hence Hesiod advises to beget one son only: *Op.* 376–77), and so on. **the results of poverty appear:** for ἔργ[α]…πέλει cf. fr. 1 n.2 on ταῦτα μέλλοι. The genitive πενίης is subjective to ἔργ[α], inasmuch as πενίη ἐργάζεται ὀδυνηρὰ ("poverty causes lamentable effects"). Cf. Solon fr. 13.41 πενίης δέ μιν ἔργα βιᾶται ("the effects of poverty constrain him"). Given that ἔργον primarily signifies human labour, perhaps poverty is personified in Mimnermus (and in Solon) and should be spelled with capital Π; cf. Alcaeus fr. 364 ἀργάλεον Πενία κάκον ἄσχετον, ἃ μέγαν | δάμνα λᾶον Ἀμαχανίᾳ σὺν ἀδελφέᾳ ("Poverty is a grievous thing, an ungovernable evil, who with her sister Helplessness lays low a great people"). Indeed, Theognis twice addresses "wretched Poverty" herself (351–54, 649–52), whom he considers worse than old age (173–74). In another Theognidean passage, poverty is clearly distinguished from old age: the former can be ignored, the latter not (1129–32 πενίης… οὐ μελεδαίνω | κλαίω δ' ἀργαλέον γῆρας, "I don't worry about … poverty but I weep for grim old age"); for the possibility of attributing this fragment to Mimnermus, see *Appendix III*. The preference for death over poverty is an un-Homeric thought: better be a labourer among the living rather than a king among the dead, says Achilles' spirit to Odysseus (*Od.* 11.488–91).

13. has no children: ἐπιδεύεται, epic form of ἐπι+δέεται = 'to be in need of', hence 'to lack'. The sorrow of childlessness for the elderly is a topos in Greek literature. Cf. *Il.* 9.444–7, 492–5 (old Phoenix on his sterility); Eur. *Alc.* 655–7 (Admetus on his old father's good fortune in having a son); *Med.* 1032–7 (Medea on her childless future); *Tro.* 1186 (Hecuba on burying her grandson); *Ion* 618–20 (Ion on Kreousa ageing yet not being a mother). It was an ancient custom – and a law, at least in Classical Athens (Plut. *Sol.* 22.1.4; Aeschin. 1.28) – that children should nurture their old parents (γηροτροφία or γηροβοσκία) as if 'paying them back' for their upbringing, respect them, and bury them with honours; see Berkel 2020: 124–200. The childless would miss these practical benefits of parenthood (cf. Isae. 2.10 for a purely utilitarian attitude), yet Mimnermus here emphasises the emotional lack: ἱμείρων. In either case, the Greeks considered children a blessing – an axiom which Aristophanes and Euripides shockingly challenged amid the moral decadence of their time, the comedian by presenting on stage a son who beats his father in *Clouds*, and the tragedian by writing a heretical ode *against* parenthood in *Medea* 1090–1115.

14. still yearning … much: the participle ἱμείρων is either concessive ("despite yearning for children so much"), or temporal, expressing the ongoing emotional state ("still yearning for children so much"). I think the latter makes a more effective meaning: even on his very way down to Hades, the childless is still craving for offspring. ἱμείρων makes a significant counterpoint to τερπόμεθα, 'we enjoy ourselves' (v.4). The only two verbs of emotion in the poem, τερπόμεθα applies to youth and ἱμείρων to old age: fulfilled desire for the young, unfulfilled for the elderly. **he passes under the earth to Hades:** passing *down* to

Hades – εἰς Ἀΐδην is a metonymy for 'the underworld' and therefore a *hendiadys* in conjunction with κατὰ γῆς – is a standard metaphor for dying (cf. *Il.* 11.164; *Od.* 10.174–75, 24.203; *Hymn. Hom. Dem.* 431; *Thebais* fr. 3.4 *GEF*). Similar to ἱμείρων *vs* τερπόμεθα, the downward course of the elderly (κατὰ…ἔρχεται) is a counterpoint to the upward course of the sun of youth (ἐπὶ…κίδναται, v.8).

15. a mind-wasting disease: here θυμοφθόρον cannot mean a 'fatal', 'deadly', or 'life-destroying' disease (*pace* Campbell 1967: 228, Falkner 1995: 133 and Sapere 2016: 43), despite Homer using the adjective in such sense (cf. *Od.* 2.329, said of φάρμακα). The reason is that the lyrical subject views death rather sympathetically, as a way to avoid the troubles of old age (v.10). Therefore, θυμοφθόρον must mean 'soul-destroying' or 'heart-breaking', Römisch 1933: 58 suggests, followed by Gerber 1970, Griffith 1975: 80, Allen 1993, Henderson 1995: 104, Faraone 2008: 21, and Allan 2019. In that sense, θυμοφθόρος also describes pain (*Od.* 4.716), labour (*Od.* 10.363), and poverty (Hes. *Op.* 717; Thgn. 155, 1129). However, a more suitable rendering, pertinent to old age, would be 'mind-consuming disease', i.e. dementia (cf. 1.7). I argued earlier that θυμῷ in v.11 means the heart rather than the mind. But now the context is substantially different; lines 9–11a offered a generic view on old age, whereas now we read the specific problems of it, which are practical and material: loss of property, lack of children, and… – the "disease of losing your mind" fits this catalogue better than a vague "soul-destroying disease", which may describe any disease, not only those affecting the elderly. For this list, Mimnermus perhaps draws inspiration from the figure of Laertes, Odysseus' father, whom old age has stricken badly (*Od.* 11.196 χαλεπὸν δ' ἐπὶ γῆρας ἱκάνει, "heavy old age has come upon him"; 24.232 γήραϊ τειρόμενον, "worn with old age"). Indeed Laertes in his old age suffers from all three misfortunes: his *oikos* is being wasted by the suitors; he is effectively a childless parent longing for his son; and as far as his mental capacity is concerned, Laertes "could be imagined as an old patient affected by dementia, terribly in need of elements outside his memory, steadily placed in his orchard (his long term memory), to accomplish the recognition of Odysseus" (Bottino 2017: 24–25). In a more explicit connection of old age to dementia, when Eurycleia announces the return of Odysseus, Penelope assumes that the gods have worn her mind out, old as she is (*Od.* 23.11–24 ἄφρονα ποιῆσαι… ἔβλαψαν… φρένας… σὲ δὲ τοῦτό γε γῆρας ὀνήσει. Cf. fr. 5 n.8). By contrast, Nestor wishes he were young again, precisely because he *can* recall the time when he was a young fighter (*Il.* 7.132–4, 11.670–1). "But whereas Nestor emphasises the fact that his θυμός remains intact despite the weight of the years, old age according to Mimnermus affects humans even in their θυμός" (Galhac 2006: 79, my transl.). Poetry aside, dementia was already discussed in the 7th century BC by Pythagoras, who took the mental decline of the elderly for granted (Stob. 4.1.49 οἱ γέροντες παραφρονοῖεν, "old men: madmen"), and was considered a dangerous enough condition for Solon to legislate that donations were not allowed for those influenced by madness, old age, or a woman (*Ath. Pol.* 35.2 ἐὰν μὴ μανιῶν ἢ γηρῶν ἢ γυναικὶ πιθόμενος).

16. There is no one … to whom Zeus does not give: like in fr. 1.10, the gods – here Zeus in particular – are to blame for the troubles of old age. Here, however, the litotes οὐδέ…μὴ makes a more categorical statement (cf. Soph. *Ant.* 2–3, where the emphasis on Zeus' blame is given with a negative rhetorical question); this difference between frr. 1 and 2 strengthens the hypothesis made above, that the two fragments may be stanzas of a single composition in climactic order. In the *Iliad*, Zeus is famously conceived as having two jars, one filled with blessings and one with evils, and distributing to the mortals either a mixture from the two – that is to the luckier ones – or evils alone (24.527–33). As far as disease is concerned in particular, both Homer and Hesiod consider Zeus to be its source, either acting directly (*Od.* 9.411) or by proxy, i.e. Pandora (*Op.* 102–105). **διδοῖ:** epic form of δίδωσι.

FRAGMENT 3

In fr. 1.9 the ageing individual is said to be unwelcome to both παισίν and women. As noted there, such a concern belongs to ageing *men* in particular, the kind of depreciation is an erotic one, and παισίν means *erômenoi* boys. Here, by contrast, παισίν means children, either sons or daughters (cf. *Il.* 1.20,443, 3.175, *pace* Allen 1993: 52), who do not respect and admire their own old father. Yet the context here is not totally unerotic: the claim to have been κάλλιστος, 'most handsome', clearly bears sexual overtones. Then there is a certain oddity: why would someone who misses his past sexual attractiveness refer to his own children as an example of the rejection he experiences? In other words, how is handsomeness relevant to how children treat their father? One could give a psychoanalytical explanation, i.e. that parents serve as sexual role models for their children, and therefore an old (i.e. necessarily unattractive, according to Mimnermus, cf. 1.6, 5.7) father is not a likeable male idol to his son – or to his daughter, who needs a handsome father on whom to model her husband idol. We should not dismiss this interpretation as being too anachronistically Freudian. Already in Homer, Telemachus has his father as a sexual idol in trying to win his mother in the bow contest (*Od.* 21.113–17; passing the arrow through the axes is a clear symbol of penetration, cf. Russo 2004: 101). A second explanation – the two are not mutually exclusive – comes from the syntactical dissociation of the two verses. Given the positioning of οὐδὲ before πατὴρ ("not even a father to his children is…"), rather than before παισὶν ("a father not even to his children is…"), πατὴρ does not have to be (even though it can be) the very subject of ἐὼν κάλλιστος. An indefinite τις may assume that role, while the participle be considered dangling and thus irrelevant to the second verse: an anacoluthon. In this reading, v.2 substitutes, in terms of meaning, a clause of comparison. The logic is: "Not even a once-gorgeous man is desirable after his season passes, in the same way that not even a father is lovable to his own children when he's old". Sexual (un)attractiveness is *equally lamentable* as filial (dis)respect, hence the gender of παισίν is irrelevant.

This fragment sounds like, and perhaps served as, a supplement to fr. 2.13–14, where old age is considered devastating to the childless. Now Mimnermus argues that even those who have children are far from blessed, for they only receive love and respect while being young parents. It seems that, whatever the conditions in one's life, old age is a misfortune *per se*. Whatever soothing arguments one may find in support of old age, the poet is ready to counter. The logically complete and linear structure of the fragment (beautiful youth > arrival of old age > negative consequences) suggests that the couplet is a complete poem or, less likely, that it comes from the very middle of a longer piece, in the same way that frr. 1 and 2 posit the coming of old age in their very centre. If the lyrical subject is to be identified with Mimnermus in old age, then perhaps the elegist conceived this couplet *ad hoc* on the occasion of a certain symposium where he received no flirting from his fellow symposiasts or the flute girls. In this scenario, τὸ πρὶν would be a performative marker, meaning "in previous symposia, when I was younger".

1. After one's prime passes: cf. fr. 2.9. **no matter how gorgeous he was:** ἐών, epic form of ὤν, is here a concessive participle. While καλός and its two other degrees in homoerotic contexts traditionally apply to the *erômenos* (cf. Thgn. 1259, 1280, 1282, 1336, 1350, 1365, and numerous archaic love graffiti: Hubbard 2003: 57–58, 82–85; Robinson and Fluck 1937), here κάλλιστος, 'gorgeous', must refer to a once young *erastês* (cf. Xen. *Mem*. 1.6.13, *Symp*. 8.11), for now he appears to miss *the younger ones*' attention. At the same time, the adjective can denote heterosexual male attractiveness (cf. Bion, *Ep. Ad. passim*; Charit. 5.1.1), which there is no reason to preclude here.
2. he's neither respected: dishonouring one's old parents is a trait of the Iron Age, according to Hesiod (*Op*. 185 αἶψα δὲ γηράσκοντας ἀτιμήσουσι τοκῆας, "They will dishonour their ageing parents at once"; cf. Thgn. 278, 821). **nor loved:** φιλέω and φίλος may apply to friends, relatives, sex partners, guests, masters, servants, the gods, animals, one's homeland, the city or fellow-citizens, even to things and situations; it is therefore a convenient choice, fitting both the erotic (v.1) and the familial (v.2) content of the couplet. **not even a father:** theoretically, οὐδὲ πατὴρ could be a hyperbaton for οὐδὲ παισὶν ("not even to his own children") or οὐδὲ τίμιος ("not even respected"), but as noted earlier, Mimnermus' word order is significant here. **by his own children:** παισὶν is dative of reference, lit. "in the eyes of his own children" (Smyth § 1496).

FRAGMENT 4

Tithonus' mythological exemplum comes to illustrate once more Mimnermus' ideas about old age: it is a fate worse than death itself (cf. frr. 1.2, 2.10) and the gods are to blame for that (cf. frr. 1.10, 2.16). The Trojan prince Tithonus is mentioned as the lover or husband of Eos already in Homer (*Il.* 11.1 = *Od.* 5.1), but the detailed story of his eternal ageing appears in the *Homeric hymn to Aphrodite*. The goddess Eos ('Dawn') fell in love with, and abducted to have as her consort, the young and handsome prince. To enjoy his beauty forever, she requested Zeus to grant him immortality, but forgot to also ask for eternal youth (218–38):

> *Zeus nodded yes to her and brought to fulfilment the words of her wish. Too bad that her thinking was disconnected! The Lady Eos did not notice in her phrenes that she should have asked for adolescence and a stripping away of baneful old age. Well, for a while Tithonus held on to adolescence, enjoying Eos* [...] *But when the first strands of grey hair started growing from his beautiful head and his noble chin, then the Lady Eos stopped coming to his bed. But she nourished him, keeping him in her palace, with grain and ambrosia. And she gave him beautiful clothes. But when hateful old age was pressing hard on him, with all its might, and he couldn't move his limbs,* [...] *she put him in her chamber and closed the shining doors over him. From there his voice pours out – it seems never to end – and he has no strength at all, the kind he used to have in his limbs when they could still bend.*
>
> (transl. Nagy)

The date of this hymn is uncertain, the suggestions ranging from the early Archaic to the Hellenistic era, but the *opinio communis* is "post-Homeric but prior to the sixth century and the earliest of the Hymns" (Faulkner 2008: 47). If so, Mimnermus' account – not a detailed one, as the fragment survives, but possibly otherwise in its original form – could be contemporary to, or even earlier than the hymn (*pace* Allen 1993: 54 who accepts Janko's too-early dating for the hymn; cf. Janko

1982: 151–69, contested by Olson 2012: 10–15). Sappho too refers to Tithonus' love story in fr. 58, as supplemented by the Cologne papyrus published in 2004 ('New Sappho'), yet she does not mention his eternal ageing:

> *Once upon a time, the tale was, rose-armed Dawn, love-smitten, carried off Tithonus to the world's end; then he was handsome and young but in time grey age overtook him, husband of immortal wife.*

Before the publication of the Cologne papyrus, it was believed that fr. 58 concluded in lines 24–25, which, we now know, form part of *a different* poem (West 2005a: 7). That couplet reads: "But I love delicacy [*lacuna*] and passionate love for the sun has provided me with brightness and beauty". As long as this was considered the conclusion of the 'Tithonus poem', Di Benedetto 1985: 157 reasonably suggested that Sappho was correcting Mimnermus' gloomy words on Tithonus and arguing that enjoying life can keep one young. Today we know that Sappho *aligns* herself with Mimnermus, at least as far as the reconstructed fr. 58 is concerned. At any rate, the popularity of the Tithonus myth in the hey-day of Greek lyric poetry (cf. Ibycus fr. 289 "Ibycus tells also how Eos carried off Tithonus") constitutes an argument in itself for dating the *Homeric hymn* near the end of the 7th century (cf. Eck 1978: 3–4). Of course, the question of which poem comes first is not essential to reading any of these passages, for their similarities may be owed to a common model, rather than to direct influence from one another (Faulkner 2008: 45–48).

Focussing on Mimnermus' fragment, Olson 2012: 243 speculates that "Τιθωνῷ μὲν was presumably balanced by a δέ-clause describing someone who got better – or at least different – treatment (*sc.* from Zeus), with Ganymede an obvious candidate". However, in his other fragments, Mimnermus reserves the worse situation, not the better, for the δέ-section. It is unlikely that Mimnermus would have wished to end his poem with the optimistic example of Ganymede, who remained eternally young and was loved by Zeus. Then what else could the δέ-section be, if we must have one? What is worse than eternal old age, which is already worse even than death? I believe this is exactly where Eos would fit perfectly: [*But even more lamentable was Eos' expectation, who foolishly believed that eternal youth was possible*] or [*…who foolishly believed that the gods are well intentioned towards men*]. Given that Mimnermus repeatedly identifies young age with sunlight (frr. 1.8, 2.2, 2.8), here too Eos ('Dawn') would symbolise youth itself, which has the delusion it will last forever. Olson 2012: 244–46 argues that, in the *Homeric hymn*, Zeus' immediate agreement to Eos' rash request implies his hostility against the goddess, whereas in Mimnermus' fragment the god is inferred to desire to inflict a terrible punishment on Tithonus himself. In my reading, according to which Eos is a personification of Tithonus' and Everyman's deluded youth, such a distinction is trivial. Of course, any speculation about the structure of the poem depends on how one restores the final foot of v.1. If <ὁ Ζεὺς> is not correct, which I doubt, then "Zeus must have been named or otherwise identified in a preceding couplet – unless, in the original setting of a symposium, 'Zeus' gifts' or the like had been the theme for song and a previous singer had named the god, so that there was no need for Mimnermus, in taking up the theme, to repeat the name" (Allen 1993: 56).

1. Zeus: I prefer <ὁ Ζεὺς> (Gesner 1559) over <αἰεὶ> (Schneidewin 1838), *pace* West 1992 and Allen 1993, and in agreement with Diehl 1949, Papademetriou 1984, Gentili and Prato 1988, and Gerber 1999. West's 1981: 1 objection that "the article with the god's name is alien to early hexameter, elegiac and lyric poetry" is not, as Allen admits, insuperable; cf. Alcaeus fr. 338.1 (ὔει μὲν ὁ Ζεῦς), Thgn. 25 (οὐδὲ γὰρ ὁ Ζεύς); and similarly, *Hymn. Hom. Ap.* 201 (ὁ Φοῖβος Ἀπόλλων), Archil. fr. 251.1 (ὁ Διόνυσος). Secondly, <αἰεὶ> seems unconvincing (also to Skiadas 1979: 140), for ἄφθιτον αἰεὶ, 'ever-unfading', may occur as an end-verse formula in Homer (*Il.* 2.46, 2.186, 13.22, 14.238) but it invariably applies to objects rather than attributes (here γῆρας, 'old age'). More importantly, αἰεὶ in Homer modifies ἄφθιτον (an ever-unfading weapon, palace, or throne), whereas in Mimnermus, <αἰεὶ>, were it correct, would modify ἔχειν ("to have forever"). Therefore, the Homeric formula is irrelevant here, both semantically and syntactically.

awful, immortal old age: stylistically, ἄφθιτον…γῆρας is an oxymoron and as such it needs no elaboration (which would fill the lacuna instead of ὁ Ζεὺς) in either constituent part; it is self-sufficient. For attaching the adjective κακὸν το γῆρας, cf. frr. 1.6–7, 2.11, 2.16. **Zeus … gave … old age:** ἔδωκεν ἔχειν = lit. "gave him old age to have it", freely translated as "gave him the attribute of old age" (cf. *Hymn. Hom. Ven.* 212 δῶρον ἔδωκεν ἔχειν). For Allen 1993: 56, "the hyperbaton which results from <ὁ Ζεὺς>, with subject distanced clumsily from verb, and appositional γῆρας in line 2 severed harshly from κακὸν ἄφθιτον, is surely unworthy of Mirnnermus". On the contrary, I consider this hyperbaton most artful (and also wonder why θανάτου ῥίγιον ἀργαλέου is not for Allen a 'clumsy' hyperbaton too). Mimnermus brilliantly interpolates <ὁ Ζεὺς> in the oxymoron, to emphatically put the blame on the particular god (cf. Smyth § 1137; Zeus' blame is also emphasised, metrically, in fr. 2.16) and also to prepare a pun: the powerful enjambment ἄφθιτον <ὁ Ζεὺς> | γῆρας highlights γῆρας, which is a witty *para prosdokian* for γέρας, 'privilege' (cf. fr. 5 n.5). Eos ('Dawn' ≈ youth) was expecting to secure a γέρας for Tithonus, but she only managed to secure γῆρας! If my hypothesis is correct, then here lies another piece of evidence for dating the *Hymn* closely to Mimnermus (cf. *Hymn. Hom. Ven.* 29 Ζεὺς δῶκε καλὸν γέρας, "Zeus granted her a fine privilege"). Janko 1990 proposes <οἶτον> ("awful immortal *doom*, that is, old age"), which is indeed attested next to the adjective κακόν (*Il.* 3.417, 8.34, 8.354, 8.465; *Od.* 1.350, 3.134). It is only because <ὁ Ζεὺς> is stylistically more effective that I reject <οἶτον>, which is still preferable to <αἰεὶ>.

2. more horrible: the comparative ῥίγιον from ῥίγος (masc. ῥιγίων is unattested) means 'colder' (cf. *Od.* 17.191: ποτὶ ἕσπερα ῥίγιον ἔσται, "it will be colder toward evening"), 'more horrible' (cf. Hes. *Op.* 703: [γυναικὸς] κακῆς οὐ ῥίγιον ἄλλο, "nothing more horrible than a bad wife"). Of all adjectives that mean 'horrible', Mimnermus picks this rare one – only here attested in early elegy – to create a macabre paradox: technically speaking, a dead body is a cold body; yet old age proves even colder! **painful death:** the poet usually attaches ἀργαλέος to old age (frr. 1.10, 2.6, 5.5) and its consequences (fr. 6.1), but here to death itself.

Looking at artefacts

Dozens of vases show winged Eos pursuing young Tithonus, who often holds a lyre "as if on his way to his lessons" (Lefkowitz 2002: 330). Some of those vases illustrate the very moment of grasping the boy, while in others Tithonus is still running away – a very literal depiction of the fleetingness of youth. But no certain representations of the *old* Tithonus survive. Gardner 1892 proposed an amphora of 480–470 BC attributed to the Berlin Painter (Oxford, Ashmolean Museum 275) and Esteban Santos 2020: 251–56 discusses it in connection with Mimnermus' and Sappho's treatments of the Tithonus myth. I wish to defend a second candidate from the same period: a neck-amphora by Oionokles Painter, with Eos pursuing young Tithonus on side A and an old man leaning on a cane on side B. Gardner categorically rejected

Attic red-figured amphora by Oionokles Painter, c. 480–460 BC. Bibliothèque Nationale de France-Cabinet des Médailles, Paris, inv. no. 358.

this vase, noting (1892: 138 n.3) that the aged man "is no doubt *not* Tithonus, but a pedagogue. He is wanting in the dignity which marks the male figure on our vase [*sc*. of the Ashmolean Museum]". However, as Mimnermus repeatedly makes explicit, there is nothing dignifying in old age, and the Oionokles Painter may have wanted to follow that very tradition. Moreover, the fact that he has inscribed his standard signature ΟΙΟΝΟΚΛΕΣ ΚΑΛΟΣ twice, beside the young man and beside the old man on the other side, invites us viewers to identify the two male figures as the same person. Thus, instead of a pedagogue, side B may represent *the future* of side A: a visual narrative. The young man, however handsome he was (τὸ πρὶν ἐὼν κάλλιστος, fr. 3.1), has now grown old and Eos no longer pursues him (ἀτίμαστος δὲ γυναιξίν, fr. 1.9); the black background that dominates side B captures his solitude. If so, then the duplicated inscription expresses the (self-)praise of youth on side A ("Oionokles [is] beautiful") but only a nostalgic recollection of it on side B ("Oionokles [was] beautiful").

FRAGMENT 5

There is no scholarly consensus on where this fragment begins: only lines 4–8 are quoted by Stobaeus as Mimnermus', while lines 1–6 feature in the Theognidean corpus with minor differentiations (1017–22). The overlapping verses 4–6 can be securely ascribed to Mimnermus, who is a century older than Theognis, and thus we are left to question about the attribution of 1–3. Those lines were first attached to the Stobaean fragment by Brunck 1784, followed by several editors including Bach 1826, Bergk 1853 and West 1992. It is, above all, the syntactical identity of, and thematical correspondence between τερπνὸν ὁμῶς καὶ καλόν, 'delightful and beautiful' (3) and ἐχθρὸν ὁμῶς καὶ ἄτιμον, 'loathsome and shameful' (7) that seems to confirm that 1–3 and 4–8 were indeed one piece (Adkins 1985: 105). Allen 1993: 59–60, on the other hand, suggests that this exactness may be suspicious, and observes an 'aspectual incongruity' between the two passages, noting that the lyrical subject of vv.1–3 must be young, if he stares at his young contemporaries (ἐσορῶν…ὁμηλικίης), whereas the speaker of vv.4–8 is evidently old. Moreover, Allen finds the 'sweaty excitement' of v.1 grotesque; it was Wilamowitz 1913: 286 who established that Mimnermus' sweat must denote an erotic excitement, in view of Sappho fr. 31 (μ' ἴδρως ψῦχρος κακχέεται, "cold sweat pours from me" ≈ Mimn. fr. 5.1). Based on such objections, editors Edmonds 1931, Diehl 1949, Campbell 1967, Papademetriou 1984, Allen 1993, Gerber 1999 and others only print the Stobaean lines as Mimnermus'. (So too Gentili and Prato 1988, who nevertheless combine this fragment with fr. 4, in what is their fr. 1, with a lacuna in between. Of course, there is no apparent connection with the story of Tithonus: Tithonus did not have short-lasting youth, but eternal old age.)

I consider the entire vv.1–8 fragment as Mimnermus', on these grounds: (*a*) *pace* Wilamowitz, ἐσορῶν may be taken metaphorically to mean 'looking back at', 'recalling', and consequently, ἄσπετος ἱδρώς as a sweat of distress, not of sexual arousal; see nn.1–2. (*b*) The supposedly suspicious isocolon is far from alien to Mimnermus' style; cf. fr. 1.9 ἀλλ' ἐχθρὸς μὲν παισίν, ἀτίμαστος δὲ γυναιξίν, "hated by boys and depreciated by women". (*c*) As Ferrari 1987: 187 admits, even though he argues *against* the unity of the fragment, the structure <adjective + ὁμῶς καὶ + adjective> that we observe in the supposedly Theognidean τερπνὸν ὁμῶς καὶ καλόν, "delightful and beautiful alike", only appears elsewhere in … Mimnermus, here in v.7, and in fr. 1.6. Ferrari's thoroughly uneconomical explanation (cf. Emiliani 2021: 123) is that this syntactical idiom betrays a line that was devised (in the style of Mimnermus) simply to 'glue' the two halves together in an earlier version of the *Theognidea*, and that Mimnermus' vv.7–8 were eventually omitted from the anthology at a later stage. I prefer the more straightforward hypothesis: the syntax is uniquely Mimnermian because the passage is written by Mimnermus! (*d*) Stobaeus may have omitted vv.1–3 not because they are not Mimnermus', but because they contain a first person singular, unsuitable for a gnomological anthology (Campbell 1984: 55; Sider 1996: 266 n.4). A less convincing argument is put forward by Burzacchini 2008: 147–48 and Nicolosi 2010: 29–30. They propose that Mimnermus' fragment inspired Euripides' *Hercules* 637–41:

> *Youth is the thing I love. But age is a burden that always lies heavier than the crags of Aetna upon the head, and over my eye it casts a veil of darkness.*
>
> (transl. Kovacs)

The Euripidean ode opens with a praise of youth, and so the source-elegy must have opened likewise, the two scholars argue. But as Emiliani 2021: 124 reasonably objects, Euripides may already be using an early version of the Theognidean pastiche, rather than Mimnermus' original piece.

Once again, the theme of the poem is youth's brevity and the pains of old age. While in frr. 1 and 2, which are long enough for a comparison to be possible, the main images providing cohesion are the sun and the leaves, the leading metaphor here is the dream (see n.6): youth is a short dream, old age is a nightmare hanging over our heads. The expression is more curt than that of frr. 1 and 2. In those fragments, for example, the sufferings awaiting the elderly unfold progressively (fr. 1 αἰεί…οὐδ'…ἀλλ'…, "at all times … he doesn't … but he…"; fr. 2 ἄλλοτε…ἄλλος…ἄλλος…, "sometimes…one is…another is…"), while here (vv.5–8) there is no such articulation – the only linking words are δέ and τε. The same applies to metre, as there are more internal pauses here: dense semicolons, weak enjambments, and short phrases which "may suggest monotony" (Adkins 1985: 102). Even the syntax seems mechanical (e.g. τερπνὸν καὶ καλόν, "delightful and beautiful"; ἀργαλέον καὶ ἄμορφον, "harsh and deformed"; ἐχθρὸν καὶ ἄτιμον, "loathsome and shameful"; ὀφθαλμοὺς καὶ νόον, "eyes and mind"). We are thus left with the impression of multiple 'snapshots', rather than a full narrative. Far from lack of inspiration, this stylistic choice betrays poetic mastery, as it perfectly serves the dream metaphor: the nightmare of old age (vv.5–8) falls upon the victim in the form of spasmodic visions (1 αὐτίκα, 'sudenly'; 6 αὐτίχ', 'now') and this intensifies the subject's panic reaction (vv.1–2) – just as horror films employ flashing scenes when the murderer attacks. The lyrical subject is a man (7) whose youth has passed (3), who is aware of its brevity (4) and who faces old age as a pressing threat (6). We may thus conclude that he is currently standing on the threshold of that age, which nevertheless remains unspecified. Allen 1993: 59, who does not accept the opening verses as Mimnermus', maintains that "the poet of lines 1–3 must be still a comparatively young man", but beside my earlier objection to the assumed meaning of ἱδρώς and ἐσορῶν, the two αὐτίκα (1, 6) and the cyclical occurrence of the eye-motif (2 ἐσορῶν, 8 ὀφθαλμοὺς) suggest a coherent, in terms of age, *view*-point.

1. Suddenly: given that growing old is a gradual procedure, its consequences appearing over years, αὐτίκα (here and in v.6) does not apply to ageing *per se*, but to that single moment when the individual looks in the mirror (or the surface of the wine, if we are to suppose a sympotic setting of inspiration) and realises the accumulated (harsh) effect of time. Of course, there are several such moments in our lives, hence this poem may be described as *iterative* in Genettian terms, i.e. it makes paradigmatic use of singulative narrative. **flows down my skin:** the verb ῥέω may take a *dative of that which flows*, e.g. πηγὴ ὕδατι ῥέει ("the fountain runs with water", LSJ); but here μοι is apparently a dative of disadvantage, which "often has to be translated as if the possessive genitive were used" (Smyth §1481), i.e. μοι… χροιὴν = "my skin". κατὰ…ῥέει is 'tmesis' for καταρρέω. In ῥέε͞ι, 'it flows', we see Mimnermus' sensational metrical skill: a word whose semantic nature is to denote duration here undergoes epic shortening, i.e. it is read faster than expected, to render (also with the aid of αὐτίκα) the exact opposite meaning, in alignment with the pragmatics of the poem. We also notice a metonymy: while the suddenness and sharpness technically apply to the lyrical subject's panic attack, they essentially describe *the reason* for it, i.e. the brevity of youth. Galhac 2006: 79–80 proposes that Mimnermus' poem echoes Odysseus' transformation into an old beggar, for in both cases old age particularly affects the skin (χροιὴν ≈ χρόα, δέρμα: *Od.* 13.430–1; see n.8). **endless sweat:** sweat flows down because youth flows away; cf. Heraclitus' comparison of life to a river (frr. 12, 49a, 91 D-K). That the sweat here does not signify sexual excitement – see my introductory note and n.2 – also follows from the fact that, when used with ῥέω, ἱδρώς always has an unpleasant cause: physical labour (*Od.* 11.599), trauma

(*Il*. 11.811) or wrestling (*Il*. 24.688, 715). After all, even the ἵδρως of Sappho fr. 31, which Wilamowitz invoked to intertextually attribute Mimnermus' ἵδρως to "excitement for the sight of beauty" (1913: 286), has itself been argued to describe a panic attack (Devereux 1970, Ferrari 2007: 172–74). The adjective ἄσπετος (<ἐνέπω), 'unspeakable' and by extension 'countless', is commonly used for liquids, e.g. ῥόος, 'stream' (*Il*. 18.403), ὕδωρ, 'water' (*Od*. 5.101), ὄμβρος, 'rain' (*Il*. 13.139, Eur. *Tr*. 78); with ἱδρώς it occurs again in Ap. Rhod. *Argon*. 2.663 (sweating during ploughing and rowing).

2. and I tremble: πτοιῶμαι (<πτοιέω) is frequently used in erotic contexts, e.g. Hes. *Op*. 447 κουρότερος γὰρ ἀνὴρ μεθ' ὁμήλικας ἐπτοίηται ("a younger man is all aflutter for his age-mates"), Sappho fr. 31.6 καρδίαν ἐν στήθεσιν ἐπτόαισεν ("my heart trembled in my breast"), Alcaeus fr. 283.3–4 κ' Αλένας ἐν στήθεσιν ἐπτόαισε θῦμον Ἀργείας, Τρọΐω δ' ὐπ' ἄνδρος ("Argive Helen's heart trembled in her breast for the Trojan man"). But here the verb must denote panic, in line with my reading above (and Dawson 1966: 55), cf. *Od*. 22.298–99 τῶν δὲ φρένες ἐπτοίηθεν· οἱ δ' ἐφέβοντο ("and the minds of the suitors were panic-stricken, and they fled in terror"), Anacr. fr. 408 οἷά τε νεβρὸν…ἀπολειφθεὶς ἀπὸ μητρὸς ἐπτοήθη ("like a fawn … frightened to have been abandoned by his mother"), Aesch. *Cho*. 535 ἡ δ' ἐξ ὕπνου κέκλαγγεν ἐπτοημένη ("She cried out in terror in her sleep"). **the flower of our generation:** for the 'flowers of youth', see fr. 1 n.4; ὁμηλικίη and ὁμῆλιξ, 'of the same age', are typically used for the young generation in particular (eg. *Il*. 3.175, *Od*. 2.158, Hes. *Op*. 444) and in our performative context, as Emiliani 2021: 129–30 notes, the word may function as an address to the poet's fellow symposiasts (cf. fr. adesp. eleg. 27.1W χαίρετε συμπόται ἄνδρες ὁμήλικες, "Cheers, mates!"). Of course, those symposiasts would not be young in reality, if they are the same age as the lyrical subject, but are momentarily envisioned as such in the speaker's recollection, and so is his own self. This leads us to the meaning of **looking back on:** ἐσορῶν, as I argued earlier, is to be taken metaphorically. More precisely, it now appears, the participle should be taken both literally *and* metaphorically; the poet is *beholding* the mature symposiasts

(LSJ 1) and *looking on them with his mind's eye* (LSJ 3) as if they were still young. The semantic ambiguity provides for performative flexibility: the symposium for which the fragment was composed, or the symposia at which it was recited, would probably have been attended by young men as well; the speaker may be beholding *those* men instead, to envision the older symposiasts (including himself) as being in *their* position. Thus the couplet would function both as a flashback for his contemporaries and, implicitly, as a warning for the younger ones. Exchanging age perspectives through beholding-and-visualising is a topos in funerary epigraphy, and this strengthens the case that the speaker's reaction here is one of suffering, not of erotic excitement. A funerary inscription of the 2nd century AD coming from Mimnermus' homeland (*CIG* 3397), composed in elegiacs, reads:

> ἄνθρωπος τοῦτ' ἔστι· τίς εἶ, βλέπε, καὶ τὸ μένον σε,
> εἰκόνα τήνδε ἐσορῶν σὸν τὸ τέλος λόγισαι
>
> *This is human nature: see what you are and what awaits you.*
> *Look at this tombstone and contemplate your end.*

3. delightful and beautiful: youth is τερπνὸν (cf. frr. 1.1, 2.4) and καλόν (cf. 3.4), and as such it ought to have lasted longer. If the two adjectives are metonymically seen as the qualities of the symposium, amusing and (homo)erotic, then the younger participants only are expected to enjoy the gathering. In v.5 the exact opposite qualities, ἀργαλέον καὶ ἄμορφον, "harsh and deformed", are attributed to old age, and therefore, following up the metonymy, the symposium is a rather painful experience to the mature participants. **it ought to have lasted longer:** the tacit conclusion is "old age ought to last shorter". On ἐπὶ πλέον ὤφελεν εἶναι the manuscripts deliver ἐπεὶ (retained by Edmonds 1931), making the sentence a causal clause, with πλέον as predicate of 'youth'; but as West 1974: 162 notes, πλέον εἶναι is not Greek for 'last longer', and he prints ἐπὶ, thus making the clause independent and ἐπὶ πλέον a predicate. For ὤφελεν + εἶναι in contrafactual wishes, cf. *Il.* 6.350 ἀνδρὸς ἔπειτ' ὤφελλον ἀμείνονος εἶναι ἄκοιτις ("I wish that I had been wife to a better man"), *Il.* 3.40 αἴθ' ὄφελες ἄγονός τ' ἔμεναι ("I wish that you had never been born").

4. short-lasting like a dream: ὄναρ is used proverbially for "anything fleeting or unreal" (LSJ) and here, in particular, as a simile (ὥσπερ, cf. n.6) for youth, which "from the viewpoint of advancing years, appears as an all too brief and pleasant dream" (Allen 1993; cf. Kessels 1978: 228). On the alliteration ὀλιγοχρόνιον…ὥσπερ ὄναρ, Silk 1974: 184 notes that it comes to link the *ground term* of the simile ('short-lasting') to its *vehicle* ('dream'), thus taking us away from the *tenor* ('youth') itself. Apart from ὀλιγοχρόνιον, the brevity of that dream is also rendered metrically, with an epic shortening in γίνετᾱι (cf. ῥέε̄ι in v.1). For the particular adjective, which is first attested here in extant Greek, cf. Simon. fr. 20.10 ὡς χρόνος ἔσθ' ἥβης καὶ βιότου ὀλίγος θνητοῖς ("how short the duration of youth and life is for mortals"), Hdt. 1.38 σε ὀλιγοχρόνιον ἔσεσθαι ("your life will be short"), Democr. 285 D-K γινώσκειν χρεὼν ἀνθρωπίνην βιοτὴν ἀφαυρήν τε ἐοῦσαν καὶ ὀλιγοχρόνιον ("it is necessary to recognise that human life is feeble and of short duration"), *AP* 5.79 σκέψαι τὴν ὥρην ὡς ὀλιγοχρόνιος ("consider how short-lived one's prime is"). And for the dream simile, cf. Theoc. *Id.* 27.8 τάχα γάρ σε παρέρχεται ὡς ὄναρ ἥβη ("like a dream, youth will pass you by"), Pind. *Pyth.* 8.95 σκιᾶς ὄναρ ἄνθρωπος ("man is only a shady dream"). While Theocritus imitates Mimnermus' simile (Campbell 1967: 228), Pindar appropriates it: for the elegist, youth is a nice dream with a premeditated end – for Pindar, the entire life is a meaningless dream with unpredictable shots of success (Theunissen 2000: 151–53; cf. fr. 1 n.8). A more complex case is Aesch. *Ag.* 79–82 τό θ' ὑπέργηρων… παιδὸς δ' οὐδὲν ἀρείων ὄναρ ἡμερόφαντον ἀλαίνει ("An all too old man, …no stronger than [i.e. as weak as] a child, is a dream-vision wandering all day"); here the dream metaphor, bearing only negative connotations unlike in Mimnermus, is *prima facie* attached to old age, but implicitly to childhood too. Also cf. Thgn. 985 αἶψα γὰρ ὥστε νόημα παρέρχεται ἀγλαὸς ἥβη ("For the splendour of youth passes by as quickly as a thought").

5. precious youth: lit. 'honourable'. Traditionally, and reasonably, *old age* was associated with honour, even if γέρας and γῆρας are only paretymologically related (Benveniste 1973: 334–45); cf. *Il.* 4.323

= 9.422 τὸ γὰρ γέρας ἐστὶ γερόντων ("honour befits the elderly"), *Od.* 13.42 χαλεπὸν δέ κεν εἴη πρεσβύτατον καὶ ἄριστον ἀτιμίῃσιν ἰάλλειν ("it would be hard to cast dishonour upon our eldest and best"). Even in Homer, however, τιμή on occasion *requires* not to be old; in *Il.* 2.447 Athena holds "the highly-prized [ἐρίτιμον] aegis, that knows neither age [ἀγήραον] nor death". In Mimnermus, youth alone (for ἥβη cf. fr. 1 n.4) can be τιμήεσσα, 'honourable', 'prestigious', 'precious', whereas old age can only be the opposite (cf. frr. 1.9, 3.2, 5.7). **Harsh and deformed:** in a familiar fashion (cf. frr. 1.5, 2.5), the semicolon marks the sharp contrast between the two ages, and, together with αὐτίχ', the abrupt transition from the former to the latter. This does not reflect the natural progression of time, according to which we age day-by-day, but the speaker's sentimental comparison between two condensed perceptions of time, one crystallised in his memory, and the other prompted by the sight of his peers. ἀργαλέον, an adjective dear to Mimnermus (cf. fr. 1 n.10), and ἄμορφον, 'misshapen' and by extension 'ugly' (cf. Hdt. 1.196, Eur. *Bacch.* 453), respectively counter youth's τερπνὸν and καλόν, "delight and beauty" (v.3).

6. old age … hangs: the position of γῆρας after enjambment echoes the position of ἥβη in the preceding verse (Adkins 1985: 104). Yet the structure of the two sentences is reverse: verb-subject-adjective for youth (γίνεται…ἥβη τιμήεσσα), adjective-subject-verb for old age (ἀργαλέον καὶ ἄμορφον γῆρας…ὑπερκρέμαται). The end-to-end positioning of the two verbs can be said to convey the much promising and the finite potential of the respective age. For the image of old age hanging over our heads, cf. Simon. fr. 520.4 ὁ δ' ἄφυκτος ὁμῶς ἐπικρέμαται θάνατος ("and death hangs inescapable over all alike"), Pind. *Isthm.* 8.14 δόλιος γὰρ αἰὼν ἐπ' ἀνδράσι κρέμαται ("for over men hangs a treacherous time"), *Eur. HF* 637–41 (quoted in the introductory note). In our case ὑπερκρέμαται is a metaphor whose *tenor* is ambiguous: does old age hang like a dream or phantom (cf. *Il.* 2.20, *Od.* 4.803, 6.21, 20.32 with Kessels 1978: 228–29), like a band, veil or skin (cf. *Il.* 9.446, *Hymn. Hom. Ven.* 5.224 with Onians 1951: 427–31), like Tantalus' rock (cf. Archil. fr. 91.14–5, Pind. *Ol.* 1.56–8, *Isthm.* 8.9 with Kessels *op. cit.*), or – to make a new suggestion – like

Sisyphus' rock (cf. *Od.* 11.593–600, esp. εἰσεῖδον ≈ Mimn. ἐσορῶν, and κατὰ δ' ἱδρὼς ἔῤῥεεν ἐκ μελέων ≈ Mimn. κατὰ μὲν χροιὴν ῥέει ἄσπετος ἱδρώς)? Tantalus was burdened with a massive stone on his head as punishment for stealing nectar and ambrosia from the gods; Sisyphus was condemned to roll such a rock eternally up a steep hill (only to watch it roll back) because he tricked Hades to escape death. In both stories the rock is a reminder of mortality, and therefore a suitable symbol for Mimnermus. There is no reason to accept only one source-imagery, but if we must prioritise them, then ἀμφιχυθέν ("spread all around" v.8), up to which the metaphor extends, singles out the dream imagery (cf. *Il.* 2.41 [Ὄνειρος] ἀμφέχυτ' ὀμφή, 14.253 [Ὕπνος] ἀμφιχυθείς). Any intertexts aside, it is only reasonable to infer that, if youth is a brief and delightful dream, then old age must be (viewed as) an eternal and awful nightmare – of course, this solution responds to our spontaneous expectation that the fragment should have the unity of a complete poem, rather than to an inviolable poetic principle that a certain imagery *must* be followed up. What *is* certain is that the simile (ὥσπερ ὄναρ, "like a dream") has now given way to a metaphor (γῆρας...ὑπερκρέμαται, "old age ... hangs"). Whereas in a simile the comparable entities are conceived separately, the lack of 'like' between *tenor* and *vehicle* in a metaphor brings immediacy to the imagery. Thus, youth as a distant memory *resembles* a good dream, but old age as a pressing threat *is* a nightmare. The old age hanging above us (γῆρας ὑπερκρέμαται) is equivalent to, and as vivid as, the Fates who stand by (Κῆρες παρεστήκασι, fr. 2.5); the difference is that the former appears 'suddenly' (v.1), whereas the Fates have been lurking beside us already since our birth.

7. loathsome and shameful: so is old age, or rather the nightmare of old age, in a construction parallel to v.3. Semantically, ἄτιμον counters ἥβη τιμήεσσα (v.5) but ἐχθρὸν does not counter anything, insofar as youth has not been described here as 'lovely' *vel sim.* Rather, the occurrence of 'loathsome' is justified as a formulaic complement to 'shameful'; cf. fr. 1.9 ἐχθρὸς μὲν...ἀτίμαστος δὲ, fr. 3.2 οὐδὲ...τίμιος οὔτε φίλος, Pind. *Ol.* 8.69 νόστον ἔχθιστον καὶ ἀτιμοτέραν γλῶσσαν ("a most hateful homecoming and words less respectful"). **it makes a**

man unrecognisable: old age makes a man ἄγνωστον, which could mean 'ignorant' (LSJ *II*; cf. the dementia in fr. 2 n.15), but most probably 'unrecognisable', compared to how he looked like in his prime, just like with Odysseus' transformation into an old beggar: *Od.* 13.189 ἄγνωστον τεύξειεν, 13.397 σ' ἄγνωστον τεύξω.

8. afflicts his eyes and his mind: this line too (cf. vv.1, 7) confirms that Mimnermus draws on Odysseus' transformation. "Athena scratched Odysseus' eyes, which once were so beautiful" (*Od.* 13.433), and so does old age βλάπτει δ' ὀφθαλμοὺς here. "But whereas in Odysseus' case, only the beauty of his eyes and therefore his outward appearance are damaged, here Mimnermus adds the mind to the eyes" (Galhac 2006: 80, my transl.) For the application of βλάπτω to νόος, cf. Hes. *Cat.* fr. 10a.88 M-W² (νόου βεβλαμμένοι, due to passion), *Hymn. Hom. Merc.* 393 (ἀβλαβίῃσι νόοιο, due to lies), Thgn. 705 (βλάπτουσα νόοιο, due to forgetfulness). But here, for the first time, it is old age – not a god – that affects the mind; cf. frr. 1.7 and 2.15 with n. (NB that Eurycleia's mind is worn out by the gods, not directly by old age: *Od.* 23.14 σε θεοὶ…ἔβλαψαν…φρένας). In Greek poetry, especially lyric, but also in medical literature and philosophy, falling in love is triggered by the sight of the love-object, either male or female (Calame 1999: 4–5, 19–23; Thumiger 2021), and therefore, having old age obscure the speaker's eyes automatically means his exclusion from love. The line may be read in connection to, and more precisely, as a sarcastic extension of, ἐσορῶν (v.2): standing on the threshold of old age, the lyrical subject suffers both from *still* being able to behold his fellow symposiasts, and from knowing that his vision *will* deteriorate – an optical dead-end. **once it's spread all around:** for the implications of ἀμφιχυθέν for the dream metaphor, see n.6; on a performative level, the word (< χέω, 'to pour'), if it actually marks the end of the poem, invites the pouring of a libation.

FRAGMENT 6

Let us begin with the reception of this fragment, which constitutes a milestone in Greek literature. Diogenes Laertius interpolates (and thus preserves for us) Mimnermus' lines into his compilation of Solonian sayings: φασὶ δ᾽ αὐτὸν καὶ Μιμνέρμου γράψαντος…ἐπιτιμῶντα αὐτῷ εἰπεῖν ("Solon is also said to have criticised the couplet of Mimnermus [= Mimn. fr. 6]…and to have replied thus [= Sol. fr. 20]…". The Solonian response reads:

> ἀλλ᾽ εἴ μοι κἂν νῦν ἔτι πείσεαι, ἔξελε τοῦτον·
>   μηδὲ μέγαιρ᾽ ὅτι σεῦ λῷον ἐπεφρασάμην·
> καὶ μεταποίησον, Λιγυαστάδη, ὧδε δ᾽ ἄειδε·
>   ὀγδωκονταέτη μοῖρα κίχοι θανάτου.

> *If you will still listen to me, delete this* [*sc*. the word 'sixty']
> *and don't hold a grudge because my thought is better than yours.*
> *Edit it, Ligyastades, and sing thus:*
> *"May my fated death come at eighty".*

This is the earliest surviving instance in Greek where a poet explicitly refers to another one, whether a contemporary or a predecessor. (Five uncertain competitors, all reported in later testimonies, are [Hesiod] fr. 357 M-W mentioning Homer; Archilochus fr. 303 mentioning Homer; Callinus T.10 G-P mentioning Homer; Stesichorus fr. 269 mentioning Hesiod; and Alcman fr. 145 mentioning Polymnestus; see Martin 2021). Whereas the Solonian 'correction' of Mimnermus is clear – better die at the age of eighty rather than sixty – its purpose is not. Does Solon only want to propose a different conception of life, more optimistic than Mimnermus', by making a philosophical statement that life is sweet and, therefore, the longer one lives the better? (Cf. Bowra 1938: 75–76; Assunção 2003: 53; Gentili and Catenacci 2007: 37–38.) Or does he admonish the younger Mimnermus – if one accepts the theory that Solon was older – for wishing to die at the age of sixty only because he (i.e. Mimnermus) was still far from it? (Cf. Wilamowitz 1913: 279; Emiliani 2021: 6.) Or does Solon just want to "protest against the famous word of a famous man", whether Mimnermus was long dead, older, younger, or the same age as – but probably alive and older than – him? (Cf. Jacoby 1918: 280.) Is Mimnermus celebrating his sixtieth birthday and Solon, who is perhaps paying him a visit in Ionia on that very occasion, invites him to reconsider his naïve past axiom? (Cf. Szádeczky-Kardoss 1942: 80; Steffen 1955:

44–47.) Or is Solon celebrating his sixtieth birthday and wishes for a twenty-year extension for himself? Equally intriguing questions arise in relation to Diogenes' source: who are those who say (φασὶ) that Solon's composition was a response to Mimnermus' poem? Was that intertextual relationship a widely known fact in Solon's day, or a later assumption initiated by the anthological tradition? Does the fame of the response hinge on the fame of the poem it corrects and tries to supersede, or does the fame of the original poem come to hinge on the response (Burton 2011: 70)?

Whatever the implications of the (unknown to us) biographical and historical data would be, what *is* certain is Solon's humorous tone. By calling the symposiast who recites Mimnermus – or even impersonates him (cf. Noussia-Fantuzzi 2010: 400) – 'Ligyastades' (<λιγὺ + ᾄδειν = 'Mr Clear Voice', cf. Diels 1902: 482), instead of his true patronymic 'Ligyrtyades' (*Suda* μ 1077), Solon presents himself as a dear colleague of Mimnermus, i.e. as someone who is confident enough to offer him a compliment in the form of a joke (Pasquali 1923: 297; Schadewaldt 1933: 284), but also confident enough to declare σεῦ λῷον, 'better than yours'. In the same spirit, the demonstrative τοῦτον, 'this [*sc*. poem/word]' – which rightly prompted West to print Mimnermus' closing line as a prelude to Solon's fragment – was probably said with (mock) contempt (LSJ *s.v.* οὗτος C.I.3). As I shall argue bellow (n.2), Solon's humorous tone might itself be due to Mimnermus. Moreover, it is a sign that Solon did not aim for a moralistic argument with his colleague, nor for 'calling dibs' on the theme of old age, but for a poetic game *for the sake of it* (Falkner 1995: 162–63). After all, it is hard to take Solon seriously, as elsewhere he proposes the age of *seventy* (fr. 27.17–18): "And if a man reaches his tenth seven-year period [δεκάτην ἑβδομάδα], having completed in turn all stages, it won't be too early for him to meet his Fate of Death"; cf. Hdt. 1.32 "For I set the limit of man's life at seventy years", with Bowie 2018a: 66. Nevertheless, I find it unwarranted to extend the poetological reading of Solon back to Mimnermus' fragment; according to Möller 2014: 49–50 (my transl.), "Mimnermus presents the subject of 'experiencing time negatively' through imaginative processing, and thus he establishes elegy as a means for coming to terms with transience… [Then Solon] explicitly builds on the goal announced by Mimnermus, that is, to survive in (and with) his own literature – and, through the *aemulatio*, to live longer than the intertext and its author". But there is nothing in Mimnermus' text to allow for a poetological reading other than its own written status; all literature employs 'imaginative processing', and with such a criterion, all literature would qualify as 'poetological'.

The comparison with Solon's response has also prompted debate on the structure of Mimnermus' fragment. For some editors (Brunck 1772, Diehl 1949, Campbell 1967) the Solonian poem continued in what is a separate fragment in West's edition (fr. 21):

μηδέ μοι ἄκλαυστος θάνατος μόλοι, ἀλλὰ φίλοισι
καλλείποιμι θανὼν ἄλγεα καὶ στοναχάς,

May death not come to me without tears, but when I die
may I leave my friends with sorrow and lamentation.
(transl. Gerber)

The reason for that conjunction is that the latter passage has been transmitted to us with Plutarch's note: οἷς πρὸς Μίμνερμον ἀντειπὼν περὶ χρόνου ζωῆς ἐπιπεφώνηκε ("In opposition to Mimnermus, this is what Solon said on the duration of life", Plut. *Publ.* 24.5). So, if Solon's frr. 20+21 have the same theme (the duration of life) and the same purpose (to respond to Mimnermus), then they must come from the same piece – a weak induction – and consequently, Mimnermus' fr. 6 must have featured an analogous, yet reverse, conclusion, i.e. a wish *not to be* lamented after death (Steffen 1955: 46). Indeed, Blass 1888 suggested a specific couplet, Thgn. 1069–70, which he (after Bergk 1853) attributed to Mimnermus:

ἄφρονες ἄνθρωποι καὶ νήπιοι, οἵ τε θανόντας
κλαίουσ', οὐδ' ἥβης ἄνθος ἀπολλύμενον.

Witless and foolish are those who weep for the dead
rather than the fading bloom of youth.

Why such a wish would suit Mimnermus is obvious: death offers redemption from the pains of old age (cf. frr. 1.2, 2.10). But this couplet's phrase ἥβης ἄνθος, 'bloom of youth', would be an awkward addition to Mimnermus' ἄνθος and ἥβη (vv.2, 5); secondly, ἄφρονες is a favourite Theognidean adjective, Allen 1993: 66 notes. "The truth may well be that Mimnermus had not expressed any wish or preference for an unmourned death", he concludes. I wish to be more categorical: the scenario that Mimnermus expressed such a wish requires not only the weak induction that the Solonian fragments must have been a single piece, but also the absurd assumption that Solon was somehow obliged to respond to the *entire* Mimnermian poem.

1. αἲ γὰρ: introducing wishes with αἲ γὰρ (= εἰ γάρ in Attic, 'And may…') + optative (κίχοι) is frequent in Homer (e.g. *Il.* 2.371, 4.189, 18.464) but not in lyric poets (excl. Archil. fr. 118, Alcm. frr. 37a, 81). **diseases … painful sorrows:** that old age comes with diseases and concerns is typical Mimnermus (cf. frr. 1.7, 2.15, 5.8), as is the wish to die (1.2, 2.10). The alternative forms ἡ μελεδώνη,-ης (*Od.* 19.517, Hes. *Op.* 66, Sappho fr. 37), ἡ μελεδών,-ῶνος/-όνος (Mimn. *hic*, Thgn. 883), ἡ μεληδών,-όνος (Simon. fr. 520.2) and τό μελέδημα, -ατος (*Il.* 23.62, *Thgn.* 789, Ibyc. fr. 288.2) always appear in plural. While the etymology is from μέλω, here perhaps a paretymological hint at μέλας is intended, i.e. understanding μελεδωνέων as 'black concerns' (cf. fr. 2.5). I do not consider the phrasing of this verse pleonastic (*pace* Möller 2014: 44): the two nouns, νούσων and μελεδωνέων, render the physical and mental aspect of ageing, and ἀργαλέων (cf. fr. 1 n.10) is a necessary specification of μελεδωνέων, insofar as 'concerns' may also be positive (cf. Eur. *Hipp.* 1103); it is νούσων that does not require – hence does not receive – such a specification, for *all* diseases are bad to have.

2. may the fate of death reach: for the phrasing μοῖρα θανάτου (gen. of explanation) + κιχάνω ('meet', 'reach', 'hit', 'overtake'), cf. Callin. fr. 1.15, Tyrt. fr. 7.2, Thgn. 340. The particular verb entails the personification of the 'Fate of Death' (Allen 1993:67), who is no other than Atropos (cf. fr. 2.5). Of course the 'irreversible' Moira will come anyway – it is the timing of her arrival that worries Mimnermus.

That timing has remained vague so far; cf. fr. 1.2 "when these matters shall no longer bother me", 1.5–6 "when painful old age is about to attack", 2.9 "once the effect of one's season passes by", 3.1 "after his season passes", 5.8 "once [old age] is spread all around". **at the age of sixty:** now Mimnermus specifies what age he counts as old, or rather, old enough to make one's life unliveable: the age of sixty. (Cf. fr. 2 n.3 for an implicit definition of the timespan of youth). However, this specification perplexes his wish even further – it is evidently a personal wish he enunciates (Burton 2011: 69), not an ideal for Everyman (West 1974: 72–73). Namely, "it seems strange that Mimnermus should wish to live *even* to sixty in view of his remarks" (Gerber 1970: 111). The poet makes a surprising stretching of the technical limits of youth (Kirk 1973: 140), given the low life expectancy in antiquity, and this "negates the pessimistic view encountered in other fragments" (Henderson 1995: 102). But whereas the latter scholar seeks "the only way out of the contradiction" he proposes that the poet's focus is on the physical and mental sufferings of v.1 rather than the age limit *per se*, and likewise Broccia 1959 claims that the poet essentially envisions not his death but an extended youth – I wish to entertain the possibility that Mimnermus *aimed* for that very contradiction. Especially if fr. 6 served as the closure of a long elegy/series of elegies on the miseries of old age (frr. 1–6), then this *para prosdokian* finale would offer a perfect narrative and emotional decompression: the poet now relinquishes his pessimist lyrical persona and returns to the cheerful tone of the symposium. In addition, the fact that most subsequent occurrences of the theme of 'deadly sixties' are comic or quasi-comic suggests that there was an established tradition – and Mimnermus may well have been its starting point! Cf. Amphis fr. 20.2 K-A ("Damn lettuce! If someone, even under the age of sixty, eats it, whenever he has sex with a woman … he won't perform"); Herod. 10 ("Gryllus, Gryllus, when you have passed your sixtieth sun, die and become ashes; for the further lap of existence is blind and the ray of life is already dimmed"); Plut. *Mor*. 136E ("Tiberius once said that a man over sixty who holds out his hand to [i.e. seeks treatment from] a doctor is ridiculous"); Luc.

Cat. 5 ("All of you who are over sixty embark [on Charon's boat] now. What's this? They don't heed me, for their ears are stopped with years"); Luc. *Peregr.*10 ("You have heard how he strangled his old father, unable to tolerate his living beyond sixty years"); Ael. fr. 110.15 ("Isidoros..., an old man..., ninety-one years old but well built and sturdy...; you wouldn't believe he is more than sixty"). It is therefore possible, to develop my earlier suggestion, that Solon wanted to compete with the already humorous tone of Mimnermus, rather than joke on his true worries, by raising the 'deadline' to make it sound even more outrageous. Demographically speaking, only 1 out of 10 newborns could reach the age of 60, and those aged ≥60 formed 6–8% of the total population (Corvisier 2018). In modern European terms, this share corresponds to those aged ≥80 (Eurostat 2021).

FRAGMENT 7

The Archilochian spirit of this fragment (cf. Archil. fr. 14: "No one, Aesimides, will be truly happy, if he worries about the people's judgement") introduces us to a more optimist Mimnermus. From 'better die' we move to 'enjoy yourself'; no age-restrictions to τέρψις are mentioned (cf. 2.3–4, 5.3); others' opinions do not matter (cf. 1.9, 3.2, 5.7); and it is *our* responsibility, and ability, to secure our well being against the external factors. Old age *is* an external factor, as is public disdain, for it comes from Zeus/the Fates in the form of an enemy/a nightmare, we read in previous fragments. Not surprisingly, the *Palatine Anthology* labels the couplet as "an exhortation to live in a relaxed manner" – the adverb ἀνέτως, only attested in medieval Greek, is a simplification of the rare ἀνετῶς (Soph. fr. 641 *TrGF*), from the adjective ἄνετος (<ἀνίημι). If in Archilochus' case "the fragment parodies traditional poetic moralising [...and] portrays the speaker as [...] a hedonistic aristocrat who seeks to corrupt others" (Swift 2019: 225), we cannot take a very different stance on Mimnermus' couplet. Of course, Archilochus explicitly speaks of sexual enjoyment (ἱμερόεντα πάθοι) where Mimnermus is more generic; but then Mimnermus is more straightforward, employing the imperative τέρπε (where Archilochus uses a conditional), for it is a necessity to enjoy ourselves, not a privilege. The second person singular (σὴν, τέρπε, σε) does not prove that Mimnermus intended to compose a gnomic couplet – only that it was extracted and anthologised as such; the original composition may well have had a specific addressee, like Archilochus had Aesimides, rather than a generalised and collective 'you' (*pace* Miralles 1988: 40). For who the specific addressee(s) may be and the potential context of performance, see p. 11.

The optimistic tone of the fragment does not preclude the possibility that it came from *Nanno*, but we should take for granted that it did *not* form part of the elegy/elegies frr. 1–6, *pace* Fränkel 1973: 211 who suggests that "a positive admonition to cheerful enjoyment must surely have followed each of them, as we see in the [fr. 7] couplet". My objection, more emphatic than Emiliani 2021: 131 who only finds the hypothesis "non demonstrable", is not that frr. 1–6 could *not* have featured a positive, even playful, ending – it is the opposite I propose in fr. 6 n.2! – but that fr. 7 in particular, with its πολιτέων ('citizens'), is incompatible with the 'boys and ladies' who have been the poet's concern in the other fragments. Even if τέρπε includes sexual pleasures of an Archilochian kind (cf. my introductory note on fr. 8), the fragment most probably belongs to socio-political rather than erotic elegy. On the contrary, the appropriation of Mimnermus' exhortation in Theoc. *Id.* 27.8, 13–14 is evidently sexual, implying masturbation; in trying to seduce a girl, the herdsman Daphnis says "Don't be too proud, your youth is passing quickly like a dream [παρέρχεται ὡς ὄναρ ἥβη]...Come here under the elms and listen to my piping" – and the girl replies "Entertain yourself [τὴν σαυτοῦ φρένα τέρψον], I don't like anything dismal" (cf. n. 1 below). The dream simile (cf. Mimn. fr. 5.4), the reference to a pipe (even though a σῦριγξ, not an αὐλός), and to dismal music leave little doubt that Theocritus had Mimnermus in mind; Daphnis resorts to the archaic poet for flirting purposes, but the girl 'calls him off' also with Mimnermus' verses – a poet for all occasions!

A Theognidean passage repeats Mimnermus' couplet (= 795–96) and continues: τοὺς ἀγαθοὺς ἄλλος μάλα μέμφεται, ἄλλος ἐπαινεῖ, | τῶν δὲ κακῶν μνήμη γίνεται οὐδεμία ("Some vehemently blame the noble and others praise them, but of the base there is no recollection at all”). A poet who bemoans the waning aristocracy of his day, Theognis, or whoever writes in his name, adapts the vocabulary and scope of Mimnermus’ exhortation: he makes a political use of the categories (moral in Mimnermus) *agathos* (Mimn. ἄμεινον) and *kakos*, and specifies his target-group, in claiming that only the noble are important enough to receive *any* public attention. If one wished to bring this Theognideum into the debate on Mimnermus’ social class (cf. p. 19) despite the ‘elephant in the room’ concerning the authorship and dating of the *Theognidea*, he would still gain no clue. For here ‘Theognis’ may be arrogantly correcting the lowborn Mimnermus – how could he think that commoners have any reputation to protect! – or he may be supplementing the ‘savoir vivre’ handed over by the aristocrat Mimnermus. As fr. 7 stands, it is equally perfunctory to call it either “a plebian […] contempt for bourgeois respectability” (Wilamowitz 1913: 280, 285) or “an aristocratic contempt for the opinions of the masses” (Emiliani 2021: 15 n.84); for δυσηλεγέων πολιτέων, ‘ruthless citizens’, neither refers to all citizens as a body (*pace* Allen 1993: 70), nor specifies which class these men come from. The tone is generic, as it is – if I may use a contemporary comparandum – in Sting’s lyrics:

> *It takes a man to suffer ignorance and smile.*
> *Be yourself, no matter what they say.*

1. **Enjoy yourself:** the manuscripts record the classic-Attic reading τὴν σαυτοῦ φρένα and Renner 1868 emends to σὴν αὐτοῦ (cf. West 1974: 101), following the late archaic *Hymn. Hom. Merc*. 565–66 “And now I am giving you my Maidens and use them as your please [σὴν αὐτοῦ φρένα τέρπε]” (which may have inspired Theocritus to adjust the phrase to his pornographic context in *Id*. 27.13–14). The wording is Homeric (e.g. *Il*. 1.474 ὃ δὲ φρένα τέρπετ’ ἀκούων, “and Apollo rejoiced with what [*sc*. the paean] he heard”) and τέρπω in particular seems to have been a dear word to Mimnermus (cf. 1.1, 1.8, 2.4, 5.3). But whereas in Homer and the *Homeric hymn* the realisation of the exhortation ‘be happy’ depends on others’ actions, i.e. granting

Maidens and singing the paean, Mimnermus appropriates the formula to advocate unconditional happiness (Miralles 1988: 40–41). **ruthless citizens:** the rare δυσηλεγής (<δυσ+ἄλγος, 'cruel'), which Homer uses only twice for death (*Od.* 22.325) and war (*Il.* 20.154), may have been chosen here as a paretymological game with *δυσ+λέγω (cf. δυσφημέω, δυστομέω, κακολογέω = 'speak ill of').

2. Of the citizens ... some ... some...: for the construction gen. part. + ἄλλος...+ ἄλλος...+ verb, cf. *Il.* 8.429 τῶν ἄλλος μὲν ἀποφθίσθω, ἄλλος δὲ βιώτω ("Of them let one perish and another live"), *Od.* 22.257–58 τῶν ἄλλος μὲν σταθμὸν ἐϋσταθέος μεγάροιο βεβλήκειν, ἄλλος δὲ θύρην πυκινῶς ἀραρυῖαν ("Of them one hit the doorpost of the well-built hall, another the close-fitting door"). **some will speak ill of you, some better:** i.e. "better than the former, but still badly!"

FRAGMENT 8

In Stobaeus' anthology, the fragment is preceded and followed by Menandrian maxims and is itself labelled as Μενάνδρου Ναννοῦς in manuscripts SMA. It is not inconceivable that Menander had a comedy named after the famous courtesan Ναννάριον (*Kolax* fr. 4 Sandbach) or Νάννιον (fr. 414 K-A), but the Ionic form ἀληθείη in our fragment (cf. ἀλήθεια Men. *Sik.* 154, with ἀ due to crasis) leaves no room for further speculation. Gaisford 1814 rightly corrected to Μιμνέρμου Ναννοῦς "without doubt".

The exhortation for sincerity may be addressed to the singer's love-target, and thus have formed part of a love elegy; justice is indeed a common desideratum in such poems (Allen 1993: 73). In that case, it is almost certain that "you and me" would refer to a heterosexual couple, given the inclusion of the fragment in *Nanno* (Gentili 1965: 381). What is hard to assume, however, is whether the lyrical subject proposes hesitantly "let us make our intentions for each other clear", or confidently "let us finally admit our feelings". If we hypothesise that the Theocritean adaptation (i.e. erotic interpretation) of fr. 7 adhered to Mimnermus' original composition more closely than the Theognidean (i.e. political) adaptation did – see my introductory note there – then fr. 8 seems to be an ideal supplement to fr. 7. Together they would have formed a 'song of seduction', for a plausible reconstruction of which I draw on Archil. fr. 23.8–16:

> *Enjoy yourself* [*sc. with me*]. *Of the ruthless citizens*
> *some will speak ill of you, some better* [*sc. anyway*].
> [*So make your heart propitious.*] *At least let's be honest*
> *with each other, the most righteous thing of all:*
> [*I know how to repay love with love* ...]

Nevertheless, the fact that Stobaeus anthologises fr. 8 in his section Περὶ ἀληθείας along with other passages none of which comes from an erotic context – insofar as we know their context – suggests that our fragment too probably comes from a non-erotic poem. The quest for sincerity "between you and me" may well apply, for example, to friends; cf. West 1974: 75; Pl. *Gorg*. 487e "For you are my friend, as you say yourself. Hence any agreement between you and me must really have attained the perfection of truth." Or the singer may be addressing his Fate of Ageing itself, in a fashion similar to that of *Anacreonteum* 40:

> *Since I was created a mortal to journey on the path of life, I can tell the years that I have gone past, but do not know the years I have to run. Let me go, worries: let there be no dealings between you and me. Before death catches up with me, I shall play, I shall laugh and I shall dance with lovely Lyaeus.*
>
> (transl. Campbell)

1. Let there be truth: Stobaeus chose not to anthologise the first half of the hexameter probably because its content did not fit well with his Περὶ ἀληθείας designation. Truth occasionally appears as a deity; cf. Pind. *Ol*. 10.4 Ἀλάθεια Διός, fr. 205 ὤνασσ' Ἀλάθεια, Bacchyl. fr. 57 Ἀλάθεια θεῶν ὁμόπολις. But here it is unlikely that ἀληθείη was thus conceived, for a third figure between 'me and you' would undermine the desired *tête-à-tête*. For the phrasing, cf. *Od*. 24.486 πλοῦτος δὲ καὶ εἰρήνη ἅλις ἔστω ("And let wealth and peace abound"), Ar. *Vesp*. 868 εὐφημία μὲν πρῶτα νῦν ὑπαρχέτω ("first let there be respectful silence now").

2. between you and me: for σοὶ καὶ ἐμοί, datives of possession, at the start of the verse, cf. *Il.* 4.37–38 "Let not this quarrel in future be | to you and me a great cause of strife" (i.e. "Let us not *have* this quarrel…"). **the most righteous thing of all:** for the claim "X is the most righteous thing/possession of all", cf. Solon fr. 2 (said of the sea), Isae. 4.22.8 (what the laws direct), Pl. *Leg.* 890a (whatever one gains by force); Philem. fr. 105.1 K-A (one's field). Justice, in its turn, is said to be "the most beautiful thing of all" (κάλλιστον τὸ δικαιότατον, Thgn. 255).

FRAGMENT 9

The theme of this fragment is historical: the migration of Pylians (Messenia, Peloponnese) to Colophon at some point in the late 11th-10th century BC, and the subsequent capture of Smyrna – a city founded by Aeolian settlers *c.* 1000 BC – by the descendants of those migrants at some point between *c.* 800–688 BC, when they were exiled from Colophon due to civic strife. In fact, this fragment is our earliest reference to the so-called Ionian Migration from mainland Greece to Asia Minor (Roebuck 1955: 25). Of course, the Peloponnese was Dorian at the time, so we have to either assume that some noble Ionian families had remained in/around Pylos after the 'Dorian Invasion' (*c.* 1200 BC) and it was *them* who settled Colophon (cf. Brillante 1993), or that Pylos' Ionian identity was a tale retrospectively invented in Asia Minor for political purposes (cf. Mongiello 2017: 208–11).

The Pylians were not the first Greeks to occupy Colophon; when they arrived, they had to come in terms with earlier settlers from Crete and, more pertinent to our discussion, from Thebes, i.e. Aeolians (Paus. 7.3.1). As Mimnermus tells us, the Pylians employed overwhelming force and provoked *hubris*, but he does not specify – nor do we know from elsewhere – whether that aggression was directed against those earlier settlers or against local natives (see n.4). Similarly, we do not know what caused, or who was involved in, the civic strife in Colophon which led to the emigration of the Pylian-Colophonians some centuries later (Hdt. 1.150). According to the historian, the fugitives gained their new homeland by trickery: they locked the

Smyrnaeans out of their own city, when they were celebrating a festival of Dionysus outside the walls. Perhaps Mimnermus' statement that Smyrna was captured "by gods' will" hints at that religious occasion, which the fugitives would have interpreted as a divine sign (Huxley 1959: 107); alternatively, the phrase may imply an oracular advice to settle in Smyrna (Steinmetz 1969: 75), or simply be a formulaic metaphor for "with good fortune". Like Colophon, Smyrna had been colonised by Greeks before: the abundant monochrome ware excavated in Old Smyrna, along with some painted Protogeometric vases, betray Aeolian influence and point to an Aeolian occupation *c.* 1000 BC. Those settlers must have been from Lesbos or Cyme (Strabo 13.3.6) and the curious Pseudo-Herodotean *Life of Homer* (38) specifies that Smyrna was founded by the Cymaeans in 1102 BC and that Homer was born there at that time. By *c.* 800 BC the predominant pottery in Smyrna was Ionian, suggesting a shift in cultural influence and, perhaps, in power (Boardman 1980: 28, Cook 1952: 104). Smyrna was already an Ionian city by 688 BC, says Pausanias, commenting on the victory of a Smyrnaean in the 23rd Olympiad (5.8.9).

Of course, in Mimnermus' treatment the line between history and fiction is not clear-cut. In fact, there was another, more popular founding myth for Colophon, which was in circulation by the 7th or 6th century BC, but perhaps even older: that the city was founded by Manto, daughter of the seer Teiresias, after receiving an oracle from Delphi, or by her husband Rhacius, or by their son Mopsus (cf. *Epigonoi* fr. 3 *GEF*; *FGrH* 115 fr. 346; Paus. 7.3.1–2, 9.33.2; Pomponius Mela 1.88). Mimnermus' account is radically different, the only common element being the motif of divine support, which is a *sine qua non* for foundation myths. In trying to reconcile the two traditions, Mac Sweeney (2013: 122) suggests that "Perhaps there was a section of the Colophonian society which sought to promote an aggressively macho view of their own past, countering the feminine mysticism of the dominant account". Similarly, there were alternative foundation myths for Smyrna, namely that it was originally occupied by an eponymous Amazon (*FGrH* 70 fr. 114a; Strabo 11.5.4) or by Ephesians, as Mimnermus' contemporary poet Callinus of Ephesus maintained (Strabo 14.1.4). Again, these conflicting tails "may be the traces of inter-city rivalry between the Ionians, where Ephesians and Colophonians vied to get one over on each other and on Smyrna" (Mac Sweeney 2013: 192). If so, then the first performance would not have been addressed to a general Smyrnaean audience (cf. Bowie 2009: 114), but to the Pylian-Colophonian faction in particular. As for the timing, Wilamowitz 1913: 283 proposes that Mimnermus composed the poem on the occasion of a contemporary crisis, namely the Lydians' attack on Smyrna under Alyattes *c.* 600 BC (cf. Cook 1985). For an alternative hypothesis, see p. 31.

Mimnermus uses the first person plural ἀφικόμεθα… ἑζόμεθ'… εἵλομεν, "we arrived… we settled… we captured", not because "the speaker or speakers took part in the migration movement of the Pylians" (Tsagarakis 1977: 27), but to refer collectively to his ancestors from two separate generations – two generations, indeed, quite distant from each other – thus affirming his contemporaries' ethnic identity. Cf. Tyrt. fr. 2.13–15 "Together with the Heraclids, we left windy Erineus and came to the Peloponnese" (Allen 1993: 81; Gehrke 2019: 97). I find it unlikely that Mimnermus was contemporary with the second migration of the Pylians, from Colophon to Smyrna, not only because that migration may well have happened before 800 BC, but also because nothing in language or metre suggests a disruption in Mimnermus' narration of a mythologised past. Indeed, the phrase 'from there' (κεῖθεν δὲ v.5), whenever used before Mimnermus, never entails a narrative leap from 'back then' to 'recently' (cf. *Il.* 15.235, 21.42; *Od.* 1.285, 13.278). In terms of expression, and comparing with other long fragments, the first impression is that of a different Mimnermus: verbs (narration) rather than adjectives (description) predominate, no metrical surprises arise, no concrete symbols or similes are employed. On a closer reading, however, the poet's rhythmical skills and playfulness manifest themselves once again. The dense use of *homoeoteleuta* allows the flow and contributes to the mythicisation of the narrative: λιπόντες–ἔχοντες–ἡγεμόνες, ἀφικόμεθα–ἑζόμεθ' ἀ…, ἱμερτὴν–ἐρατὴν, Ἀσίην–βίην, ὕβριος–Ἀλήεντος.

Bowie 2009: 113 suggests that Mimnermus "uses perhaps clichéd eroticising language", but I wish to develop this observation into a positive, even if exaggerated, hypothesis. Apart from the openly erotic adjectives ἱμερτὴν, 'longed-for', and ἐρατὴν, 'lovely', which indeed apply to cities in a formulaic manner (e.g. Solon fr. 1.1 ἱμερτῆς Σαλαμίνος, *Hymn. Hom. Ap.* 477 πόλιν ἐρατὴν), the phrase βίην… ἔχοντες, 'we took by force', inevitably bears sexual connotations (cf. Henderson 1991 §§222, 231, 383), as does the naval imagery (cf. Kanellakis 2022: 428–30). Moreover, the name of Pylos itself can be a *double entendre* (< πύλη = 'the gate', cf. Ar. *Lys*. 1163; Anaxandr. fr. 33.17 K-A) and its qualification as αἰπεῖάν, 'rugged', only intensifies this ambiguity (cf. Archil. fr. 331 συκῆ πετραίη, with Swift 2019: 432). The participle ἀπορνύμενοι ('having set off') may also be read as a vaginal metaphor (cf. n.5) or humorously (mis)read as "having left the prostitute" (α+πόρνη). The verb εἵλομεν (< αἱρῶ, 'we seized') may be understood – especially in view of Smyrna being an Amazon's name – as "we picked her as a sex slave" (cf. *Il*. 9.139, 272, 281). Therefore, instead of a serious historical lesson on *hubris* that aims at either reassuring or censuring Mimnermus' contemporaries in view of a current crisis (cf. n.4; Steinmetz 1969: 76–77; Allen 1993: 78), and far from "an almost dry piece of narrative" (Bowra 1938: 28), the fragment offers a cheerful, if implicit, pornographic mythology of the Pylian-Lydian (or Pylian-Aeolian) conflict. In fact, it resembles the Herodotean attribution of the conflict between Europe and Asia to reciprocal rapes, and the parody of that tale in Ar. *Ach*. 524–39; for more potential influences of Mimnermus on Herodotus, see Bowie 2018a: 64–67. Mimnermus' suggestive language allows such a re-reading of the fragment:

Abandoning the rugged Front Door that is Neleus' city,
we approached sexy Asia with full mast
and in taking passionate Colophon forcefully
we found our position, we masters of hard violence.
And then, leaving that whore behind, through the Ales river
we took Smyrna the Aeolian girl, by the gods' will.

In this subtext, the Pylian migration is rendered as a departure from boring sex with an old Nelean woman (Messenia), to violent sex with a prostitute (Colophon), and then to pleasant sex with a young girl (Smyrna); with the latter, the Pylians could finally ‘settle down’. Such an erotic version of history can explain how a fragment which we would expect to find in *Smyrneis* actually comes from *Nanno*, a collection named after a *hetaira*! (Cf. Bowie 2009: 113 n.11, who proposes that the fragment may be “a reworking for sympotic performance of a part of the *Smyrneis*”.) This provocative reading is a less eccentric solution than imagining *Smyrneis* as a section of, or even another name for, *Nanno* (cf. Gerber 1970: 113; ruled out by Bowie 1986: 30).

1. Pylos, the city of Neleus: Neleus was son of Poseidon and the Thessalian princess Tyro, and twin brother of Pelias; the two brothers fought for the crown of Iolcus, Pelias won and banished Neleus to Messenia, where he became king of Pylos. He bequeathed the throne to his son Nestor, the king known for his wisdom in Homer. **steep Pylos:** at the start of the line, the manuscripts deliver αἰπὺ τε Πύλον and ἐπεί τε Πύλον, which are both unmetrical – we need more syllables. Of the numerous corrections proposed, I consider αἰπειἄν τε Πύλον (Hiller 1888: 132) the most economical; cf. *Od.* 3.485 = 15.193 Πύλου αἰπὺ πτολίεθρον, *Il.* 9.668 Σκῦρον ἑλὼν αἰπεῖαν, Ἐνυῆος πτολίεθρον. Other proposals see a reference to Aipy, a city also belonging to Neleus’ kingdom (e.g. Αἰπὺ < > τε Πύλον, West 1992; Αἰπύτιόν τε Πύλον, Huxley 1959; Αἶπύ τε καὶ τὸ Πύλου, Steinmetz 1969); but there is no good reason why Mimnermus would have mentioned any other city along with Pylos as the point of departure. Other proposals try to combine the two readings delivered by the manuscripts (e.g. αἰπὺ δ’ ἐπεί τε Πύλον, Szádeczky-Kardoss 1959; αἰπὺ δ’ ἐπεί τε Πύλου, Edmonds 1931; αἰπὺ δ’ ἔπειτα Πύλον, De Falco 1946), but such solutions violate the stemmatic method, for two wrongs do not make a right (cf. Emiliani 2021: 159).

2. to longed-for Asia: initially the term ‘Asia’ referred exclusively to western Anatolia, as it does here in Mimnermus, and it was only later, during the course of the 6th century, that the term came to designate an entire continent (Mac Sweeney 2017: 384; cf. *Il.* 2.461, Hes. *Cat.* fr. 180.3 M-W, Archil. fr. 227). Asia is here called ‘desired’ probably for its alleged lavishness and effeminacy – a stereotype fixed by Herodotus' time with particular reference to the Lydians and later the Persians (Hdt. 1.71) but already evidenced in Sappho (cf. Nagy 1990: 285). It is indeed "hard to imagine that the poet [*sc.* Mimnermus] who celebrated Smyrna's resistance to Gyges [*sc.* in *Smyrneis*] could have spoken of 'desirable Asia' if the name still evoked memories of Lydian aggression"; but this should not make us assume (*pace* Allen 1993: 80–81) that in Mimnermus' time 'Asia' meant the Anatolian coast rather than western Anatolia in general – the two meanings probably coexisted, in the same way that today 'Athens' means both the city of Athens and the Attica Basin. The word 'Asia' would not evoke warlike associations *only*, and the very adjective ἱμερτὴν suggests that the poet aimed for the erotic nuances of the toponym.

3. lovely Colophon: this is the first attestation of the toponym. **with our overwhelming force:** for the expression cf. Hes. *Theog*. 670 βίην ὑπέροπλον ἔχοντες, said of the Titans, and for the sexual overtones of the phrase, as well as of ἐρατὴν, 'lovely', see the introductory note. The intertext with the Titans seems more appropriate if the Pylians attacked other Greek settlers, i.e. people of the same 'kin', rather than indigenous people – but as mentioned above, this is unknown. Whether 'overwhelming force' is an objective description of the size of the Pylian troops and their heavy armour, or a euphemistic description of their excessive violence (a massacre?) is also unclear; but in view of *hubris* in next line, which must be associated with the 'overwhelming force' (cf. Jacoby 1918: 273), the latter scenario appears more likely than generally accepted (cf. Allen 1993: 77).

4. we settled: for ἕζομαι, and more frequently καθέζομαι, in the sense 'to occupy a country', cf. Thuc. 2.18, 7.77. The morphology of the particular form ἑζόμεθ[α] has been debated, but its tense-value is certainly the aorist, as it is in Homer. **instigators of painful hubris:** that Mimnermus characterises his ancestors 'leaders/instigators of painful *hubris*/violence' has been read, almost invariably after Wilamowitz 1913: 283, as an expression of regret for, and condemnation of their shameful deeds – and by extension, an example to be avoided by all next generations – and what remains debatable is whether that *hubris* referred to violence inflicted upon other Greek settlers or upon the natives. Extending Wilamowitz's train of thought, Jacoby 1918: 267–75 argued that the current (in Mimnermus' day) aggression of the Lydians (under Alyattes) against Smyrna would have been viewed as a retribution for the Pylians' past *hubris*, which must therefore refer to violence exercised against 'Asian' people in Colophon. But there are counterarguments too: apart from the Titans-intertext above, the most serious objection is that *hubris* (a moral assault, apart from physical) against *barbarians* is something unconceivable; cf. Immisch 1890: 143, Lenschau 1944: 229. The pornographic subtext which I propose for the fragment fits better with the scenario of 'Asian' inhabitants: given that tales of Euro-Asian rapes were already an old tradition in Herodotus' time, then Mimnermus too must have mythicised thus (i.e. as a rape) the violence against *natives* of Colophon. Note that *hubris* does apply to sexual harassment and rape of women (cf. *Od.* 4.321; Hes. *Theog.* 307, fr. 148a M W; Thuc. 8.74.3; Lys. fr. 79 Carey; Aeschin. *de falsa leg.* 4; Isoc. *Ep.* 9.10; Polyb. 6.8.5).

5. setting out from the Ales river: the manuscripts deliver κεῖθεν †διαστήεντος†..., which needs to be corrected so as to specify the river. Whether the reference was to Colophon's river Ales, mentioned by Paus. 7.5.10, 8.28.3 (hence δ' Ἀλήεντος, Brunck 1776: 10), or some otherwise unattested Asteeis river (hence δ' Ἀστήεντος, Brunck 1772: 62; cf. *BAtlas*, map 56: E5), or Smyrna's river Meles (hence δ' αὖτε Μελήτος, Cook 1965: 150) is uncertain. See further discussion in Emiliani 2021: 160–67. Considering this debate to be of geographical rather than literary interest, I have adopted the most popular emendation, δ' Ἀλήεντος. For the humorous potential of ἀπορνύμενοι see introductory note and cf. *Hymn. Hom. Ap.* 29: "Leto bore you ... in Delos... From there you went forth [ἔνθεν ἀπορνύμενος] and became lord over all humankind"; technically speaking, Apollo went forth not only from Delos, but also from his mother's 'harbour'.

6. Smyrna the Aeolian city: for Smyrna's Aeolian past and the sexual hint in εἵλομεν, 'we took', see introductory note, and cf. Tyrt. fr. 5.2–3 Μεσσήνην εἵλομεν εὐρύχορον, Μεσσήνην ἀγαθὸν μὲν ἀροῦν, ἀγαθὸν δὲ φυτεύειν· ("We seized Messene, the wide one, Messene which is good to plough and good to sow"). **by the gods' will:** the phrase θεῶν βουλῇ, for whose possible meanings see the introductory note, might cause confusion: how could the gods ever favour the *hubristic* settlers? The phrase is "comprehensible only if the capture of Smyrna by the poet's ancestors is favourably contrasted with his Pylian great-ancestors' forceful settling at Colophon" (Allen 1993: 11). This is not the only possible explanation. In fact, Mimnermus may well have aimed for that (im)moral confusion: in his thought, values do not seem to bother the gods; the same gods who want men to suffer are unlikely to care about *hubris*. In Mimnermus, moral criteria are "completely dispensed with" (Snell 1953: 177).

FRAGMENTS 11+11a

The theme of this poem is mythological: the quest of Jason and the Argonauts for the golden fleece, a myth already known in some form to Homer (*Od.* 12.69–72) and to other, now lost, early epics (*Corinthiaca* fr. 23 *GEF*; *Carmen Naupactium* frr. 5–9 *GEF*). Hesiod too has some explicit references, but those come from sections which are considered later additions (*Theog.* 956–62, 992–1002; West 2005b: 40 n.3). Lyric poets other than Mimnermus who deal with Jason are Simonides (fr. 576), Ibycus (fr. 301) and Pindar (*Pyth.* 4.70 f.) All this material, and especially the fact that Homer calls Argo πασιμέλουσα, 'a ship known to all', suggest the existence of a pre-Homeric *Argonautica* (Huxley 1969: 60); since no testimony of any *Argonautica* of that period has reached us, we must assume that it only existed in oral form (West 2005b: 39–40). As for the place and purpose of Jason's story in Mimnermus' oeuvre, the current fragments seem to offer a mythological parallel to fr. 9: the Pylians reached Smyrna with divine aid and with erotic motivation, as did the Argonauts reach Aea (cf. n.1). Jason's journey was different in many respects indeed – most importantly, he went to Aea for a specific task rather than to settle – but the parallelism for which Mimnermus seems to be aiming is the element of divine support. The concept of *hubris* also permeates both fragments: the Pylians were violent towards the Colophonians (fr. 9.4) as was Pelias towards Jason (fr. 11.3); and as Pelias was later punished for his *hubris*, so were the Pylians' descendants exiled from Colophon. For a possible context of performance, cf. p. 33.

We do not know how many couplets have been omitted in between the two fragments. Sometimes Strabo uses ὑποβάς, "and he says below", to mean 'in the next line' (cf. Str. 8.3.28 quoting *Il.* 11.757–60, with only half a verse omitted); but elsewhere he means 'several lines below' (cf. Str. 13.1.36 quoting *Od.* 14.469 and 14.496, with almost thirty verses omitted). On one occasion (Str. 7.3.4) he makes the specification καὶ ὑποβάς μικρὸν ("And *a bit* further down he says"), which suggests that ὑποβάς alone was expected to be understood either as "immediately afterwards" or as "long further down". At any rate, the omitted section would refer to the challenges of the journey in more detail and/or to the aid which Jason received. Gemin 2020 finds some striking verbal and syntactical echoes of fr. 11 in *Medea* 6–10, the difference being that, while Mimnermus focuses on Jason and the outward journey, Euripides shifts focus onto Medea and the return trip to Greece. I reproduce Gemin's table, with minor adjustments:

	Mimn. fr. 11	**Eur. *Med.* 6–10**
Apodosis	οὐδέ κοτ' ἂν μέγα κῶας ἀνήγαγεν αὐτὸς Ἰήσων ἐξ Αἴης (*Jason himself would never have brought back the great fleece from Aea*)	οὐ γὰρ ἂν δέσποιν' ἐμὴ Μήδεια πύργους γῆς ἔπλευσ' Ἰωλκίας (*My lady Medea would not have sailed to the towers of Iolcus*)
Subordinate participle	τελέσας ἀλγινόεσσαν ὁδόν (*accomplishing a painful journey*)	ἔρωτι θυμὸν ἐκπλαγεῖσ' Ἰάσο-νος· (*having her heart smitten with love for Jason*)
Subordinate participle	ὑβριστῇ Πελίῃ τελέων χαλε-πῆρες ἄεθλον, (*accomplishing a difficult labour for shameless Pelias*)	κτανεῖν πείσασα Πελιάδας κό-ρας πατέρα (*having persuaded Pelias' daughters to kill their father*)
Apodosis	οὐδ' ἂν ἐπ' Ὠκεανοῦ καλὸν ἵκοντο ῥόον (*nor would they have reached Oceanus' fair stream.*)	οὐδ' ἂν…κατῴκει τήνδε γῆν Κορινθίαν (*nor would she be inhabiting this land of Corinth now.*)

I cannot find similar echoes of fr. 11a in *Medea*'s prologue, which would have given us a clue to how many verses Strabo omitted in his quotation.

1. the great fleece: the fleece, more often τό δέρος or δέρας (< δέρω, 'to flay') but here τό κῶας (uncertain etym.; irreg. without gen.; pl. τά κώεα; dimin. τό κώδιον) is called μέγα in the sense 'precious', rather than 'big in size', given its golden colour (cf. Hes. *Cat.* fr. 68 M-W; Pind. *Pyth.* 4.231; Eur. *Med.* 5; Theoc. *Id.* 13.16; Ap. Rhod. *Argon.* 1.889). **would never have … nor would…:** lines 1–4 are the apodosis to a missing protasis, with the conditional expressing the counterfactual, insofar as Jason *did* come back with the golden fleece, and the Argonauts *did* enter the Oceanus river on the way towards Aea, where the fleece was kept. These two events of the journey are mentioned in *hysteron proteron*, i.e. the more important comes first, even though it happened second. The protasis of the conditional (with εἰ+indic. past) is not preserved, but obviously it meant "If X had not helped", and could either precede the apodosis, as is the case with *Medea* 1–6, or follow it. The identity of X is debatable. **Jason himself:** at first glance, the phrase 'Jason himself' or 'Jason alone' – we must assume a bucolic diaeresis emphasising αὐτὸς – could make one think that the protasis perhaps mentioned the aid he received from the Argonauts, but since the latter too are said to have been beneficiaries (v.4), then this scenario seems improbable. Theoretically, we could imagine a chiastic structure praising their bilateral support (i.e. [*If the Argonauts had not participated*], *Jason alone would not have brought back the fleece, nor would the Argonauts have reached Oceanus,* [*if Jason was not a good leader*]). But the fact that fr. 11a returns to Jason (v.7) suggests that the poet did not aim for a 'democratic' representation. Other candidates proposed for the X-factor in the protasis are Medea (Bowra 1938: 27), Aphrodite (Pfeiffer 1928: 143), Hera (Dräger 1996: 38–41), and the gods' will in general (Allen 1993: 89). According to Ap. Rhod. *Argon.* 3.23–29, it was Hera who persuaded Aphrodite to send Eros to make Medea fall in love with, and therefore help, Jason; but an archaic poet might not have had this exact sequence in mind. For certain, Medea is the least likely candidate, for she only helped with the seizure of the fleece and the escape from Aea. Aphrodite does not seem to have been involved in the outward journey either (Pind. *Pyth.* 4.213–23). Hera, on the contrary, is said to have 'escorted' the Argo, being a steady ally of Jason (Ἥρη παρέπεμψεν, ἐπεὶ φίλος ἦεν Ἰήσων, *Od.* 12.72) and to have instilled the Argonauts with *passion* for joining the enterprise in the first place (ἡμιθέοισιν πόθον ἔνδαιεν Ἥρα ναὸς Ἀργοῦς, Pind. *Pyth.* 4.184–5). Hera's divine support in the form of erotic motivation for sailing is a perfect fit for the protasis, both in view of the apodosis, and of fr. 9 as interpreted earlier. Also, the fact that 'the Argonauts' are absent from the apodosis – they are only implied as subject of ἵκοντο, '[they] have reached' (v.4) – strengthens the case that they were mentioned in the protasis. To appropriate Pindar, I propose the reconstruction: [*If Hera had not kindled in these demigods* (= the Argonauts) *that most seducing, sweet longing for the ship Argo*,] *Jason himself would never…*

2. from Aea: in his *hysteron proteron*, Mimnermus first mentions the return *from* Aea – ἐξ Αἴης is aptly positioned in enjambment, so as to qualify both ἀνήγαγεν ("he brought back from Aea") and ὁδόν ("journey from Aea") – and will then (vv.4–7) describe Argo's outward route. One may reasonably wonder, "Did the Argonauts sail out to Aea on the Ocean, or to Colchis on the Black Sea? […] Colchis appears to have come rather late to the Jason myth, first mentioned only in Eumelus in the sixth century BC [fr. 17 *GEF*]. Prior to him, Jason's journey was instead said to be the fabulous land of Aea. Later writers tried to harmonise the divergent traditions by making Aea the capital of Colchis, but this is a rather late development. […] The land of Aea may take its name from the Akkadian and Babylonian goddess of the dawn, Aya, wife of the sun, or from an Indo-European word for the sun's radiance, so in this sense Aeëtes may be some garbled transmission of an old name or epithet for a sun god. This suspicion finds confirmation in the universal description of Aeëtes as the son of Helios, the Greek sun god" (Colavito 2014: 101, 141, 151). Aea does not appear in Homer, who only uses the adjective Αἰαίη ('the Aeëan') for Circe and her island (*Od.* 12.3, 268) – the sorceress was Aeëtes' sister. **a painful journey:** we do not know what exactly Jason's ἀλγινόεσσαν ὁδόν back to Iolcus comprised in the archaic tradition, other than the Argo's passing through the Planctae Rocks (*Od.* 12.71), which may or may not be identified with the Clashing Rocks (whose passing, however, is placed by Pindar *Pyth.* 4.207–10 during the Argo's *outward* journey to Aea). Apollonius makes a clear but probably invented geographical distinction to avoid confusion (*Argon.* 2.420–22, 4.860): passing the Clashing Rocks (the Bosporus) on the way to Aea, and the Planctae (somewhere in the Ionian Sea) on the way back.

3. for shameless Pelias: Πελίῃ is dative of advantage ("in the interest of Pelias"). A jealous and power-hungry man, hence a ὑβριστής, Pelias had usurped the throne of Iolcus from his half-brother Aeson, whom he imprisoned in the dungeons of the city. To avoid any retaliation, Pelias banished his brother Neleus, who then founded Pylos in Messenia (cf. fr. 9 n.1), and half-brother Pheres, who then founded Pherae in Thessaly. While imprisoned, Aeson begot Jason and sent him to Mount Pelion, to protect him from Pelias, where he was raised by the centaur Chiron. When Jason came of age and visited Iolcus, Pelias ordered him to retrieve the golden fleece from Aea only to ensure his death, because Jason was the legitimate heir to the throne. **fulfilling a difficult labour:** contrary to Pelias' expectation, Jason succeeded in his task (cf. n.5); there is a clear touch of surprise in the phrase τελέων χαλεπῆρες ἄεθλον, enhanced by the *hapax* adjective and the emphatic repetition τελέσας-τελέων. Upon the return of Jason from Aea with Medea and the fleece, Pelias still refused to surrender the throne of Iolcus, and so Medea conspired to have his own daughters slay and boil him, supposedly to rejuvenate him. Thus did Pelias pay for his *hubris*.

4. reached the fair stream of Oceanus: hereafter (part of) the Argo's outward trip is described. The Argonauts entered the Black Sea from Bosporus and sailed east, along the coastline (north of Turkey), until they reached Aea (Georgia). That was Strabo's understanding too, as we gather from his comment that Mimnermus placed Aea at Oceanus, far towards the sunrise (πρὸς ταὶς ἀνατολαῖς ἐκτός). Not yet known to be an enclosed sea, the Black Sea was thought of as a river, the Ocean river, which surrounded the flat earth and provided all waters on it; cf. *Il.* 18.399, 607; Hes. *Theog.* 337, 368–69.

5. To Aeëtes' city: Aeëtes, the first mythical king of Aea/Colchis, was the son of the god Helios and father of Medea (cf. *Od.* 10.138; Hes. *Theog.* 958–61; Pind. *Ol.* 13.53 with *schol.* 74a; on his name cf. n.2). Here Helios, who is described as **swift** (ὠκύς) in line with Mimnermus' usual view on the passing of time (cf. frr. 2.7–8, 14.11), is not explicitly referred to as Aeëtes' father; but the fact that his rays are stored in Aea (*sc.* as heirlooms) allows such an implication. Aeëtes agreed to concede the golden fleece if Jason managed to complete three tasks, which he did with some magical help from Medea: to yoke a pair of fire-breathing oxen, to sow a field with dragons' teeth, and to overcome the sleepless dragon who guarded the fleece. Some elements of this narrative would probably feature in the missing lines.
6. Sun's rays: the sunrays are sometimes thought of as a body part of Helios, namely his eyes (*Od.* 11.16), and sometimes as a throwing weapon, not unlike the lighting bolt of Zeus (*Od.* 5.479) – here in the latter sense, insofar they are kept inside a room (κεέαται = Ionic form of κεῖνται). **rest in a … chamber:** why are they stored? Either because the sun needs new rays to throw on earth every day (Allen 1993: 92), or because he keeps his (permanent) rays locked while he is sleeping – "in Near Eastern belief, derived from a geocentric model of the cosmos, the sun passed the night-time hours beneath the earth, in the underworld, where he was also the judge of the dead" (Colavito 2014: 159) – or because, as suggested earlier, he has inherited them to Aeëtes. **golden chamber:** the chamber is 'golden' either because it was conceived as made of gold, or (metonymically) because of the rays it hosted – the sunlight is traditionally thought of as gold in colour (cf. *Od.* 18.296; Aesch. *Ag.* 288; Eur. fr. 771.3 *TrGF*; Hdt. 2.132.1). At any rate, the pleasant imagery provides relief from the anxiety built up in the preceding lines. According to Apollonius, Hephestus had crafted marvellous decorations for Aeëtes' palace, "in payment of thanks to Helios, who had taken the god up in his chariot when faint from the Phlegraean fight" (*Argon.* 3.233–34).
7. at the edge of Oceanus: Aeëtes' city is located at the end of Oceanus, i.e. at the edge of the world (cf. n.4), insofar as "Aea was still a fantastic, mythical land in the seventh century, not yet part of

the real world of the Black Sea the Greeks were starting to colonise" (Colavito 2014: 92). If I am right in seeing a parallelism with fr. 9, then Mimnermus claims that Smyrna was as exotic a destination for the Pylians, as Aea was for the Argonauts. **glorious Jason:** lit. 'divine' (in beauty; cf. Ap. Rhod. *Argon.* 3.443–57; Val. Flac. *Argon.* 8.26–31).

Looking at artefacts

Even though Ἰάσων means 'healer', almost nothing survives to highlight that aspect of the hero. Conceivably, that tradition vanished early because it would be hard to reconcile with Medea's expertise in herbs – for e.g. he would be able to cure his new wife of Medea's poisons. The archaic 'Argonauts krater' is not only one of the earliest surviving depictions of Jason in Greek pottery, but also our sole testimony of Jason as a healer. Specifically, Jason, whose name is inscribed vertically behind his head, appears treating the blind seer

Corinthian krater, c. 575 BC. Archaeological Museum of Thessaloniki, inv. no 3656.

Phineus, who in return shakes hands with (i.e. provides his prophetic services to) the Argonauts Castor and Pollux. Indeed, it was Phineus who instructed Jason how to safely pass through the Clashing Rocks (Ap. Rhod. *Argon.* 2.309–44). But the healing episode itself is unattested in literature, while in Apollonius' version, Phineus says that there is no remedy for his blindness (*Argon.* 2.441–47; for more detailed analyses, see Vojatzi 1982: 71–87; Mackie 2001; Kefalidou 2008). Mackie, in particular, discusses at length how unparalleled in art and in literature this representation of Jason is, but ignores Mimnermus' account. While it is true that fr. 11+11a does not mention the episode with Phineus, v.2 τελέσας ἀλγινόεσσαν ὁδόν does allow for some medical associations, i.e. that Jason "executed a painful course [*sc.* of treatment]" (cf. Gal. *Meth. Med.* 5.390 Kühn ὁ τὴν ὁδὸν ἅπασαν ἐπιστάμενος τῆς θεραπείας) or that he "brought the painful course [*sc.* of the disease] to an end" (cf. LSJ *s.v.* τελέω A6). The lost verses could explicitly refer to Phineus, but this we cannot know. What we *can* assume rather safely is that the Argonauts krater did have some poetic precedent; cf. Wachter 2001: 293–94, 335.

FRAGMENT 12

This fragment offers an aetiological myth for the daily route of the sun. The full concept, if we fill the narrative gaps with modest speculation, is that every time Eos ('Dawn') appears in the horizon, Helios ('Sun') has to mount a chariot (sunrise) and travel west across the sky (daytime); tired as he is from the journey, he falls asleep (sunset) and a cup-shaped bed carries him back to the far east (night-time), where his chariot and horses stand by, until Eos appears again. Only the nightly voyage is described in sufficient detail, whereas the other parts are deductively inferred. Helios' back-and-forth route and the 'elegiac' tone of the opening lines (1–3a) invite us to compare Helios to poor Sisyphus (on whose toil cf. fr. 5.6), but what follows is an allusive diversion to humour, as suggested below. The first who spoke of the sun's journey in a cauldron was the poet of the *Titanomachy* (fr. 10 *GEF* ἐπὶ λέβητος…διαπλεῦσαι), according to Athenaeus, and later fragments by Pherecydes (fr. 18a *FGrH*), Stesichorus (fr. 185) and

Aeschylus (fr. 69 *TrGF*) confirm that such a vehicle (there specified as a cup, δέπας) was used for Helios' *nightly* voyage in particular. Philodemus, 1st century BC, offers a testimony to Mimnermus' fragment (= fr. 23), which confirms that the voyage described happens each night (καθ' ἑκάστην νύκτα). He also says that Mimnermus is one among many poets and mythographers to present Helios as long-suffering (πολύμοχθον): "Mimnermus does *not* seem to disagree [*sc.* with those poets], saying that Helios sleeps every night". (Allen 1993: 105 ignores the negative οὐ in his translation, even though on p. 94 he prints the same text as I do in *Appendix II.*)

The paradoxicality of this statement – essentially, the paradoxicality of fr. 12 itself – has been ignored even by modern critics: how is sleeping a toil (πόνος, v.1)? The few attempts to address that contradiction are rather in the direction of covering it up: "Strictly speaking, the toil is continual, not continuous" (Allen 1993: 100); "The peace now enjoyed by the sun is only the ultimate result of tiredness, of abandonment, of resignation in the face of fatigue" (Bonelli 1977: 67, my transl.). But the text itself, with the metrical emphasis on πόνον, 'pain', and the hyperbole οὐδέ ποτ'...οὐδεμία, 'no ... ever ... at all', does not allow any reconciliation with the 'luxurious idleness' that follows. Only Euripides, for whom "to live is to die" (fr. 833 *TrGF*), or Aristophanes, who parodied such oxymora (*Ran.* 1477–8), could have envisioned that! Indeed Aristophanes offers a valuable gauge for the comic potential of our fragment. In *Acharnians*, some corrupt ambassadors, who receive their stipend but never actually go on a mission, fabricate a blatantly fake story of how they 'suffered' in having to ... sleep in luxurious chariots, and how they were 'forced' to ... drink wine from golden cups (*Ach.* 68–75 with Kanellakis 2020: 70–71). Similarly in Mimnermus, and for reasons explained below, Helios' cruise-and-sleep on a golden bed appears *para prosdokian* after "no rest is ever possible at all for him" (v.2); the same is true of his horses, who are also said to take no rest, but apparently they do so (vv.9–10).

Where did this fragment belong? Judging from other passages quoted nearby by Athenaeus, Lavagnini 1950: 6–8 proposed that fr. 12 formed part of an elegy dedicated to the labours of Hercules, who in various sources is said to have borrowed Helios' cup in order to reach Erytheia, in his quest for the cattle of Geryon (cf. Pherecydes and Stesichorus, cited earlier; Panyassis fr. 12 *GEF*; Aesch. fr. 74 *TrGF*; Apollod. 2.5.10–11). Alternatively, the motif of painful journey suggests a connection with Jason's expedition, which Mimnermus thematises in fr. 11+11a, which indeed concludes with a reference to Helios (Ercole 1929: 490 n.3). After all, Jason's love affair with Medea makes the Argonautic myth more appropriate for inclusion in *Nanno* than Hercules' labours (Suárez de la Torre 1985: 7–8, 17–19). A connection with fr. 4 could also work, since it mentions Tithonus, the husband of Eos (Szádeczky-Kardoss 1968: 944). Other scholars envisage fr. 12 in a philosophical rather than mythological context, perhaps introduced as "proof (note γάρ in v.1) that not only men, but even gods, must endure hardships" (Gerber 1970: 111; cf. Bowra 1938: 27 "Not even a great god like this is free from toil and trouble"); the poet seems to reflect on "the steady, incessant flight of days in which youth and life escape us" and therefore we are induced to feel "friendly sympathy" for Helios (Fränkel 1973: 213).

In my reading, on the other hand, it is envy rather than sympathy that comes forth. West 1997: 507 has proposed that Mimnermus' purpose was to *contrast* the eternal course of Helios with the numbered days of man, and the way in which Catullus (5.4–6) receives this fragment confirms that scenario: *soles occidere et redire possunt: | nobis cum semel occidit brevis lux, | nox est perpetua una dormienda* ("Suns can set and rise again; for us, once our brief light has set, there is one eternal night for sleeping"). I believe that this is precisely what the ironic *para prosdokian* (ἔλαχεν πόνον…εὕδονθ' ἁρπαλέως) comes to express. For unlike humans, whose daytime (youth) is unrepeatable (cf. fr. 2 n.8) and night-time (old age) irreversible, Helios will always have another day to shine – and still he complains, in what is essentially *a parody of mournful elegy*, for having to 'go to work' every morning! According to this reading, vv.1–4 represent Helios' *free indirect speech* (≈ "I suffer every day and I take no rest"), while vv.5–11 are the poet's/humans' sarcastic response (≈ "Indeed… you sleep all night, and wake up fresh each day"). The lavishness of the bed-cup, described with accumulated adjectives (vv.5–7), the delicate imagery which renders Helios a 'snowflake' (τὸν…φέρει, ἐφ' ὕδωρ, ἁρπαλέως), the possible *double entendre* about Eos (v.4), and the majestic address 'son of Hyperion' (v.11) also contribute to the ironic tone. Stylistically remarkable is also the perfect ring composition of vv.5–9a, schematically presented by Suárez de la Torre (1985: 11, 15–16), who connects it to Helios' circular route and sees it as offering mimetic possibilities for public performance.

1. γάρ does not necessarily mean (*pace* Gerber 1970: 111) that our fragment was preceded by lines now missing – it may just be a performative marker (cf. δέ in fr. 1 n.1). **has been assigned:** with ἔλαχεν Helios is presented as a passive instrument of the Fates (cf. fr. 2 n.5), who were indeed believed to be superior to the gods (Hes. *Theog.* 220), even Zeus himself in some sources (Aesch. *PV* 516–8; cf. Paus. 1.40.4). For the idea that the gods assumed their duties and realms of authority by lot, cf. *Il.* 15.187–92. **daily pain:** those who sympathise with Helios will perceive the epicism ἤματα πάντα (which is reserved for the end of the hexameter as almost invariably in Homer) as 'day by day', and synecdochally as 'eternally'; it may also have a spatial value here, pertinent to "the arc of the sky in whose vastness the sun is carried" (Bonelli 1977: 66, my transl.), i.e. 'across the day span'. However, for a sarcastic reader, ἤματα πάντα is understood as "all his days (as opposed to his nights)", which, Davies 1981: 169 explains, is an unusual sense but compatible with the contradiction introduced by v.5 ff. The bucolic diaeresis after, and perhaps a secondary hepthemimeral caesura before πόνον come to metrically render Helios' fatigue, but also to highlight πόνον as the concept soon to be contradicted – an exhausted exhale by Helios, and at the same time, an ironical pause for us, so that the key-word stands out.

2. no rest … at all: because the second negative (οὐδεμία) is compound, it simply confirms the first negative (οὐδέ ποτ') in a phenomenon called *negative concord*, thus producing the meaning "He never takes *any* rest" (Smyth §2761). Cf. Dem. 20.23 οὐδὲν ἔπασχε δεινὸν οὐδείς ("None suffered any evil"); Pl. *Phlb.* 19b.7–8 οὐδεὶς εἰς οὐδὲν οὐδενὸς ἂν ἡμῶν οὐδέποτε γένοιτο ἄξιος ("None of us can ever be of any use in anything”). Mimnermus subverts the epic description Ἠέλιον δ’ ἀκάμαντα, ‘Helios the untiring’ (*Il.* 18.239, 483; fr. adesp. 937.9 *PMG*), insofar as his Helios is, or at least claims to be, tired.

3. for him and his horses: according to Suárez de la Torre 1985: 11, the enjambment from the previous line underlines the unceasing toil – neither Helios nor the metre get a break! – but more likely it is only a symptom of space restrictions in v.2 (i.e. Mimnermus prioritised the emphasis on the negatives). A chariot is synecdochally inferred from ἵπποισίν τε καὶ αὐτῷ (Bonelli 1977: 66) and confirmed by ἅρμα in v.9. For the imagery, which is absent from Homer and probably imported from the East (West 1997: 507), cf. *Hymn. Hom. Dem.* 88, *Hymn. Hom. Merc.* 69, and a plethora of archaic vases. According to the poet of the *Titanomachy*, Helios had two male and two female horses (fr. 11 *GEF*). **rosy-fingered Dawn:** the formulaic adjective ῥοδοδάκτυλος for Eos is either a metaphor for the grades of colours (red, pink, orange, yellow) which spread across the sky like the fingers of an open hand, or just another way to say ‘beautiful’, ‘sexy’ (cf. Irwin 1994). **as soon as:** the manuscript reading ἐπὴν is perfectly satisfactory (ἐπεὶ + ἄν + subjunctive εἰσαναβῇ = present general, cf. frr. 2.9, 3.1), hence West was right to revoke his initial (*IEG*[1] 1972) correction to ἐπεὶ. At any rate, the temporal arrangement is accurate, for during a sunrise we first see the colours of the dawn in the horizon, and then appears the sun itself.

4. Oceanus ... sky: if the earth is surrounded by Oceanus river (cf. fr. 11 nn.4, 7) and covered by a hemispherical sky (cf. Hes. *Theog.* 127; Kirk *et al.* 1983: 9), then it is only logical why Eos is here said to emerge from the former and reach the latter – a conception which seems valid if one watches the sunrise from the beach. Cf. *Od.* 3.1–2 Ἠέλιος δ’ ἀνόρουσε, λιπὼν περικαλλέα λίμνην, οὐρανὸν ἐς πολύχαλκον (“And the sun, leaving the beautiful water surface, sprang up into the brazen heaven”); Hes. *Op.* 565–67 ἀστὴρ Ἀρκτοῦρος προλιπὼν ἱερὸν ῥόον Ὠκεανοῖο πρῶτον…ἐπιτέλλεται (“The star Arcturus leaves behind the holy stream of Oceanus and rises first”). **mounts the sky:** given Eos’ insatiable lust for men (including Tithonus, Cleitus, Cephalus and

Orion), her description as rosy-fingered/sexy (n.3), and the inclusion of the fragment in *Nanno*, it would not be far-fetched to read the line as a *double entendre*: "every time she abandons Oceanus and mounts Uranus"! For the verb in that sense, cf. *Il.* 8.291 ἠὲ γυναῖχ', ἥ κέν τοι ὁμὸν λέχος εἰσαναβαίνοι ("...or a woman who will go up into your bed").

5. Indeed ... carries him: for the *para prosdokian* introduced hereafter, see introductory note. For the ironic use of γὰρ ("Sure...", "Indeed..."), to pretentiously support but actually to undermine a statement – here, that Helios indeed suffers – cf. *Od.* 21.402 (with Monro §296); Eur. *Med.* 309; Ar. *Ach.* 71 (with Kanellakis 2020: 82). It is unclear whether the bed transports Helios alone, or his horses too (cf. n.10): at first glance τὸν μέν seems to suggest the former (West 1974: 176; Allen 1993: 103) but the singular may just result from the poet's focalisation on Helios (Bonelli 1977: 66); in fact, Pherecydes (fr. 18a *FGrH*) specified that Helios was carried σὺν ταῖς ἵπποις. In Mimnermus' conception, what matters is that Helios' nightly voyage is comfortable, with or without his horses. **a lovely bed:** the noun εὐνή describes any surface on/inside which one lies, not only a bed in the narrow sense, and therefore it is not unsuitable for Helios' cup. From his perspective, and for those who sympathise with him, the bed is πολυήρατος in the sense 'much longed for' (cf. *Od.* 23.354); but taking into consideration his fixed sleep-schedule, one can read the adjective as 'much enjoyed'. Cerri's suggestion 2014: 170 that the adjective signifies a nuptial bed in particular, on which Helios and his wife (i.e. Perseis: Hes. *Theog.* 956–57) have sex during the predawn hours, presupposes an absurd connection with Odysseus and Penelope's πολυήρατον εὐνήν (*Od.* 23.354). **over the waves:** harder to speculate is whether διὰ κῦμα is supposed to mean "(sailing) across the waves" or "(flying) above the waves"; ὑπόπτερος and ἄκρον ἐφ' ὕδωρ facilitate either sense (cf. n.7), while no iconographical evidence survives. There is no known representation in pottery of Helios *in a cup*, with or without his horses. Two vases proposed by Schauenburg 1962: 51–52 (Boston lekythos 93.99 and Vienna neck-amphora 815) depict a construction which is hardly identifiable with a cup –

indeed the scholar himself admits "we must assume that the painter is dependent on a model that he himself did not fully understand" (my transl.)

6. an adorned: the manuscripts deliver κοίλη, 'hollow', which lacks one syllable to fit the metre. Most editors accept Meineke's 1840: 417 correction to κοιίλη, an otherwise unattested form (hence accepted with reservation by Emiliani 2021: 189), by analogy to ὅμοιος = ὁμοίιος, *Il.* 4.315. I prefer ποικίλη, 'adorned' (Kaibel 1890: 33, also printed by West 1992 and Papademetriou 1984), not because 'hollow' would be "a surprising epithet for a bed" (West 1974: 175) – on the contrary, this is precisely the shape of Helios' εὐνή by convention – but because it makes more sense with the description that follows in v.7: any technician would produce a *hollow* cup, but only Hephaestus, who also decorated (ποίκιλλε, *Il.* 18.590) the magnificent shield of Achilles, would forge such a *splendid* one. Indeed, ποικίλη may be taken with the specific sense 'many-coloured' (LSJ, I), to encompass the colours of the sunset as counterpoint to the colours of the dawn (n.3). That Athenaeus introduces Mimnermus' fragment with the comment αἰνισσόμενος τὸ κοῖλον τοῦ ποτηρίου ("*alluding to* the hollowness of the cup, Mimnermus writes…") is not evidence that the words 'hollow' and/or 'cup' actually featured in the pom – it rather suggests the opposite. For that same reason I dislike ἀγκύλη ('curved'), proposed by Pace 1999: 241–43. **forged by Hephaestus' hands:** Aeschylus too attests that the cup was made by Hephaestus (fr. 69.2 *TrGF*) of gold (fr. 74.4 *TrGF*). For ἐληλαμένη (<ἐλαύνω) as 'forged', cf. *Il.* 12.295–96 ἀσπίδα…ἣν ἄρα χαλκεὺς ἤλασεν.

7. of precious gold: a genitive of material, χρυσοῦ qualifies ἐληλαμένη ('forged of gold') after enjambment, hence I delete West's comma between vv.6–7. Allen 1993: 104 attaches χρυσοῦ to εὐνή ('bed of gold'), claiming that ὑπόπτερος, 'winged', would be otherwise left 'unbalanced' in an 'top-heavy' appositional sequence. But syntax is not the only way a word receives emphasis: like πόνον, 'pain' (v.1), ὑπόπτερος is *metrically* highlighted, with a penthemimeral caesura before and a bucolic diaeresis after it. For the conception of the sun (and here, synecdochally, of his bed) as golden, cf. fr. 11 n.6. For the phrase 'precious gold', cf. *Il.* 18.475 (said of weapons), *Od.* 8.393 (of coins), 11.327 (of jewellery), Simon. fr. 16.2 (of the sun itself). **and winged:** all editors agree (after Heyne 1783) that we must correct ὑπόπτερον presented by the manuscripts to ὑπόπτερος, so as to qualify εὐνή, 'the bed', rather than Helios. The adjective qualifies the cup-bed as having wings (Allen 1993: 105), or oars (Gerber 1970: 112), or handles (Allan 2019: 127), or simply as 'speedy' (Suárez de la Torre 1985: 14; cf. θοὸν in v.9). I consider the last reading the least likely, because if Helios enjoys sleep in respect of luxury and comfort, he must also enjoy it in respect of duration – realistically speaking, night-time (excluding twilight) in this part of the planet lasts 6–12 hours, depending on season. Instinctually, 'with wings' sounds more probable, by analogy to Helios' chariot/horses. **on the surface of the waters:** ἄκρον ἐφ' ὕδωρ = "(flying) *over* the surface of the water" or "(sailing) *across* the surface of the water", or "(flying/sailing) *as far as* the edge of the waters" (cf. *CGL s.v.* ἐπὶ A3, A4, B10). The only other occurrence of the phrase is [Hes.] *Sc.* 317 οἵ ῥά τε πολλοὶ νῆχον ἐπ' ἄκρον ὕδωρ ("and many [swans] were swimming on/above/across the surface of the water"), but on that occasion ἐπί is largely dictated by the fact that the swans are represented *on the surface of a shield* (Koopman 2018: 36, 125 n.194, 169–72, 258). In other contexts, the same preposition denotes purpose or destination, e.g. Xen. *Cyr.* 5.49 Ἴτω τις ἐφ' ὕδωρ ("Someone go get water!").

8. while he's sleeping: in a striking hyperbaton which would be "unthinkable in Homer [and] stands as vivid witness to the literary rather than oral pedigree of Mimnermus' poetry" (Allan 1993: 102–103), εὕδονθ' (= εὕδοντα) qualifies τὸν μὲν…φέρει (v.5), either as a participle of time ("it carries him … while he's sleeping") or a supplementary predicate ("it carries him … asleep") – the latter is more difficult to grasp because of the distance from the verb. **delightfully:** for ἁρπαλέως cf. fr. 1 n.4, but here obviously used in a positive sense. **the place of Hesperides:** the (unspecified) far west, where Helios' nightly voyage begins, i.e. where the sunset takes place. Daughters of Night, who guard the golden apples beyond Ocean (Hes. *Theog.* 213–16), the Hesperides are the nymphs of evening, and by extension, of the west itself (cf. LSJ: ἑσπέρα ὥρα/χώρα; Servius on Virg. *Aen.* 4.484).

9. from the place ... to the land...: note the poetic placement of the prepositions in χώρου ἀφ' Ἑσπερίδων and in γαῖαν ἐς Αἰθιόπων (Smyth §1664). The two phrases are rhythmised by *isocolon* and *homoeoteleuton* to support the mythical narrative, but are spatially separated by enjambment to render the length of Helios' journey. **the land of the Ethiopians:** the (mythical) Ethiopians lived in the far east, where Helios' nightly voyage finishes, i.e. where the sunrise will take place. Their king was Memnon, son of Eos (Hes. *Theog.* 984), and their name signifies their colour and relation to the sun (<αἴθω, 'to burn'). Cf. Aesch. *PV* 807–8 "You will then come to a land at the furthest bounds of earth, to a black tribe [κελαινὸν φῦλον] that dwells at the sources of the sun, where flows the River Aethiops". For a detailed monograph, see Snowden 1970 (esp. 3–5 on their colour and 144–55 on mythology). On **δή** see next note. **his swift chariot and horses:** for the phrase 'chariot and horses' cf. *Il.* 8.438, 23.334, 24.440; for the application of 'swift' to this group, cf. Hes. fr. 30.6 M-W, [Hes.] *Sc.* 97; for Helios' horses in particular, cf. n.3 and the discussion below.

10. chariot and horses rest: are these horses and chariot the same as those of v.3, or does Helios employ a new set each day? The decision affects how we perceive ἑστᾶσ[ι]: the tired horses of the previous day would be 'resting', while a fresh crew would be 'awaiting'. In the former scenario, it is left unexplained how the horses return to the east at night – do they fly unguided or do they use the same bed as Helios? – while in the latter scenario it is left unexplained who provides endless chariots or what happens to the expiring ones (cf. n.5). The former scenario fits better my overall reading: if both Helios and his horses are said to take no rest (vv.2–3), then both Helios and his horses must appear resting for the *para prosdokian* to sound totally outrageous. This poetic intention is also signalled by **δή** (v.9) which may be used ironically: "...where *of course* his fast chariot and horses rest!" (cf. LSJ, A.II). And to make sure irony passes through, Mimnermus adds θοὸν near ἑστᾶσ(ι): the swift horses stand ... still! **early-born Dawn:** the epicism Ἠὼς ἠριγένεια occurs almost thirty times in Homer.

11. mounts his other vehicle: manuscript A, our sole witness for this line, delivers the erroneous reading ἐπεβη ἑτερεων ὀχέων. I prefer the correction to ἐπέβη ἑτέρων ὀχέων, already found in the aldine edition (Musurus 1514) and accepted by West, Allen, and Allan; the misspelling ἑτερεων was formed by analogy with ὀχέων, we must assume. Schneidewin's conjecture ἐπεβήσεθ' ἑῶν ὀχέων (accepted by Gentili-Prato, Gerber, Campbell, Diehl, and Emiliani) would require greater deviation from the manuscript, without providing better meaning. Each morning (ἐπέβη is gnomic aorist) Helios rides his "other vehicle", i.e. his day-chariot as opposed to his night-bed, or less likely "another vehicle", i.e. a new chariot as opposed to his expired one (Allen 1993: 109). **he 'son of Hyperion':** Hyperion was the father of Helios, Eos, and Selene (Hes. *Theog*. 371–74), but Homer also used the name as an epithet for Helios himself (*Il*. 8.480, 19.398; *Od*. 1.8, 12.133). Here I take "the son of Hyperion" to be an ironical address to Helios. Patronymics are often used in scornful contexts, e.g. Odysseus is sometimes referred to as the "offspring of Sisyphus" (a euphemism for 'bastard': Soph. *Phil*. 417; Eur. *IA* 524, *Cyc*. 104). In our case, of course, the patronymic is not used to laugh at Helios' ancestry, but to pretentiously glorify him. Similarly, in Aristophanes' *Frogs* Xanthias refers to Hercules as "the son of Alcmene" not out of honest reverence for him, but with fake reverence for Dionysus, who tries to pass off as Hercules (530–31, 582–83 with Kanellakis 2020: 188). Mimnermus appears to acknowledge and perhaps envy how privileged Helios is, just like Xanthias envies Dionysus: of course will "the son of Hyperion" rise up again tomorrow ("as opposed to us mortals", I suspect v.12 would continue).

Looking at artefacts

Our earliest certain representations in pottery of Helios, identified from the solar disk above his head, are on late 6th century lekythtoi. The pattern is fixed: Helios is shown frontally, riding his biga drawn by winged horses, which are shown in profile, either entire or as protomes; the zone under the horses represents the ocean, either rendered realistically with fish, or in a more abstract manner. This

Theran amphoriskos, c. 650 BC. British Museum 1950,1112.1. Drawing from Coldstream 2010: PLATE 78. ©The Trustees of the British Museum.

Attic black-figured lekythos attributed to Leagros Group, c. 520–500 BC. National Archaeological Museum, Athens, inv. no 513.

trend lasted until the middle of the 5th century, when showing Helios and his whole chariot in profile became the norm (also in sculpture, judging from Helios' tethrippa at the left corner of the Parthenon's east pediment). However, Coldstream 1965 proposes that this development was not unprecedented and that the earliest representation of Helios was actually in profile, on a Sub-Geometric vase from Thera datable to *c.* 650 BC, i.e. contemporary with Mimnermus' childhood. If Coldstream's identification of the Theran horseman with Helios is accepted, then that vase provides further support for how pioneering Mimnermus' poetic conception was for its time. By granting Helios free indirect speech (vv.1–4), Mimnermus moves towards bringing this mythical figure *vis-à-vis* with his audience, thus anticipating (and perhaps inspiring) the frontal depiction of Helios in late-archaic and proto-classical art.

FRAGMENT 13a

This is the only surviving fragment which is reported to come from *Smyrneis* – as is also the *sine versibus* fr. 13 (*Appendix II*). It is the opening of a battle scene, most probably the battle in the Hermus valley between Smyrnaeans and Lydians under Gyges, at some point in the 680s or 670s BC, which Mimnermus also thematises in fr. 14. Indeed, the champion who is eulogised in the latter fragment could be the most prominent of the men who are here said to fling themselves into the fight, or even the *basileus* himself – if the present fragment describes the Smyrnaeans, as I maintain below, and not the Lydians. (See also the introductory note on fr. 14.) The couplet appears to be the *tenor* of a simile ("…so did Z"), whose preceding *vehicle* ("Similar to X…") is missing. By standards of epic language, the *basileus*' men would have rushed into the battle like folks of bees (*Il.* 2.87) or flies (2.469) or birds (2.459) or stormy waves (2.144) or black clouds (4.275) or mountain streams (4.452) or lions (5.161) or stallions (6.506) or hunting dogs (8.338) or wild boars (12.41) or wolves (16.156) etc. It is generally assumed that the phrase ἐνεδέξατο μῦθον, 'when he gave the order' – for the verb, see below – implies that the *basileus*' command preceded in direct speech (Treu 1968: 105; West 1974: 74; Allen 1993: 23, 112; Bowie 2016: 28) but this is far from certain. The word μῦθος in Homer can refer to a direct speech which is about to begin (*Il.* 1.24 "And Agamemnon laid on Chrysis a stern *word*: «blah-blah-blah»); or to a direct speech which has just been completed (*Il.* 1.33 "«blah-blah-blah». So did Agamemnon spoke, and the old man obeyed his *word*"); or to an indirect speech (*Il.* 5.715 "We pledged *words* to Menelaus, that he would blah-blah-blah"); or even to a non-reported speech (*Il.* 3.212 "They began to weave the web of *words* and of devices in the presence of all").

1. the commander's men: οἳ πὰρ βασιλῆος, lit. "those [*sc.* men] beside the *basileus*"; cf. Xen. *Anab.* 1.1.5 τῶν παρὰ βασιλέως. In Homer, *basileus* designates any noble commander in a region, as opposed to *anax*, the King. Thus Ithaca has many *basileis* but only Telemachus is entitled to become *anax* after his father (*Od.* 1.394-8). In the *Iliad*, the title *anax* is mainly reserved for Agamemnon and Priam, while minor (in hierarchy) figures are occasionally called thus due to their prominence – more frequently, of course, Achilles; cf. Palaima 2020. It is unclear whether in Mimnermus' fragment *basileus* retains its Homeric sense, in which case it could either refer to the Smyrnaean or the Lydian commander-in-chief, or constitutes "the earliest extant application of βασιλεύς to any historical monarch", in which case it refers to Gyges. The latter scenario has monopolised scholars' attention (Hammond 1950: 52; Adrados 1956: 223 n.3; Mazzarino 1973: 40; Allen 1993: 112; Sider 2006: 334), even though contemporary sources suggest that the word did *not* yet mean a 'monarch', at least in Sparta where two *basileis* ruled (Tyrt. frr. 4.3, 5.1). **upon his order:** lit. "when of course [ῥ' = ἄρα] he gave [ἐνεδέξατο < ἐνδέκνυμι, Att. ἐνδείκνυμι = 'he declared'] the order". For μῦθος as 'military command', cf. *Il.* 16.83 πείθεο δ' ὥς τοι ἐγὼ μύθου τέλος ἐν φρεσὶ θείω (Achilles orders Patroclus to push the Trojans away from the Greek ships: "But obey, as I put in your mind the sum of my counsel").

2. so did (they) rush: ἤϊξαν < ἀΐσσω = 'to rush'. **fenced behind**

hollow shields: Tyrtaeus (fr. 19.7) applies the same phrase to the three Dorian tribes/army units of Sparta, i.e. to his compatriots, whom he imagines fighting together against a common enemy: ……]ạị κοίλης ἀσπίσι φραξ̣ά̣μ[ενοι. Indeed he describes them with the simile ……] ν ἔθνεσιν εἰδομ[ένους ("like hordes of…", 19.3) – the crucial word is lost, but σφηκῶ]ν, 'wasps', might be the most apt supplement (West 1967: 175). Given the near-identity of Tyrt. fr. 19.7 to Mimn. 13a.2, it is increasingly likely that Mimnermus too referred to his compatriots (and the Smyrnaean commander-in chief) rather than the Lydians (and Gyges), and also that he employed the same *vehicle* as Tyrtaeus – be that 'wasps' or something else. The epithet 'hollow' may denote either a pre-hoplite shield, usually round (cf. εὔκυκλος, *Il.* 5.797), with a central hand-grip for free manoeuvring and a baldric to hang from; or the hoplite type, also round but narrower, with double grip to keep the shield attached to the owner's forearm, and without baldric. Cf. Hammond 1950: 51–55, who nevertheless denies any reference to the hoplite shield here (*pace* Lorimer 1947: 122), taking for granted that Mimnermus speaks of Gyges and his men. In fact, 'fencing behind shields' is consistent with both pre-hoplite (mass combat in open formation) and hoplite tactics (the *phalanx* arrangement), hence our fragment does not help much in dating the introduction of hoplite warfare in Smyrna; cf. Wees 1994: 3–5.

FRAGMENT 14

This fragment is an encomium (cf. Jacoby 1918: 303) of a distinguished soldier, a Smyrnaean who routed the Lydian cavalry (under Gyges) in the Hermus valley in the 680s or 670s BC. The lyrical subject has learnt about that hero from his elders (v.2), who had witnessed him in the battlefield (i.e. were his contemporaries) and who might have died by the time of the poem's composition – the generation of men who were 20 to 40 years old in 670 BC was deceased by 610 BC. Not much can be deduced in respect to the dating issue: the only certainty is that Mimnermus cannot have been grown enough (i.e. a teenager) in 670 BC to have met that man in person. And because that man might have lost his life in (or soon after) the Hermus battle, the elegy may have been composed as early as *c.* 660 BC, when the fame of the recent hero would have excited a young poet, or as late as *c.* 600 BC, when all witnesses were long dead and a poet would have wished to preserve their memoirs. But the lyrical subject does not even have to be Mimnermus: he may just be a speaker within a battle narrative (Bowie 1986: 29 n.88). The battle is described in Homeric fashion – a one-man show without regard to the *phalanx* (Jacoby 1918: 287; cf. n.6) – indeed with "a larger number of epicisms than is normal in this poet" (Fowler 1987: 46; for a possible explanation see p. 1). But unlike Homer, who gains knowledge from the Muses to sing of distant mythical heroes, the lyrical subject draws on his fellow citizens to speak of the recent past (Swift 2015: 101; Allan 2019: 128).

Promoting the stereotype of 'Asianic hedonism', Pasquali 1923: 298–300 made the unfounded suggestion (cf. Miralles 1988: 37) that Mimnermus praised the legendary warrior only to declare his own impossibility of acting as heroically: like another Archilochus, he would readily drop off his shield! Yet the common reading is that Mimnermus here reproaches his contemporary Smyrnaeans for failing to imitate the bravery of their legendary ancestor who repelled Gyges, or that he exhorts them to fight likewise – the present threat must be Alyattes' attack, *c.* 600 BC. The decline of mankind from a golden past is a common archaic trope (Swift 2015: 101) but the specific model would be *Il.* 4.370–80, where Agamemnon reproaches Diomedes for being less brave than his father Tydeus (Jacoby 1918: 288–89; Fränkel 1973: 208; West 1974: 74; Allen 1993: 117; Allan 2019: 128). However compelling the theory, it is based on the weak assumption that τοῖον, 'similar/such' (v.2), must mean 'similar *to your spirit* / such *as your spirit*'. Yet the adjective may well be used absolutely (cf. LSJ, III and my translation), and also it is quite exceptional for Mimnermus to address his audience as 'you' (Miralles 1988: 39; cf. fr. 7 with introductory note). The fragment possibly comes from *Smyrneis* (a 'tempting' allocation for Bowie 1986: 29, which Diehl 1949, Steffen 1955: 9, Adrados 1956, and Szádeczky-Kardoss 1968: 945 accept) and conceivably from the same context as fr. 13a. The Smyrnaean hero praised here may be the *basileus* (commander-in-chief) or one of his men mentioned there. Allen 1993: 23 n.11 objects that fr. 14 "is too concise and personal to have come [from] a lengthy narrative elegy… [Instead, it] probably comes from a poem which was hortatory rather than narrative" (cf. n.2). But Bowie 1986: 29 rightly says that *Smyrneis* may well have featured exhortatory bits and passing comparisons with the present world *without* losing its narrative character, and that fr. 14 is not un-narrative, after all. Whether the fragment "is part of a shortish poem composed for sympotic performance" or part of *Smyrneis* "composed for first performance in public festivals" indeed remains inconclusive (Bowie 2010a: 59), but the association with fr. 13a proposed here offers further support to the latter scenario.

1. that man's: the verses preceding our fragment would specify whom κείνου refers to. **Nothing…:** the multiple negatives οὐ μὲν… οὔ ποτε (v.5) …οὐ γάρ τις (v.9) underline the uniqueness of the hero as it has been crystallised in the witnesses' memory, i.e. not necessarily in the most objective way, but invested in nostalgia. **power and noble spirit:** the phrasing is grandiose to render the nostalgia, with μένος and θυμὸς constituting a formulaic *hendiadys*; cf. *Od.* 11.562 δάμασον δὲ μένος καὶ ἀγήνορα θυμόν ("tame your power..."), *Il.* 20.174 ὣς Ἀχιλῆ' ὄτρυνε μένος καὶ θυμὸς ἀγήνωρ ("thus he roused Achilles' power…").

2. like: for the implications of τοῖον, see introductory note. **I learn from:** an εἶναι is implied as object to πεύθομαι ("I learn from my elders [that there is] nothing like that man's spirit"), even though I preferred to render v.1 as direct speech, syntactically independent from v.2. **from my elders:** ἐμέο προτέρων (gen. of source to πεύθομαι) = "from those before me"; cf. *Il.* 10.124. **who saw him:** the relative pronoun οἵ here introduces a relative clause *of cause*: "I learn from my elders, who/because they saw him…" (Smyth §2555). ἴδον entails "a visual narrative, with the details of location, military equipment, and the hero's dynamic movement through the battleline" (Swift 2015: 101). Grethlein 2007: 103–105 proposes, after Meineke 1857: lvii, that οἵ μιν ἴδον ("my elders, who saw him...") should be corrected to ὅς μιν ἴδον ("I who saw him". By mistake he prints ὡς, but his intention is clarified in Bowie 2010a: 59 n.5). The meaning would change drastically, with the lyrical subject appearing to *have* witnessed the brave warrior and to *ignore* his elders ("It is *not* from my elders that I learned of that man's bravery, *I* who saw him routing..."). I find this proposal improbable, for the word order ought to be οὐ μὲν προτέρων. As v.1 stands, the emphasis clearly lies on κείνου: "Nothing like *that* man's bravery", as opposed to any other's.

3. the Lydian cavalry: because the enemy is here specified to be the Lydians, we deduce that the hero, the witnesses, and the speaker must be Smyrnaeans. The Lydian cavalry was formidable (cf. Hdt. 1.79.3, speaking of Croesus' reign), which makes our protagonist's achievement even greater, all the more so considering the numerical disparity. **saw him routing:** κλονέοντα is a supplementary participle dependent on ἴδον. Cf. *Il.* 5.93–4 πυκιναὶ κλονέοντο φάλαγγες Τρώων. **the dense ranks:** πυκινὰς...φάλαγγας is a hyperbaton (unlike in my translation). πυκινός = poetic form of πυκνός. Of course in Homer, and here in Mimnermus, φάλαγξ does not mean the hoplite *phalanx* but a 'rank' of soldiers – here cavalrymen – and it almost invariably appears in plural; cf. Latacz 1977: 45–49.

4. at the plain of Hermus: the river (today Gediz) flows about 25km north of Smyrna, so we must assume that the Lydians were advancing from the highlands and the Smyrnaeans moved up the valley to repel them, hence the preposition ἂμ (apocope of ἀνὰ). Both Homer (*Il.* 20.392) and Hesiod (*Theog.* 343) mention Hermus. **Spearman:** modelled on the Homeric ἐϋμμελίης, 'armed with good ashen spear', the adjective φερεμμελίης (<φέρω + μελίη), 'bearing the ashen spear', is a *hapax* possibly devised for its alliterative effect near φῶτα (Gerber 1970: 114). I translate 'Spearman' after 'Superman'. **φῶτα φερεμμελίην:** ascriptive appositive qualifying μιν (v.2), distanced by hyperbaton. The preference for poetic φώς,-τός ('man', here in accusative) over ἀνήρ *vel sim.* is not only due to the Homeric tone of the fragment, but also to its significance – hence its repetition in v.9 – for decoding the sun metaphor (cf. nn.9, 11).

5. Never at all did...: for the negative, cf. *Od.* 11.258 κεῖνον δ' οὔ ποτε πάμπαν ἐγὼν ἴδον ὀφθαλμοῖσιν ("but never did my eyes see his handsome face grow pale at all"), and for the accumulative effect, cf. n.1. **Pallas Athena:** Athena is the most appropriate judge for our protagonist's courage, not only as the goddess of martial skill but also as patron of Smyrna. A magnificent temple dedicated to her was built in the early 7th century, located on the north-east side of the city. Thus Athena could be thought of as looking out towards Hermus river. If our elegy is hortatory, the message for the audience would be that Athena *still* witnesses the Smyrnaean's (lack of) bravery; Allen 1993: 119. **τοῦ μὲν:** genitive of possession to κραδίης ("the power of *his heart*") or genitive subjective to μένος ("*his power* of heart" v.6), separated in hyperbaton for emphasis.

6. his heart's fierce power: δριμὺ μένος κραδίης is equivalent to the *hendiadys* μένος και ἀγήνορα θυμὸν, "power and noble spirit" (vv.1–2), but this time the wording is purely Mimnermian (*pace* Allan 2019: 129 who lists the phrase among epicisms, yet without citing any parallels. The only possible candidate, *Od.* 24.318–9 ἀνὰ ῥῖνας δέ οἱ ἤδη δριμὺ μένος προὔτυψε, "and up through his nostrils shot a keen pang", is evidently unrelatable, both syntactically and semantically). The initial description of the hero by the first-hand witnesses, who as such employ Homeric language, has now given way to a more personal impression, as if Athena has mediated her autopsy to the lyrical subject. **whenever he hasted:** the use of optative in εὖθ'...σεύαιθ' (= εὖτε σεύαιτο < σεύω, 'every time he rushed') suggests that the narrative is iterative, i.e. that our hero had not fought only one battle against the Lydians. **among the fore-fighters:** as in Homer, here πρόμαχοι probably refers to the élite champions fighting individually before the eyes of the rest of the army, rather than to the front of the hoplite *phalanx*; cf. Gerber 1970: 72 on Tyrt. fr. 10.1 (= fr. 6–7 in his numbering).

7. the battle of bloody war: αἱματόεντος...πολέμοιο is hyperbaton (cf. *Il.* 9.650); πολέμοιο is appositional genitive (elsewhere called 'of designation' or 'of explanation') to ὑσμίνῃ. The qualification is pleonastic.

8. bitter darts: πικρὰ...βέλεα is also a hyperbaton (unlike in my translation). **repelling:** here βιαζόμενος cannot mean "being pressed hard/overwhelmed by the arrows", for that would require a dative (cf. *Il.* 11.589 ὅς βελέεσσι βιάζεται). With βέλεα in the accusative, better read "repelling the arrows" (cf. Xen. *Anab.* 1.4.5 καὶ βιασάμενοι τοὺς πολεμίους παρέλθοιεν, "they might dislodge the enemy and pass through") or "ignoring the arrows" (cf. Thuc. 8.53 τοὺς νόμους βιασάμενος, "defying the laws").

9. And none of his enemies: the adjective δήιος (Att. δάϊος/δᾷος), 'hostile', is here treated as a noun – a genitive partitive to τις in particular – and as such it takes the genitive possessive (κείνου) instead of a dative objective (cf. Smyth §1499a). **more eminent (a man):** for the idiomatic use of the double comparative ἀμεινότερος instead of ἀμείνων, cf. *Il.* 14.81 βέλτερος, *Il.* 1.376 λωίτερος, *Il.* 20.436 χειρότερος. Further emphasis is given with ἔτι (LSJ, II2): "yet more better". Only the best of the best would deserve such a description; thus Achilles is said to be ἀμείνων φώς than Agamemnon (*Il.* 2.239), or Hector compared to Menelaus (*Il.* 7.111), or Hercules compared to his maternal half-brother Iphicles ([Hes.] *Sc.* 51). In our context, the precise meaning of ἀμεινότερος, I believe, is 'more eminent / brilliant' (≈ ἐπιφανέστερος), in connection to the apparent employment of **φὼς** ('man'), here and in v.4, as a near-paronomasia on φάος (φῶς by contraction, whence φόως by diectasis = 'light'), so that our hero emerges as a 'star' (cf. n.11). A similar pun is attempted by Pindar, who compares his encomium for victorious Callicles to a lucent statue (*Nem.* 4.82–5): "Refined gold displays all its radiance [αὐγὰς], and a hymn for fine [ἀγαθῶν] achievements makes a man [φῶτα] happy as a king". The reverse semantic relation, i.e. 'light' as a metaphor for 'man', is much better attested; cf. *Od.* 6.23 ἦλθες, Τηλέμαχε, γλυκερὸν φάος – of course 'light' here stands for a 'long-desired man', rather than a glorious one. Euripides' *Ion* 1439 facilitates both meanings: ὦ φῶς μητρὶ κρεῖσσον ἡλίου ("O my child, light/person dearer than the sunlight to your mother").

10. And none … was: ἔσκεν = epic imperfect of εἰμί (= ἦν). **going about the task:** cf. *Il.* 6.492, *Od.* 1.358 ἔργον ἐποίχεσθαι (< ἐπὶ + οἴχομαι, lit. 'going towards'), always used thus at the beginning of the hexameter, but here separated in hyperbaton. Because of the next line's φέρετ[ο], which implies arriving, the most appropriate translation for the infinitive here is 'setting/going about', rather than e.g. 'taking up'. **of mighty fighting:** φυλόπιδος κρατερῆς is genitive of explanation to ἔργον; cf. *Il.* 18.242, *Od.* 16.268. φύλοπις, 'battle', is a strictly epic – parodied as such in Ar. *Pax* 1076 – pre-Greek word of unknown etymology. "In antiquity, it was interpreted as a compound from φῦλον and ὄπα (ὄσσα), 'voice', which convinces neither semantically nor formally (one would have expected *φυλωπις)"; *EDG*.

11. since he was borne by the … sun: this line has caused much ado, with most scholars considering it troublesome and/or inconclusive. Some propose that the next, missing verse would start with εἴκελος ('similar': Bergk 1853, Meineke 1857: lvii) or εἴκελα ('similarly': West 1992) or οἰκὼς (= ἐοικὼς, 'similarly': Defradas 1962), which would govern the dative αὐγῇσιν, so that the meaning would be "when he advanced *similarly to* (i.e. as fast as) the rays of the swift sun" (Edmonds 1931: 101; Gerber 1970: 115; Bowie 2010a: 59). In West's more elaborate supplement, in particular (<εἴκελα χαλκείοις τεύχεσι λαμπόμενος>), the meaning becomes "when he advanced, his bronze armour gleaming like the swift sun's light" (seconded by Allan 2019: 130). However, I doubt that the anthologist would have 'chopped' the fragment in v.11, if v.12 indeed began with a word so intrinsically linked to αὐγῇσιν – no other fragment of Mimnermus quoted by Stobaeus is syntactically inconclusive. Other scholars do not require a supplement but emend φέρετ' to τρέφετ' (Klinger 1930: 79) or to θέρετ' (McKay 1975) to produce "when he was *nourished/warmed* by the rays of the swift sun", which of course would be a metaphor for "when he was still alive" (cf. Wilamowitz 1913: 276–77). I find these solutions equally uneconomical. In fact, there is nothing wrong with the line as it stands; the key is ὅτ[ε], which here introduces a *causal* temporal clause (LSJ, B) to explain why our hero is ἀμεινότερος, 'more eminent' (v.9). He is such – whether that means 'more eminent', as I have suggested in n.9, or simply 'better' – *since/as long as* (cf. Swift 2015: 100) he *is borne by* the rays of the swift sun. For φέρετο in that sense (rather than in the active sense 'he advanced/rushed') with instrumental dative (here αὐγῇσιν), cf. *Od.* 10.54 ἐφέροντο κακῇ ἀνέμοιο θυέλλῃ ("the ships were borne by an evil blast of wind"), 9.82 φερόμην ὀλοοῖς ἀνέμοισιν ("I was borne by savage winds"). In our fragment, the meaning is that the Smyrnaean hero appears at the battlefield on the rays of swift Helios (cf. fr. 11.5) – either a metaphor for arriving on a chariot, or a general auspicious image – and for that reason he outshines everyone else; he receives support from, and thus the splendour of, his patron. For Helios as a war patron in Anatolian cult, see introductory note on fr. 17. That could also explain why the formidable Lydian cavalry has no hope: the very horses of Helios serve the Smyrnaeans!

FRAGMENTS 15+16

The two pentameters, which I print together after Diehl 1949 and Gentili and Prato 1988, probably come from the same elegy, as they are anthologised together, in immediate succession, by the same source. (On the *Etymologicum Genuinum*, its sources and significance, see Dickey 2007: 91.) They may even derive from two consecutive couplets – i.e. with a single hexametric verse separating them – given that placing βάξις and βάξιος as close would not be troublesome to Mimnermus (cf. fr. 1.5–6 ἀνδράσιν / ἄνδρα, 6–7 κακὸν / κακαὶ). The first impression is that fr. 15 concerns the bad reputation of a certain individual while fr. 16 includes a general statement on people's evilness. However, it could well be the case that μιν, 'him', (fr. 15) refers to a common noun (e.g. ἀνήρ, 'a man') and the plural ἱέμενοι, 'are eager', (fr. 16) to a specific group of people. The content could be similar to fr. 1.9 (women and boys speaking badly of aged men) or to fr. 7 (fellow citizens speaking badly of one another). At any rate, the now-lost hexametric lines which preceded the two pentameters would specify the respective subjects. For Broccia 1972–1973, Mimnermus draws on Hes. *Op.* 760–64:

> *Act this way: avoid the wretched talk* [φήμην] *of mortals. For talk is evil: it is light to raise up quite easily, but it is difficult* [ἀργαλέη] *to bear, and hard* [χαλεπὴ] *to put down. No talk is ever entirely gotten rid of, once many people talk it up.*
>
> (transl. Most)

The combination of the two adjectives here and in Mimnermus is indeed conspicuous. But given that Hesiod makes φήμη a goddess in his next phrase (764 θεός νύ τίς ἐστι καὶ αὐτή), i.e. a proper name, and that Mimnermus too wanted a *personified* subject-noun (to judge from ἕχει, 'reputation *follows*'), it is improbable that the elegist would have replaced Φήμη with βάξις, for the former would perfectly fit his purpose and metre (with epic shortening Φήμη ἕχει).

1. **Bad reputation follows him:** lit. bad reputation 'occupies' (ἕχει) him and circulates 'among' (ἐπὶ) the people, exactly as good fame (κλέος) does; cf. *Il.* 17.143; *Od.* 1.299. βάξις (<βάζω = 'to speak') is absent from Homer and Hesiod but increasingly used in lyric and tragedy. Cf. Thgn. 1298 θεῶν δ' ἐποπίζεο μῆνιν βάξιν τ' ἀνθρώπων ("Respect the wrath of the gods and the talk of men"), Aesch. *Ag.* 10 ἁλώσιμόν τε βάξιν ("the rumour of Troy's capture"), Soph. *Aj.* 494–95 βάξιν ἀλγεινὴν λαβεῖν ("suffering painful words"), Eur. *Hel.* 224 διὰ δὲ πόλιας ἔρχεται βάξις ("and throughout the cities of Greece runs the rumour").

2. **They're always eager:** ἱέμενοι < ἵεμαι = 'to hasten' and metaphorically 'to be eager/to long for'. **for harsh judgement:** because verbs signifying 'to desire' take the genitive, here βάξιος is the participle's object. Cf. *Il.* 23.370–71 πάτασσε δὲ θυμὸς ἑκάστου νίκης ἱεμένων ("Each man's heart was athrob as they strove for victory"). For ἀργαλέης, cf. fr. 1 n.10.

FRAGMENT 17

The Paeonians, a mixed Thraco-Illyrian tribe living in the Axios River basin, were allies of the Trojans (*Il.* 2.848). Their leader Pyraichmes was attacked by Patroclus (16.287) but elsewhere Asteropaeus claims to be their leader (21.155). The explanation given by the scholiast is that Pyraichmes led their cavalry, as Mimnermus' fragment also suggests, whereas Asteropaeus their archers. That Thracian tribes had a long tradition in horse breeding is evidenced by the legendary white horses of King Rhesus of Thrace, which are described as unusually beautiful, big, and shinny (*Il.* 10.436, 544–60), as well as the man-eating mares of King Diomedes of Thrace which Hercules was sent to steal – they were *trained* to devour human flesh (Diod. Sic. 4.15.3–4). The Thracians themselves are called ἱπποπόλοι, 'herding horses' (*Il.* 13.4, 14.227), and φίλιπποι, 'loving horses' (Soph. fr. 582 *TrGF*), and they worshipped Sabazius envisioned as a horseman, the so-called 'Thracian Rider'. In Ps.-Oppian's *Cynegetica*, 3rd C AD, Thracian horses are listed among the best breeds (1.166–72).

How this hexameter line fits in Mimnermus' oeuvre is certainly uncertain. Because it is preserved in a Iliadic scholium, its original context might be a Troy-themed work (cf. Bowie 2010a: 60). If it comes from *Smyrneis*, the context might have been the 652 or 644 BC attack on Lydia and the killing of Gyges by the Cimmerians, who were assisted by, or even identified with, a Thracian tribe (cf. Adrados 1956: 224 n.2; Allen 1993: 126). The subject of ἄγων would thus be the Cimmerian commander-in-chief. A third possibility is that the line came up in connection with the sun, whom Mimnermus thematises so often. "The Paeonians worshipped the Sun in the form of a little disk attached to the top of a long pole" and the Thracian Rider too "must have had a well-marked solar aspect, […for he] is portrayed on some monuments with rays about his head" (Pettazzoni 1967: 85 n.28; 88). Mimnermus would have been familiar with these cults, since the Phrygians migrating to Anatolia *c.* 1200 BC (and settling north of the Lydians) brought Sabazius with them. So perhaps it is Helios "who guides the Paeonians", whose famous horses might have been associated with Helios' own horses.

1. He leads men from Paeonia: for the wording, cf. *Il.* 2.848 Πυραίχμης ἄγε Παίονας, *Il.* 21.155 Παίονας ἄνδρας ἄγων, Hdt. 5.23 ἄγων τοὺς Παίονας. **a famous breed:** cf. Pind. *Nem.* 6.61 κλειτᾷ γενεᾷ.

APPENDIX I: METRICAL NOTES

Epic shortening: καὶ εὐνή (fr. 1.3), γίνεται ἁρπαλέα (1.4), τέρπεται ἠελίου (1.8), αὔξεται ἠελίου (2.2), γίνεται ἥβης (2.7), κίδναται ἠέλιος (2.8), παραμείψεται ὥρης (2.9), γίνεται· ἄλλοτε (2.12), ἐπιδεύεται, ὧν (2.13), ἔρχεται εἰς (2.14), παραμείψεται ὥρη (3.1), ῥέει ἄσπετος (5.1), γίνεται ὥσπερ (5.4), καὶ ἄμορφον (5.5), καὶ ἄτιμον ... τιθεῖ ἄνδρα (5.7), καὶ ἀργαλέων (6.1), καὶ ἐμοί (8.2), κείαται ἐν (11+11a.6), γίνεται οὐδεμία (12.2), καὶ αὐτῷ, ἐπὴν (12.3), ποικίλῃ, Ἡφαίστου (12.6), χώρου ἀφ' (12.8), καὶ ἵπποι (12.9), καὶ ἀγήνορα (14.1), πεύθομαι, οἵ (14.2), δηίων (14.9; cf. West 1987: 14).

Attic shortening: Ἀφροδίτης (1.1), τεθνάναι (2.10), ἀ]σπίσι φραξάμενοι (13a.2).

Synizesis: ἄνθεα (1.4), ἔαρος (2.2), θεῶν (2.4), μελεδωνέων (6.1), πολιτέων (7.1), θεῶν (9.6), χρυσέῳ (11+11a.6), ἐμέο (14.2).

Probable combination of caesurae, or of caesura and diaeresis:
- τίς δὲ βίος, | τί δὲ τερπνὸν | ἄτερ χρυσῆς Ἀφροδίτης; (1.1)
- Ἠέλιος μὲν γὰρ ἔλαχεν | πόνον ‖ ἤματα πάντα, (12.1)
- χρυσοῦ τιμήεντος, | ὑπόπτερος, ‖ ἄκρον ἐφ' ὕδωρ (12.7)
- ἔνθ' ἐπέβη | ἑτέρων ὀχέων | Ὑπερίονος υἱός. (12.11)

Peculiarities in quantities (cf. the respective *lemmata* in LSJ):
- γᾰ̀ρ (2.11; 6.1) but γᾱ̀ρ (12.1). And *long by position* in γᾰ̀ρ διὰ (12.5) and γᾰ́ρ τις (14.9).
- κᾱλόν (5.3; 11+11a.4). The adjective comes with ᾱ in epic and early iambus, with ᾰ in lyric and tragedy, and with ᾰ or ᾱ in elegy, epigram and bucolic poetry.
- ᾰ̓πορνῡ́μενοι (9.5). Active ὄρνῡμι but Middle ὄρνῠμαι.
- ῑ̔έμενοι (16). The verb ἵημι usually comes with ῐ in Homer and ῑ in Attic authors, but sometimes it is the other way round.

APPENDIX II: TESTIMONIA OF LOST FRAGMENTS

F10 Source: Strabo 14.1.3

Κολοφῶνα δὲ Ἀνδραίμων Πύλιος (κτίζει), ὥς φησι καὶ Μίμνερμος ἐν τῇ *Ναννοῖ.*

F13 Source: Paus. 9.29.4 + Comm. in Alcm. *P. Oxy.* 2390 (= *PMG* 5, fr. 2 col. i)

Μίμνερμος δὲ ἐλεγεῖα ἐς τὴν μάχην ποιήσας τὴν Σμυρναίων πρὸς Γύγην τε καὶ Λυδούς, φησὶν ἐν τῷ προοιμίῳ θυγατέρας Οὐρανοῦ τὰς ἀρχαιοτέρας Μούσας, τούτων δὲ ἄλλας νεωτέρας εἶναι Διὸς παῖδας.
Γῆς [μὲν] Μούσα[ς] θυγατέρας ὡς Μίμνερμ[ος αὐ]τὰς ἐγε̣[νεαλόγησε [*sc.* Ἀλκμάν].

F18 Source: Ath. 4.174a

ὁ δὲ αὐτὸς [*sc.* Δημήτριος ὁ Σκήψιος] ἱστορεῖ κἀν τῷ τετάρτῳ καὶ εἰκοστῷ τῆς αὐτῆς πραγματείας Δαίτην ἥρωα τιμώμενον παρὰ τοῖς Τρωσίν, οὗ μνημονεύει<ν> Μίμνερμον.

F19 Source: Ael. *VH* 12.36

ἐοίκασιν οἱ ἀρχαῖοι ὑπὲρ τοῦ ἀριθμοῦ τῶν τῆς Νιόβης παίδων μὴ συνᾴδειν ἀλλήλοις. Ὅμηρος μὲν ἓξ λέγει <ἄρρενας> καὶ τοσαύτας κόρας, ... Μίμνερμος εἴκοσι, καὶ Πίνδαρος τοσούτους.

F20 Source: Plut. *de facie lun.* 19.931e

Θέων ἡμῖν οὗτος τὸν Μίμνερμον ἐπάξει καὶ τὸν Κυδίαν καὶ τὸν Ἀρχίλοχον, πρὸς δὲ τούτοις τὸν Στησίχορον καὶ τὸν Πίνδαρον ἐν ταῖς ἐκλείψεσιν ὀλοφυρομένους, "ἄστρον φανερώτατον κλεπτόμενον" καὶ "μέσῳ ἄματι νύκτα γινομέναν" καὶ "τὴν ἀκτῖνα τοῦ ἡλίου σκότους ἀτραπὸν <ἐσσυμέναν>" φάσκοντας.

F10 From Strabo's *Geography*

Andraemon from Pylos has founded Colophon, as indeed Mimnermus says in *Nanno*.

F13 From Pausanias and a *Commentary on Alcman*

Mimnermus, who wrote an elegy about the battle of the Smyrnaeans against Gyges and the Lydians, says in his prologue that Uranus' daughters are the oldest Muses, whereas the other, the younger Muses, are Zeus' offspring.
Like Mimnermus, Alcman designated these Muses as daughters of Earth in his genealogy.

F18 From Athenaeus' *Learned Banqueters*

In the 24th book of his treatise, Demetrius of Scepsis records Daites, the hero honoured among the Trojans, and that Mimnermus mentions him.

F19 From Aelianus' *Various History*

The ancient authors don't seem to agree with each other on the number of Niobe's children. Homer speaks of six sons and as many daughters… Mimnermus of twenty, and Pindar of the same number.

F20 From Plutarch's *Face on the Moon*

Theon here will recite for us Mimnermus and Cydias and Archilochus and, in addition to them, Stesichorus and Pindar, who during eclipses lament by saying "the brightest star has been stolen" or "night emerged in the middle of the day" or "the sun's ray is running the path of darkness".

F21 Source: Sall. *Argum.* ii in Soph. *Ant.*

στασιάζεται δὲ τὰ περὶ τὴν ἡρωίδα ἱστορούμενα καὶ τὴν ἀδελφὴν αὐτῆς Ἰσμήνην. ὁ μὲν γὰρ Ἴων ἐν τοῖς διθυράμβοις καταπρησθῆναί φησιν ἀμφοτέρας ἐν τῷ ἱερῷ τῆς Ἥρας ὑπὸ Λαοδάμαντος τοῦ Ἐτεοκλέους· Μίμνερμος δέ φησι τὴν μὲν Ἰσμήνην προσομιλοῦσαν Περικλυμένῳ ὑπὸ Τυδέως κατὰ Ἀθηνᾶς ἐγκέλευσιν τελευτῆσαι.

F21a Source: Zenob. (recensio Athoa, cod. Athen.) 3.17 ed. Crusius and Kugéas 1910.

"ἄριστα χωλὸς οἰφεῖ". φησὶν ὅτι αἱ Ἀμαζόνες τοὺς γιγνομένους ἄρσενας ἐπήρουν, ἢ σκέλος ἢ χεῖρα περιελόμεναι· πολεμοῦντες δὲ πρὸς αὐτὰς οἱ Σκύθαι καὶ βουλόμενοι πρὸς αὐτὰς σπείσασθαι ἔλεγον ὅτι συνέσονται τοῖς Σκύθαις εἰς γάμον ἀπηρώτοις καὶ οὐ λελωβημένοις· ἀποκριναμένη δὲ πρὸς αὐτοὺς ἡ Ἀντιάνειρα ἡγεμὼν τῶν Ἀμαζόνων εἶπεν· "ἄριστα χωλὸς οἰφεῖ". μέμνηται τῆς παροιμίας Μίμ<ν>ερμος.

F22 Source: *Schol.* ad Lycoph. *Alex.* 610

ἡ Ἀφροδίτη, καθά φησι Μίμνερμος, ὑπὸ Διομήδους τρωθεῖσα παρεσκεύασε τὴν Αἰγιάλειαν πολλοῖς μὲν μοιχοῖς συγκοιμηθῆναι, ἐρασθῆναι δὲ καὶ ὑπὸ Κομήτου τοῦ Σθενέλου υἱοῦ. τοῦ δὲ Διομήδους παραγενομένου εἰς τὸ Ἄργος ἐπιβουλεῦσαι αὐτῷ· τὸν δὲ καταφυγόντα εἰς τὸν βωμὸν τῆς Ἥρας διὰ νυκτὸς φυγεῖν σὺν τοῖς ἑταίροις καὶ ἐλθεῖν εἰς Ἰταλίαν πρὸς Δαῦνον βασιλέα, ὅστις αὐτὸν <δόλῳ> ἀνεῖλεν.

F23 Source: Philod. *de pietate*, *P. Herc.* 1088+433 ed. Boserup, *ZPE* 8, 1971: 110.

[.... καὶ τὸν] Ἥλιον [καὶ ἄλλους] τινὰς [θεοὺς πολυ]μόχθο[υς πεποιή]κασι … Μί]μνερ[μος] μ[ὲν οὐ δι]ạφωνεῖν δ[οκ]εῖ, [κα] θ' ἑκάστ[η]ν [νύκ]ṭα καθεύ[δειν αὐ]τὸν λέγων.

F21 From Sallustius' *hypothesis* to Sophocles' *Antigone*

There is conflict between the stories concerning the heroine [Antigone] and her sister Ismene. Ion says in his dithyrambs that both were burned to death by Laodamas, son of Eteocles, in Hera's temple. But Mimnermus says that Ismene was killed by Tydeus while she was having sex with Periclymenus, upon Athena's command.

F21a From Zenobius. On this fr. see Colantonio 1993.

"A cripple fucks the best". They say that the Amazons used to cripple their male children by cutting off either a leg or a hand. When the Scythians were at war with them and wanted to make a treaty, they promised the Amazons that the latter would now be married to Scythians, who are neither crippled nor mutilated! Responding to them, the leader of the Amazons Antianeira said "a cripple fucks the best". Mimnermus recalls this proverb.

F22 From scholia on Lycophron's *Alexandra*

Aphrodite, as Mimnermus says, because she had been wounded by Diomedes, made [his wife] Aegialeia sleep with many lovers and have sex even with Cometes, son of [Diomedes' best friend] Sthenelus. And when Diomedes returned to Argos [after Troy's fall], she plotted against him. He took refuge at the altar of Hera and fled in the middle of the night with his companions and went to Italy, to king Daunus, who killed him by a trick.

F23 From Philodemus' *On Piety*

[Several poets and mythographers] have presented the Sun and some other gods as suffering much. Mimnermus does not seem to disagree, saying that the Sun sleeps every night.

APPENDIX III: THEOGNIS' OR MIMNERMUS'?

The *Theognidea* incorporates fragments by poets other than Theognis, both subsequent and earlier elegists. On several occasions, other sources allow us to identify the actual authors, e.g. lines 227–32 and 585–90 are quoted by Stobaeus as Solon's (= fr. 13.65–76), lines 935–38 and 1003–6 as Tyrtaeus' (= fr. 12.13–16, 37–42), and lines 1017–22 as Mimnermus' (= fr. 5.1–6); and it is thanks to the *Palatine Anthology* that we know that lines 795–96 actually belong to Mimnermus (= fr. 7). But those instances of luck aside, not much can be said conclusively for the rest of the *Theognidea*; even the attribution to Theognis himself of those fragments which mention Cyrnus (an *erômenos* whose name is supposedly used by the poet as a 'seal') is a hypothetical convention (cf. West 1974: 41–42).

The following lines from the *Theognidea* were marked by Bergk 1853 as "fortasse Mimnermi sunt" or "Mimnermi videntur": vv.567–70, 877–78, 939–42, 983–88, 1007–12, 1023–24, 1055–58 (assuming the conjecture <Ναννοῖ> after σοὶ καὶ ἐμοὶ), 1063–70 and 1129–32. Several of these proposals were followed by Hartung 1859, who also printed vv.1013–16 under Mimnermus, and by Renner 1868, who also contested vv.527–28. These amount to 46 lines claimed for Mimnermus, which would make a significant addition to our poet's slim corpus. In his first scholarly article, Friedrich Nietzsche (1867: 1858–6) went even further, ascribing to Mimnermus the entire Book II of the *Theognidea* (vv.1231–1388); he suggested that, by inserting those 'soft' verses to the anthology, the compiler wanted to slander Theognis as a pederast. Modern scholarship has abandoned the reattribution enterprise, the verdict being that "the topical, almost never concrete content of the [Theognidean] verses as well as the uncertainty of stylistic judgments usually make attempts to recognise such passages, or even to assign them to a certain poet, futile" (Selle 2008: 224; my transl.). But such axioms usually betray a reluctance to 'get down to business', as indeed has happened in our case. I agree that Mimnermus' corpus cannot be expanded under our present knowledge of the *Theognidea*, but I wish to openly address, rather than ignore, the relevant proposals. The evident, if unexplicit, criterion for the above-listed attributions was the occurrence of the word ἥβη ('youth') in those passages (vv.527, 877, 985, 1007, 1063, 1069). Indeed, these are nearly all the passages in the *Theognidea* (excl. vv.1119–22, 1323–26) where this word appears, while only three of the contested passages do *not* contain it (vv.939–42, 1023–24, 1055–58). The unacknowledged assumption that only Mimnermus could have thematised youth undermines the credibility of the proposals. The reason (also unexplicit but obvious) for that assumption was that one other passage which contains ἥβη indeed comes from Mimnermus, according to Stobaeus' testimony (vv.1017–22 = fr. 5.1–6; see introductory note). But to conclude that "therefore, every Theognidean passage with ἥβη must originate from Mimnermus" is pure nonsense, which in fact hindered an actual stylistic evaluation.

Here I shall only review one of the contested passages, the only one (to my knowledge) to have passed down to more recent bibliography. Following Bergk and Renner, van Groningen 1966: 413 notes on vv.1129–32 "On a évidemment voulu attribuer ces vers à Mimnerme". The statement is rather vague: does it actually endorse, or indirectly avoid the attribution to Mimnermus? Given that in all other contested passages van Groningen is openly critical towards Bergk's ungrounded readiness to remove lines from the *Theognidea* (1966: 335, 357, 371, 378, 383, 392, 395), his silence here rather suggests a hesitant agreement. The text reads:

> ἐμπίομαι· πενίης θυμοφθόρου οὐ μελεδαίνω,
> οὐδ' ἀνδρῶν ἐχθρῶν οἵ με λέγουσι κακῶς.
> ἀλλ' ἥβην ἐρατὴν ὀλοφύρομαι, ἥ μ' ἐπιλείπει,
> κλαίω δ' ἀργαλέον γῆρας ἐπερχόμενον.

I'll drink my fill, without a thought for soul-destroying poverty or enemies who speak ill of me. But I bewail the lovely youth that is leaving me and weep at the approach of grim old age.

(transl. Gerber)

It should go without saying that general thematic echoes with Mimnermus' oeuvre do not suffice to establish Mimnermian authorship; on the contrary, over-concentration of such themes (here: lovely youth + devastating poverty + enemies who speak ill + the grim of old age) seems rather suspicious. Instead, it is the thematic and verbal *details* which must be examined, in comparison both with Mimnermus' corpus *and* with the rest of the *Theognidea*.

(a) ἐμπίομαι (1129): Mimnermus' surviving poetry is sober – no mention of drinking (Fränkel 1973: 213 n.10) – whereas the *Theognidea* are rather alcoholic (e.g. 33, 211–12, 261, 263, 413, 473, 484, 487, 492, 498, 501, 509–10, 533, 763, 840, 879, 883, 959, 971, 989, 1042).

(b) θυμοφθόρος (1129) is used for poverty elsewhere in the *Theognidea* (155), whereas Mimnermus only applies this adjective to νοῦσος (fr. 2.15).

(c) πενίης (1129): poverty is here distinguished from old age – the lyrical subject can ignore the former but grieves for the latter – as it is elsewhere in the *Theognidea* (cf. 173–78: poverty is harsher than old age). On the contrary, poverty in Mimnermus is an *aspect* of old age (fr. 2.12).

(d) The verb μελεδαίνω (1129) is found again in the *Theognidea* (185) but nowhere in Mimnermus, who only has the noun μελεδώνη (fr. 6.1). The *Theognidea* has both μελεδώνη (883) and μελέδημα (789).

(e) λέγουσι κακῶς (1130): the advice to ignore public slander is found in both Mimnermus (fr. 7 ἄλλός τίς σε κακῶς…ἐρεῖ) and the *Theognidea*: do not trust someone who speaks ill behind your back (93–96 γλῶσσαν…κακήν) and do not waste your friendships for bad rumours (323–24 χαλεπῇ…διαιβολίῃ).

(f) The adjective ἐρατὸς (1131) occurs once in Mimnermus (fr. 9.3) but multiple times in the *Theognidea* (569, 778, 790, 984, 1044, 1348), where indeed it applies to youth (242 νέοι ἄνδρες… ἐρατοὶ).

(g) ὀλοφύρομαι and ἐπιλείπω (1131) neither exist elsewhere in the *Theognidea*, nor in Mimnermus.

(h) κλαίω (1132) is very frequent in the *Theognidea* (931, 1041, 1070, 1217, 1267) but absent from Mimnermus.
(i) ἀργαλέον γῆρας (1132) is formulaic in Mimnermus (frr. 1.10, 2.6, 4.2, 5.5), whereas this adjective appears nowhere else in the *Theognidea* with reference to γῆρας, which is instead described as οὐλόμενον (272, 527, 768, 1012, 1021), ἄμορφον (1021), κακὸν (728). In the *Theognidea*, ἀργαλέος applies to things such as γνώμη (832), θυμὸς (1091), μόχθος (1338) and μνῆμα (1358).
(j) γῆρας ἐπερχόμενον (1132) fits the style of both Mimnermus (fr. 1.5) and the *Theognidea* (528, 728).

Of these observations, only one supports Mimnermian authorship (*i*), six suggest that the passage better fits in the *Theognidea* (*a*, *b*, *c*, *d*, *f*, *h*), while three are ambivalent (*e*, *g*, *j*). Far from 'futile', stylistic analysis has finally helped us safely reject – rather than merely ignore – the potential admission of vv.1129–32 into Mimnermus' corpus. It is hoped that this methodological exercise will inspire students and colleagues to put more passages to the test.

BIBLIOGRAPHY

Acosta-Hughes, B. (2002) *Polyeideia: The Iambi of Callimachus and the Archaic Iambic Tradition*, Berkeley.

Adkins, A. W. H. (1985) *Poetic Craft in the Early Greek Elegists*, Chicago.

Adrados, F. R. (1956) *Líricos griegos: elegíacos y yambógrafos arcaicos*, vol. 1, Barcelona.

Aldine ed. [=Aldus Manutius' unknown editor] (1495) *Τάδε ἔνεστι ἐν τῇδε τῃ βίβλῳ. Θεοκρίτου εἰδύλλια [...]*, Venice.

Aldine ed. [=Aldus Manutius' unknown editor] (1516) *Στράβων περὶ γεωγραφίας*, Venice.

Allan, W. (2019) *Greek Elegy and Iambus: A Selection*, Cambridge.

Allen, A. (1993) *The Fragments of Mimnermus: Text and Commentary*, Stuttgart.

Aloni, A. (2009) 'Elegy: Forms, Functions and Communication', in F. Budelmann (ed.) *The Cambridge Companion to Greek Lyric*, Cambridge, 168–88.

Anderson, J. K. (1958) 'Old Smyrna: The Corinthian Pottery', *ABSA* 53/54, 138–51.

Anhalt, E. K. (1993) *Solon the Singer: Politics and Poetics*, Lanham, MD.

Assunção, T. R. (1998–1999) 'Juventude e velhice: Mimnermo', *Kleos* 2/3, 158–71.

Assunção, T. R. (2003) 'Nota sobre a correção de Mimnermo por Sólon (26 G. e P.)', *Clássica* (São Paulo) 15, 51–62.

Astoreca, E. (2021) *Early Greek Alphabetic Writing: A Linguistic Approach*, Oxford.

Babut, D. (1971) 'Sémonide et Mimnerme', *REG* 84, 17–43.

Bach, N. (1826) *Mimnermi Colophonii carminum quae supersunt*, Leipzig.

Barigazzi, A. (1956) 'Mimnermo e Filita, Antimaco e Cherilo nel proemio degli *Aitia* di Callimaco', *Hermes* 84, 162–82.

Barnes, H. R. (1995) 'The Structure of the Elegiac Hexameter', in M. Fantuzzi and R. Pretagostini (eds) *Struttura e storia dell'esametro omerico*, vol. 1, Rome, 135–61.

Bartol, K. (1993) *Greek Elegy and Iambus: Studies in Ancient Literary Sources*, Poznań.

Bartol, K. (1998) 'Two in One: A Note on the Mimnerman Couplet by Stobaeus (Fr. 3 W = 9 G-P)', *Euphrosyne* 26, 151–53.

Bartol, K. (2022) 'Elegy', in Swift 2022: 221–33.

Bastianini, G. (1996) 'Κατὰ λεπτόν in Callimaco (Fr. 1.11 Pfeiffer)', in M. S. Funghi (ed.) *Le vie della ricercar: studi in onore di F. Adorno*, Florence, 69–80.

Bechtel, F. von (1917) *Die historischen Personennamen der Griechischen bis zur Kaiserzeit*, Halle.

Bekker, I. and Gigon, O. (eds) (1987) *Aristotelis Opera, vol. III: Librorum deperditorum fragmenta*, Berlin.

Benveniste, E. (1973) *Indo-European Language and Society*, London.

Bergk, T. (1853)[2] *Poetae Lyrici Graeci*, Leipzig.

Berkel, T. van (2020) *The Economics of Friendship*, Leiden/Boston.

Blass, F. (1888) 'Solon und Mimnermos', *Neue Jahrbücher für Philologie und Paedagogik* 137, 742.

Boardman, J. (1980) *The Greeks Overseas: Their Early Colonies and Trade*, London.

Boisacq, E. (1916) *Dictionnaire étymologique de la langue grecque*, Paris.

Bonelli, G. (1977) 'Lettura estetica dei lirici greci', *Rivista di Studi Classici* 25, 65–94.

Bottino, A. P. (2017) 'Space, Time and Remembering in the Orchard of Laertes: A Cognitive Approach', *Classics@*. https://chs.harvard.edu/firstdraftsclassics/

Bowie, E. (1986) 'Early Greek Elegy, Symposium and Public Festival', *JHS* 106, 13–35.

Bowie, E. (2009) 'Wandering Poets, Archaic Style', in R. Hunter and I. Rutherford (eds) *Wandering Poets in Ancient Greek Culture: Travel, Locality and Pan-Hellenism*, Cambridge, 105–36.

Bowie, E. (2010a) 'The Trojan War's Reception in Early Greek Lyric, Iambic and Elegiac Poetry', in L. Foxhall, H.-J. Gehrke and N. Luraghi (eds) *Intentional History: Spinning Time in Ancient Greece*, Stuttgart, 57–87.

Bowie, E. (2010b) 'Stobaeus and Early Greek Lyric, Elegiac and Iambic Poetry', in M. Horster and C. Reitz (eds) *Condensing Texts – Condensed Texts*, Stuttgart, 587–617.

Bowie, E. (2012) 'An Early Chapter in the History of the *Theognidea*', in X. Riu and J. Pòrtulas (eds) *Approaches to Archaic Greek Poetry*, Messina, 121–48.

Bowie, E. (2016) 'Cultic Contexts for Elegiac Performance', in Swift and Carey 2016: 15–32.

Bowie, E. (2018a) 'The Lesson of Book 2', in T. Harrison and E. Irwin (eds) *Interpreting Herodotus*, Oxford, 53–74.

Bowie, E. (2018b) 'The Performance Contexts of Trochaic Tetrameters Catalectic', *Classica* 31, 31–43.

Bowra, C. M. (1938) *Early Greek Elegists*, London.

Brillante, C. (1993) 'Pilo e i Neleidi in un frammento di Mimnermo', in R. Pretagostini (ed.) *Tradizione e innovazione nella cultura greca da Omero all'eta ellenistica*, vol. 1, Rome, 267–78.

Broccia, G. (1959) 'Il voto di Mimnermo', in his *Ricerche di filologia greco-latina*, Rome, 29–31.

Broccia, G. (1969) 'Mimnermo', in his *Tradizione ed esegesi*, Brescia, 93–106.

Broccia, G. (1972–1973) 'Mimn., 9 D. < Hes., *Erga* 762 e appunti sul Mimnermo "esiodeo"', *AFLM* 5/6, 502–10.

Brunck, R. F. P. (1772) *Analecta veterum poetarum Graecorum*, vol. 1, Strasbourg.

Brunck, R. F. P. (1776) 'Lectiones et emendations in volumen I', in his *Analecta veterum poetarum Graecorum*, vol. 3, Strasbourg, 1–120.

Brunck, R. F. P. (1784) *Ἠθικὴ ποίησις sive Gnomici poetae Graeci*, Strasburg.

Budelmann, F. and Power, T. (2013) 'The Inbetweeness of Sympotic Elegy', *JHS* 133, 1–19.

Burgess, J. S. (2001) *The Tradition of the Trojan War in Homer and the Epic Cycle*, Baltimore.

Burton, D. (2011) 'Response and Competition in Archaic Greek Poetry', *Antichthon* 45, 58–76.

Burzacchini, G. (2008) 'Osservazioni su alcuni luoghi dell' *Eracle* di Euripide', in P. Arduini *et al.* (eds) *Studi offerti ad Alessandro Perutelli*, vol. 1, Rome, 143–58.

Calame, C. (1999) *The Poetics of Eros in Ancient Greece*, Princeton.

Calori, C. (1964) *I frammenti di Mimnermo*, Milan.

Cameron, A. (1995) *Callimachus and His Critics*, Princeton.

Campbell, D. A. (1964) 'Flutes and Elegiac Couplets', *JHS* 84, 63–68.

Campbell, D. A. (1967) *Greek Lyric Poetry: A Selection of Early Greek Lyric, Elegiac and Iambic Poetry*, London.

Campbell, D. A. (1982) *Sappho and Alcaeus (Loeb Classical Library)*, Cambridge, MA.

Campbell, D. A. (1984) 'Stobaeus and Early Greek Lyric Poetry', in D. Gerber (ed.) *Greek Poetry and Philosophy: Studies in Honour of Leonard Woodbury*, California, 51–57.

Card, T. (2004) 'Cory, William Johnson', in *Oxford Dictionary of National Biography*.

Carey, C. (2011) 'Alcman: From Laconia to Alexandria', in L. Athanassaki and E. Bowie (eds) *Archaic and Classical Choral Song*, Berlin, 437–60.

Casanova, A. (2012) 'Una precisazione per Mimnermo nel Prologo degli *Aitia*', *Prometheus* 38, 128–30.

Cerri, G. (2014) 'L'Ade ad Oriente, viaggio quotidiano del carro del Sole e direzione della corrente dell'Oceano', in L. Breglia and A. Moleti (eds) *Hespería: tradizioni, rotte, paesaggi*, Paestum, 165–79.

Colantonio, M. (1993) 'Contributi epigrafici a Mimnermo, fr. 24 Gent.-Pr.', in R. Pretagostini (ed.) *Tradizione e innovazione nella cultura greca da Omero all'eta ellenistica*, vol. 1, Rome, 279–83.

Colavito, J. (2014) *Jason and the Argonauts Through the Ages*, Jefferson, NC.

Coldstream, J. N. (1965) 'A Theran Sunrise', *BICS* 12, 34–37.

Coldstream, J. N. (2010) *Greek Geometric Pottery (Corpus Vasorum Antiquorum: Great Britain 25 / The British Museum 11)*, London.

Colonna, A. (1952) 'Mimnermo e Callimaco', *Athenaeum* 30, 191–95.

Cook, J. M. (1952) 'Archaeology in Greece, 1951', *JHS* 72, 92–112.

Cook, J. M. (1965) 'Mimnermus' River', in *Χαριστήριον εἰς Ἀναστάσιον Κ. Ὀρλάνδον*, vol. 1, Athens, 148–52.

Cook, J. M. (1985) 'On the Date of Alyattes' Sack of Smyrna', *ABSA* 80, 25–28.

Cook, J. M. and Nicholls, R. V. (1998) *Old Smyrna Excavations: The Temples of Athena*, London.

Cook, R. M. and Dupont, P. (1998) *East Greek Pottery*, London.

Corrêa, P. (2009) 'Musical Instruments and the Paean in Archilochus', *Synthesis* 16, 99–112.

Corvisier, J. N. (2018) 'La vieillesse dans le monde antique: aspects démographiques et conséquences sociales', *CEA* 55, 17–36.

Crahay, R. (1968) 'Questions et réponses', *Otia: Association des classiques del'Université de Liège* 16, 28.

Crielaard, J. P. (2009) 'Cities', in Raaflaub and Wees 2009: 349–72.

Cross, N. D. (2020) 'The Panionia: The Ritual Context for Identity Construction in Archaic Ionia', *Mediterranean Studies* 28, 1–22.

Crusius, O. and Kugéas, S. (1910) *Paroemiographica: Textgeschichtliches zur alten Dichtung und Religion*, Munich.

Dallas, G. (2011) 'Ο Ελύτης και ο αρχαίος λυρισμός. Ένας ενδογλωσσικός διάλογος', in P. M. Minucci and C. Bintoudis (eds) *Ο Ελύτης στην Ευρώπη*, Athens, 171–89.

Darcus Sullivan, S. (1981) 'The Function of θυμός in Hesiod and the Greek Lyric Poets', *Glotta* 59, 147–55.

Davies, M. (1981) [Review of Gentili and Prato 1979[1]], *JHS* 101, 167–9.

Dawson, C. M. (1966) 'Σπουδαιογέλοιον: Random Thoughts on Occasional Poems', *YCS* 19, 42–50.

De Falco, V. (1946) 'Note ai lirici greci', *PP* 1, 347–59.

De Marco, V. (1939–1940) 'Studii intorno a Mimnermo', *RIL* 73, 311–50.

Defradas, J. (1962) *Les élégiaques grecs*, Paris.

Della Corte, F. (1965) [Contribution] in F. Della Corte, V. De Marco, A. Garzya, A. Colonna, L. Alfonsi and B. Gentili, 'Mimnermo', *Maia* 17, 366–87.

Devereux, G. (1970) 'The Nature of Sappho's Seizure in fr. 31 L-P as Evidence of Her Inversion', *CQ* 20, 17–31.

Di Benedetto, V. (1985) 'Il tema della vecchiaia e il fr. 58 di Saffo', *QUCC* 19, 145–63.

Dickey, E. (2007) *Ancient Greek Scholarship*, Oxford.

Diehl, E. (1949)[3] *Anthologia lyrica graeca: poetae elegiaci*, Leipzig.

Diels, H. (1902) 'Onomatologisches', *Hermes* 37, 480–83.

Dihle, A. (1962) 'Zur Datierung des Mimnermos', *Hermes* 90, 257–75.

D'Ippolito, G. (1993) 'Compattezza e novita nella poesia di Mimnermo (auto- e intertestualità)', in R. Pretagostini (ed.) *Tradizione e innovazione nella cultura greca da Omero all'eta ellenistica*, vol. 1, Rome, 285–300.

Dräger, P. (1996) 'Ein Mimnermos-Fragment bei Strabon (11/11a W, 10 G/P, 11 A)', *Mnemosyne* 49, 30–45.

Eck, J. van (1978) 'The Homeric Hymn to Aphrodite: Introduction, Commentary and Appendices', PhD Diss., University of Utrecht.

Edmonds, J. M. (1931) *Elegy and Iambus (Loeb Classical Library)*, vol. 1, Cambridge, MA.

Emiliani, A. (2021) 'Studi per una nuova edizione critica commentata dei frammenti di Mimnermo', PhD Diss., University of Messina.

Ercole, P. (1929) 'Ancora sulle elegie di Mimnermo', *RFIC* 57, 478–94.

Espenak, F. (2022) 'Solar Eclipses of Historical Interest', *NASA* [website in progress] https://eclipse.gsfc.nasa.gov/SEhistory/SEhistory.html

Esteban Santos, A. (1985) 'Estructura y estilo en los fragmentos de Mimnermo sobre la vejez', *EClás* 89, 21–32.

Esteban Santos, A. (2020) 'Iconography of Themes in Greek Lyric: The

Example of Anacreon's Poetry', in A. Cantarero de Salazar *et al.* (eds) *Greek Lyric Poetry and Its Influence*, Newcastle upon Tyne, 213–60.

Evans, J. (1998) *The History and Practice of Ancient Astronomy*, New York.

Falkner, T. M. (1995) *The Poetics of Old Age in Greek Epic, Lyric, and Tragedy*, Norman, OK.

Faraone, C. A. (2008) *The Stanzaic Architecture of Early Greek Elegy*, Oxford.

Farrar, F. (1870) *A Brief Greek Syntax,* London.

Farrell, J. (2012) 'Calling Out the Greeks: Dynamics of the Elegiac Canon', in B. Gold (ed.) *A Companion to Roman Love Elegy*, Malden, MA.

Faulkner, A. (2008) *The Homeric Hymn to Aphrodite: Introduction, Text and Commentary*, Oxford.

Ferrari, F. (1987) 'Sulla ricezione dell'elegia arcaica nella silloge teognidea. Il problema delle varianti', *Maia* 39, 177–97.

Ferrari, F. (2007) *Una mitra per Kleis: Saffo e il suo pubblico*, Pisa.

Fileni, M. G. (1977) 'Mimnermo (fr. 26 West) o Menandro (fr. 937 KTh)?', *QUCC* 26, 83–86.

Föllinger, S. (2005) 'Geschlecht und Körperwahrnehmung in der frühgriechischen Dichtung', in F. Stahnisch and F. Steger (eds) *Medizin, Geschichte und Geschlecht*, Stuttgart, 27–39.

Fowler, R. L. (1987) *The Nature of Early Greek Lyric: Three Preliminary Studies*, Toronto.

Frame, D. (2009) *Hippota Nestor*, Washington, DC.

Fränkel, H. F. (1973) *Early Greek Poetry and Philosophy*, New York.

Froben ed. [=Johann Froben's unknown editor] (1533) *Διογένους Λαερτίου περὶ βίων, δογμάτων καὶ ἀποφθεγμάτων...*, Basel.

Frouzakis, K. (2011) 'Γιώργος Γεραλής: μια όψιμη φωνή του μετασυμβολισμού στην πρώτη μεταπολεμική γενιά', PhD Diss., Aristotle University of Thessaloniki.

Gaisford, T. (1814) *Poetae minores graeci*, vol. 1, Oxford.

Galhac, S. (2006) 'La représentation de la vieillesse dans les fragments 1, 2 et 5 (ed. West) de Mimnerme et dans les poèmes homériques', *REG* 119, 62–82.

Gardner, P. (1892) 'Tithonus on a Red-Figured Vase', *JHS* 13, 137–38.

Garner, R. S. (1990) *From Homer to Tragedy: The Art of Allusion in Greek Poetry*, London.

Garner, R. S. (2010) *Traditional Elegy: The Interplay of Meter, Tradition, and Context in Early Greek Poetry*, Oxford.

Garzya, A. (1965) [Contribution] in F. Della Corte, V. De Marco, A. Garzya, A. Colonna, L. Alfonsi and B. Gentili, 'Mimnermo', *Maia* 17, 366–87.

Gehrke, H. J. (2019) 'Intentional History and the Social Context of Remembrance in Ancient Greece', in W. Pohl and V. Wieser (eds) *Historiography and Identity*, vol. 1, Turnhout, 95–106.

Gemin, M. (2020) 'Mimn., fr. 11 West e Eur., *Med.* 1–10', *GIF* 72, 19–23.

Genette, G. (1992) *The Architext: An Introduction*, Berkeley.

Gentili, B. (1965) [Contribution] in F. Della Corte, V. De Marco, A. Garzya, A. Colonna, L. Alfonsi and B. Gentili, 'Mimnermo', *Maia* 17, 366–87.

Gentili, B. and Catenacci, C. (2007) *Polinnia: poesia greca arcaica*, Florence.

Gentili, B. and Prato, C. (1988)[2] *Poetarum elegiacorum testimonia et fragmenta*, Leipzig.

Gerber, D. E. (1970) *Euterpe: An Anthology of Early Greek Lyric, Elegiac, and Iambic Poetry*, Amsterdam.

Gerber, D. E. (1975) 'Mimnermus, Fragment 2.4–5', *GRBS* 16, 263–68.

Gerber, D. E. (1997) 'Elegy', in *idem* (ed.) *A Companion to the Greek Lyric Poets*, Leiden/Boston, 89–132.

Gerber, D. E. (1999) *Greek Elegiac Poetry (Loeb Classical Library)*, Cambridge, MA.

Gerber, D. E. (2003) 'Mimnermus, Fragment 1.3 W.', in A. F. Basson and W. J. Dominik (eds) *Literature, Art, History: Studies on Classical Antiquity and Tradition in Honour of W.J. Henderson*, Frankfurt am Main, 193–95.

Gesner, C. (1559)[3] *Ioannis Stobaei sententiae ex thesauris Graecorum delectae*, Zurich.

Giannini, P. (1977) 'La giovinezza ignara del bene e del male: Mimnermo 2 D., 2 West, vv.4–5', *QUCC* 25, 23–27.

Goethe, J. W. (1819) 'Naturformen der Poesie', in his *Noten und Abhandlungen zu besserem Verständnis des Westöstlichen Divans*, Stuttgart, 379–85.

Gosse, E. (1891) *Gossip in the Library*, London.

Grethlein, J. (2007) 'Diomedes redivivus: A New Reading of Mimnermus fr. 14 W', *Mnemosyne* 60, 102–11.

Griffith, M. (1975) 'Man and the Leaves: A Study of Mimnermos fr. 2', *CSCA* 8, 73–88.

Groningen, B. A. van (1966) *Theognis. Le premier livre*, Amsterdam.

Hadjimichael, T. (2019) *The Emergence of the Lyric Canon*, Oxford.

Halleran, M. R. (1988) '*Bacchae* 773–4 and Mimnermus fr. 1', *CQ* 38, 559–60.

Hammond, N. G. L. (1950) 'The Lycurgean Reform at Sparta', *JHS* 70, 42–64.

Hartung, J. A. (1859) *Die Griechischen Elegiker*, vol. 1, Leipzig.

Hartwig, P. (1893) *Die griechischen Meisterschalen der Blüthezeit des strengen rothfigurigen Stiles*, Stuttgart.

Hasluck, M. (1912–1913), 'Dionysos at Smyrna', *ABSA* 19, 89–94.

Hearn, L. (1917) *Life and Literature*, New York.

Hegel, G. W. F. (1835) *Vorlesungen über die Aesthetik*, Brlin [transl. T. M. Knox (1975) *Hegel's Aesthetics: Lectures on Fine Art*, vol. 2, Oxford.]

Henderson, J. (1991) *The Maculate Muse: Obscene Language in Attic Comedy*, Oxford.

Henderson, W. J. (1995) 'Mimnermus' Images of Youth and Age', *Akroterion* 40, 98–105.

Hermann, G. (1822) 'Appendix', in F. Vigeri, *De praecipuis Graecae dictionis idiotismis liber*, Leipzig 1822, 929.

Hertel, I. (ed.) (1561) *Theognidis Megarensis sententiae elegiacae [...] Accesserunt et horum poetarum opera sententiosa [...] Mimnermi [...]*, Basel.

Heyne, C. G. (1783) *Ad Apollodori Atheniensis Bibliothecam notae*, Göttingen.

Hiller, E. (1888) 'Jahresbericht über die griechischen Lyriker (mit Ausschluss Pindars) und die griechischen Bukoliker für 1886 und 1887', *Jahresbericht über die Fortschritte der classischen Altertumwissenschaft* 54, 129–203.

Holzberg, N. (2000) 'Lesbia, the Poet, and the Two Faces of Sappho: "Womanufacture" in Catullus', *PCPhS* 46, 28–44.

Hubbard, T. K. (1994) 'Elemental Psychology and the Date of Semonides of Amorgos', *AJPh* 115, 175–97.

Hubbard, T. K. (2001) 'New Simonides or Old Semonides? Second Thoughts on *POxy* 3965 fr. 26', in D. Boedeker and D. Sider (eds) *The New Simonides*, Oxford, 226–31.

Hubbard, T. K. (2002) 'Pindar, Theoxenus, and the Homoerotic Eye', *Arethusa* 35, 255–96.

Hubbard, T. K. (2003) *Homosexuality in Greece and Rome: A Sourcebook of Basic Documents*, Berkeley.

Hunt, A. S. (1927) *The Oxyrhynchus Papyri: Part XVII*, London.

Hunter, R. (2008) *On Coming After: Studies in Post-Classical Greek Literature and its Reception*, Berlin/New York.

Hunter, R. (2012) 'Callimachus and Roman Elegy', in B. Gold (ed.) *A Companion to Roman Love Elegy*, Oxford, 155–71.

Hunter, R. (2013a) 'One Verse of Mimnermus? Latin Elegy and Archaic Greek Elegy', in T. Papanghelis, S. Harrison and S. Frangoulidis (eds) *Generic Interfaces in Latin Literature*, Berlin/Boston, 337–50.

Hunter, R. (2013b) 'Greek Elegy', in T. Thorsen (ed.) *The Cambridge Companion to Latin Love Elegy*, Cambridge, 23–38.

Huxley, G. L. (1959) 'Mimnermus and Pylos', *GRBS* 2, 103–107.

Huxley, G. L. (1969) *Greek Epic Poetry from Eumelos to Panyassis*, London.

Immisch, O. (1890) 'Klaros. Forschungen über griechische Stiftungssagen', *Jahrbücher für classische Philologie Supp*. 17, 125–210.

Irwin, E. (1994) 'Roses and the Bodies of Beautiful Women in Early Greek Poetry', *EMC* 13, 1–13.

Jacoby, F. (1918) 'Studien zu den älteren griechischen Elegikern. II. Zu Mimnermos', *Hermes* 53, 262–307.

Janko, R. (1982) *Homer, Hesiod and the Hymns. Diachronic Development in Epic Diction*, Cambridge.

Janko, R. (1987) *Aristotle: Poetics I, With the Tractatus Coislinianus: A Hypothetical Reconstruction of Poetics II. The Fragments of the On Poets*, Indianapolis.

Janko, R. (1990) 'Mimnermus, Fragment 4 West: A Conjecture', *AJP* 111, 154–55.

Jeffreys, P. (2015) *Reframing Decadence: C. P. Cavafy's Imaginary Portraits*, New York.

Johnson, M. (2009) 'A Reading of Sappho Poem 58, Fragment 31 and Mimnermus', in E. Greene and M. Skinner (eds) *The New Sappho on Old Age: Textual and Philosophical Issues*, Washington, DC, 162–75.

Josserand, C. (1967) 'Questions et réponses', *Otia: Association des classiques del' Université de Liège* 15, 131–32.

Kaibel, G. (1890) *Athenaei Naucratitae Dipnosophistarum libri XV*, vol. 3, Leipzig.

Kanellakis, D. (2020) *Aristophanes and the Poetics of Surprise*, Berlin/Boston.

Kanellakis, D. (2022) 'Seminal Figures: Aristophanes and the Tradition of Sexual Imagery', in A. Serafim, G. Kazantzidis and C. Demetriou (eds) *Sex and the Ancient City*, Berlin/Boston, 425–44.

Kantzios, I. (2010) 'Marginal Voice and Erotic Discourse in Anacreon', *Mnemosyne* 63, 577–89.

Kassel, R. (1969) 'Kritische und exegetische Kleinigkeiten III', *RhM* 112, 97–103.

Kazantzidis, G. (2018) 'Doctors in a Comic Costume: Medical Language and Mass Audience in the Comedy of Menander', *ICS* 43, 25–57.

Kefalidou, E. (2008) 'The Argonauts Krater in the Archaeological Museum of Thessaloniki', *AJA* 112, 617–24.

Kelly, A. (2015) 'Stesichorus' Homer', in P. J. Finglass and A. Kelly (eds) *Stesichorus in Context*, Cambridge, 21–44.

Kerschner, M. (2017) 'East Greek Pottery Workshops in the Seventh Century BC: Tracing Regional Styles', in X. Charalambidou and C. Morgan (eds) *Interpreting the Seventh Century BC*, Oxford, 100–13.

Kessels, A. H. M. (1978) *Studies on the Dream in Greek Literature*, Utrecht.

Kirk, G. S. (1973) 'Old Age and Maturity in Ancient Greece', *Eranos-Jb* 40, 123–58.

Kirk, G. S., Raven, J. E. and Schofield, M. (1983) *The Presocratic Philosophers. A Critical History with a Selection of Texts*, Cambridge.

Klinger, W. (1930) 'Un fragment de l'élégie guerrière de Mimnerme: Son importance et l'époque où elle fut composée', *Bulletin International de l'Académie Polonaise de Sciences et des Lettres* 4–6, 78–83.

Koopman, N. (2018) *Ancient Greek Ekphrasis: Between Description and Narration*, Leiden/Boston.

Kröhnert, O. (1897) 'Canonesne poetarum scriptorum artificium per antiquitat-em fuerunt?', PhD Diss., University of Königsberg.

Lambert, S. D. (1993) *The Phratries of Attica*, Ann Arbor.

Landor, W. S. (1836) *Pericles and Aspasia*, vol. 1, London.

Lardinois, A. (1995) 'Wisdom in Context: The Use of Gnomic Statements in Archaic Greek Poetry', PhD Diss., Princeton University.

Laskaris, J. (ed.) (1494) *Ἀνθολογία διαφόρων ἐπιγραμμάτων [...]*, Florence.

Latacz, J. (1977) *Kampfparänese, Kampfdarstellung und Kampfwirklichkeit in der Ilias, bei Kallinos und bei Tyrtaios*, Munich.

Lavagnini, B. (1950) *Da Mimnermo a Callimaco: contributi esegetici e critici ai lirici greci*, Turin.

Lear, A. (2014) 'Ancient Pederasty: An Introduction', in T. K. Hubbard (ed.) *A Companion to Greek and Roman Sexualities*, Chichester, 102–27.

Lefkowitz, M. R. (2002) '"Predatory" Goddesses', *Hesperia* 71, 325–44.

Lenschau, T. (1944) 'Die Gründung Ioniens und der Bund am Panionion', *Klio* 36, 201–37.

Livingstone, N. and Nisbet, G. (2010) *Epigram*, Cambridge.

Lightfoot, J. (2009) *Hellenistic Collection (Loeb Classical Library)*, Cambridge, MA.

Lobel, E. and Page, D. L. (1963)[2] *Poetarum lesbiorum fragmenta*, Oxford.

Lorimer, H. L. (1947) 'The Hoplite Phalanx with Special Reference to the Poems of Archilochus and Tyrtaeus', *ABSA* 42, 76–138.

Mac Sweeney, N. (2013) *Foundation Myths and Politics in Ancient Ionia*, Cambridge.

Mac Sweeney, N. (2017) 'Separating Fact from Fiction in the Ionian Migration', *Hesperia* 86, 379–421.

Mackie, C. J. (2001) 'The Earliest Jason. What's in a Name?', *G&R* 48, 1–17.

Maehler, H. (2003)[11] *Bacchylidis carmina cum fragmentis*, Munich.

Margulies, Z. (2021) 'Like Golden Aphrodite: Grieving Women in the Homeric Epics and Aphrodite's Lament for Adonis', *CQ* 70, 485–98.

Martin, R. (2021) 'Stesichorus and the Name Game', in M. Fantuzzi, H. Morales and T. Whitmarsh (eds) *Reception in the Greco-Roman World: Literary Studies in Theory and Practice*, Cambridge, 48–71.

Martinazzoli, F. (1946) *Ethos ed eros nella poesia greca*, Florence.

Masson, O. (1990) *Onomastica graeca selecta*, vol. 2, Paris.

Matthäus, H. (1999) 'The Greek Symposion and the Near East: Chronology and Mechanisms of Cultural Transfer', in R. Docter and E. M. Moormann (eds) *Proceedings of the XVth International Congress of Classical Archeology*, Amsterdam, 256–60.

Matthews, V. J. (1979) 'Antimachos in the *Aitia* Prologue', *Mnemosyne* 32, 128–37.

Matthews, V. J. (1995) *Antimachus of Colophon*, Leiden/New York.

Mazarakis Ainian, A. and Leventi, I. (2009) 'The Aegean', in Raaflaub and Wees 2009: 212–38.

Mazzarino, S. (1973) *Il pensiero storico classico*, vol. 1, Bari.

McKay, K. J. (1975) 'Mimnermos fr. 13.9 ff. Diehl (fr. 14 West)', *Hermes* 103, 373.

Meineke, A. (1840) *Fragmenta comicorum graecorum*, vol. 3, Berlin.

Meineke, A. (1841) *Fragmenta comicorum graecorum*, vol. 4, Berlin.

Meineke, A. (1857) *Ioannis Stobaei Florilegium*, vol. 4, Leipzig.

Meister, K. von (1921) *Die homerische Kunstsprache*, Leipzig.

Mele, A. (2019) 'Colofone, Diomede e Glauco', in L. Vecchio (ed.) *Colofone città della Ionia: Nuovi studi e ricerche*, Salerno, 35–76.

Méndez Dosuna, J. (2007) 'Una lectura menos negativa de Mimnermo, fr.

2.4–5 *IEG*²', in G. Hinojo Andrés and J. C. Fernández Corte (eds) *Munus quaesitum meritis*, Salamanca, 595–605.

Merisio, E. N. (2021) 'Semonides or Simonides? A Century-Long Controversy Over the Authorship of a Greek Elegiac Fragment (Simonides, fr. 8 W. = frr. 19–20 W²)', in R. Berardi, M. Filosa and D. Massimo (eds) *Defining Authorship, Debating Authenticity*, Berlin/Boston, 11–24.

Miralles, C. (1988) 'La poesia di Mimnermo', *Lexis* 1, 35–52.

Mitchell, L. (2009) *Maurice Bowra: A Life*, Oxford.

Möller, M. (2014) 'Das Spiel mit der Zeit: Beobachtungen zur agonalen Struktur in den 'Alters'-Elegien des Mimnermos und des Solon', *Philologus* 158, 26–52.

Mongiello, V. (2017) 'I racconti di fondazione di Colofone', *Erga-Logoi* 5, 193–214.

Monro, D. B. (1891) *A Grammar of the Homeric Dialect*, Oxford.

Müller, C. W. (1988) 'Die antike Buchausgabe des Mimnermos', *RhM* 131, 197–211.

Murray, G. (1897) *A History of Ancient Greek Literature*, London.

Murray, O. (1990) *Sympotica: A Symposium on the Symposion*, Oxford.

Murray, O. (1994) 'Nestor's Cup and the Origins of the Greek Symposion', in B. D'Agostino and D. Ridgway (eds) *Apoikia*, Naples, 47–54.

Murray, O. (2009) 'The Culture of the Symposion', in Raaflaub and Wees 2009: 508–23.

Musurus, M. (ed.) (1499) *Ἐτυμολογικὸν μέγα κατὰ ἀλφάβητον πάνυ ὠφέλιμον*, Venice.

Musurus, M. (ed.) (1514) *Ἀθηναίου Δειπνοσοφιστοῦ τὴν πολυμαθεστάτην πραγματείαν [...]*, Venice.

Nagy, G. (1985) 'Theognis of Megara: A Poet's Vision of His City', in T. Figueira and G. Nagy (eds) *Theognis of Megara: Poetry and the Polis*, Baltimore, 22–81.

Nagy, G. (1990) *Pindar's Homer: The Lyric Possession of an Epic Past*, Baltimore.

Nagy, G. (2010) 'Ancient Greek Elegy', in K. Weisman (ed.) *The Oxford Handbook of the Elegy*, Oxford, 13–45.

Nelson, T. J. (2019) '"Most Musicall, Most Melancholy": Avian Aesthetics of Lament in Greek and Roman Elegy', *Dictynna* 16: *http://journals.openedition.org/dictynna/1914*

Neri, C. (2011) *Lirici greci: età arcaica e classica*, Rome.

Nicolosi, A. (2010) 'Imagery e motivi ricorrenti nell' *Eracle* di Euripide', *Maia* 1, 28–40.

Nietzsche, F. (1867) 'Zur Geschichte der Theognideischen Spruchsammlung', *RhM* 22, 161–200.

Nobili, C. (2011) 'Threnodic Elegy in Sparta', *GRBS* 51, 26–48.

Noussia-Fantuzzi, M. (2010) *Solon the Athenian: The Poetic Fragments*, Leiden/Boston.

Obbink, D. (2001) 'The Genre of Plataea: Generic Unity in the New Simonides', in D. Boedeker and D. Sider (eds) *The New Simonides*, Oxford, 65–85.

Olson, S. D. (2012) *The Homeric Hymn to Aphrodite and Related Texts*, Berlin/Boston.

Onians, R. B. (1951) *The Origins of European Thought*, Cambridge.

Pace, N. (1999) 'Mimnermo F 5 G.-P', in F. Conca (ed.) *Ricordando Raffaele Cantarella. Miscellanea di studi*, Bologna, 239–46.

Page, D. L. (1955) *Sappho and Alcaeus: An Introduction to the Study of Ancient Lesbian Poetry*, Oxford.

Page, D. L. (1962) *Poetae melici graeci*, Oxford.

Palaima, T. G. (2020) '*Basileus* and *Anax* in Homer and Mycenaean Greek Texts', in C. Pache (ed.) *Cambridge Guide to Homer*, Cambridge, 300–303.

Papademetriou, I. T. (1984) *Ελεγεία και Ίαμβος*, Athens.

Papanikolaou, D. (2005) '"Words That Tell and Hide": Revisiting C. P. Cavafy's Closets', *Journal of Modern Greek Studies* 23, 235–60.

Papanikolaou, D. (2014) *'Σαν κ' εμένα καμωμένοι': Ο ομοφυλόφιλος Καβάφης και η ποιητική της σεξουαλικότητας*, Athens.

Parry, M. (1929) 'The Distinctive Character of Enjambement in Homeric Verse', *TAPhA* 60, 200–20.

Paspalakis, A. (2018) 'Ν. Γ. Πεντζίκης: η τέχνη της διακειμενικής αναφοράς', PhD Diss., Aristotle University of Thessaloniki.

Paspalas, S. A. (2017) 'Old Smyrna: A Window Onto the Seventh-Century Painted Wares From the Anglo-Turkish Excavations (1948–1951)', in X. Charalambidou and C. Morgan (eds) *Interpreting the Seventh Century BC*, Oxford, 114–22.

Pasquali, G. (1923) 'Mimnermo', *SIFC* 3, 293–303.

Patocchi, M. (1983) 'A proposito della patria di Mimnermo', *QUCC* 15, 75–82.

Percy, W. A. (1996) *Pederasty and Pedagogy in Archaic Greece*, Urbana/Chicago.

Perotti, P. A. (2013) 'Vecchiaia e morte in Mimnermo: Nota A 1 W., 2', *REC* 40, 129–40.

Perseus Digital Library (n.d.) 'Smyrna, Temple of Athena (Building)', Tufts University: http://www.perseus.tufts.edu/hopper/artifact?name=Smyrna,+Temple+of+Athena&object=building

Perysinakis, I. N. (2012) *Ἀρχαϊκὴ λυρικὴ ποίηση. Ἠθικὲς ἀξίες καὶ πολιτικὴ συμπεριφορὰ στὴν ἀρχαία ἑλληνικὴ λογοτεχνία*, Athens.

Pettazzoni, R. (1967) 'The Religion of Ancient Thrace', in his *Essays on the History of Religions*, Leiden, 81–94.

Pfeiffer, R. (1928) 'Gottheit und Individuum in der frühgriechischen Lyrik', *Philologus* 84, 137–52.

Pironet, J. M. (1968) 'Questions et réponses', *Otia: Association des classiques del' Université de Liège* 16, 27.

Podlecki, A. J. (1984) *The Early Greek Poets and Their Times*, Vancouver.

Privitera, G. A. (2004) 'Inizio e fine del fr. 8 G.-P. di Mimnermo', *AION (filol)* 26, 223–26.

Prothero, G. W. (1888) *A Memoir of Henry Bradshaw*, London.

Puelma, M. (1957) 'Kallimachos-Interpretationen, I: Philetas und Antimachos im Aitienprolog', *Philologus* 101, 90–100.

Raaflaub, K. A. and Wees, H. van (eds) (2009) *A Companion to Archaic Greece*, Malden, MA.

Reitzenstein, R. (1893) *Epigramm und Skolion*, Giessen.

Renner, J. G. (1868) 'Quaestiones de dialecti antiquioris Graecorum poesis elegiacae et iambicae', in G. Curtius (ed.) *Studien zur Griechischen und Lateinischen Grammatik*, Leipzig, vol. 1.1, 134–235 and vol. 1.2, 1–62.

Ricks, D. (1989) *The Shade of Homer: A Study in Modern Greek Poetry*, Cambridge.

Robinson, D. M. and Fluck, E. J. (1937) *A Study of the Greek Love-Names Including a Discussion of Paederasty and a Prosopographia*, Baltimore.

Roebuck, C. (1955) 'The Early Ionian League', *CPh* 50, 26–40.

Romilly, J. de (1985) *A Short History of Greek Literature*, Chicago.

Römisch, E. (1933) *Studien zur älteren griechischen Elegie*, Frankfurt.

Rosenmeyer, T. G. (1968) 'Elegiac and elegos', *California Studies in Classical Antiquity* 1, 217–31.

Rösler, W. (1980) *Dichter und Gruppe: Eine Untersuchung zu den Bedingungen und zur historischen Funktion früher griechischer Lyrik am Beispiel des Alkaios*, Munich.

Rostagni, A. (1928) 'Nuovo Callimaco, I: Il Prologo degli *Aἴτια*, testo e interpretazione', *RFIC* 56, 1–35.

Rotstein, A. (2010) *The Idea of Iambos*, Oxford.

Russo, J. (2004) 'Odysseus' Trial of the Bow as Symbolic Performance', in A. Bierl, A. Schmitt and A. Willi (eds) *Antike Literatur in neuer Deutung*, Leipzig, 95–101.

Sanz Morales, M. (2000) 'La cronología de Mimnermo', *Eikasmos* 1, 29–52.

Sapere, A. V. (2016) 'Τίς δὲ βίος, τί δὲ τερπνὸν ἄτερ χρυσῆς Ἀφροδίτης: una interpretación de los fragmentos 1–6 de Mimnermo', *Anuari de Filologia Antiqua et Mediaevalia* 6, 41–54.

Sbardella, L. (2017) 'Dai canti simposiali alla "grande donna": Mimnermo e i suoi epigoni nel prologo dei Telchini di Callimaco', *RFIC* 145, 47–74.

Sbardella, L. (2018) 'Aulodes and Rhapsodes: Performance and Forms of Greek Elegy from Mimnermus to Hermesianax', *Aitia* 8: http://journals.openedition.org/aitia/2247

Schadewaldt, W. (1933) 'Lebenszeit und Greisenalter im frühen Griechentum', *Die Antike* 9, 282–302.

Schauenburg, K. (1962) 'Gestirnbilder in Athen und Unteritalien', *AK* 5, 51–64.

Schlegel, F. (1797) *Kritische*, vol. 1, Paderborn.

Schlegel, F. (1798) *Geschichte der Poesie der Griechen und Römer*, Berlin.

Schmiel, R. (1974) 'Youth and Age: Mimnermus 1 and 2', *RFIC* 102, 283–89.

Schneidewin, F. G. (1838) *Delectus poesis graecorum elegiacae, iambicae, melicae*, vol. 1, Göttingen.

Segal, C. (1976) 'Pindar, Mimnermus, and The "Zeus-Given Gleam": The End of *Pythian* 8', *QUCC* 22, 71–76.

Selle, H. (2008) *Theognis und die Theognidea*, Berlin.

Sider, D. (1996) 'As Is the Generation of Leaves in Homer, Simonides, Horace, and Stobaios', *Arethusa* 29, 263–82.

Sider, D. (2006) 'The New Simonides and the Question of Historical Elegy', *JHS* 127, 327–46.

Sider, D. (2020) *Simonides: Epigrams and Elegies*, Oxford.

Silk, M. S. (1974) *Interaction in Poetic Imagery With Special Reference to Early Greek Poetry*, Cambridge.

Sittig, E. (1911) *De graecorum nominibus theophoris*, Halle.

Skiadas, A. D. (1964) *Γλυκὺς βίοτος-μείλιχος αἰών. Ἔρευνα εἰς τοὺς πρώτους Ἕλληνας λυρικοὺς ποιητάς*, Athens.

Skiadas, A. D. (1979) *Αρχαϊκός λυρισμός*, vol. 1, Athens.

Slater, W. J. (1969) *Lexicon to Pindar*, Berlin.

Slings, S. R. (2000) *Symposium, Speech and Ideology: Two Hermeneutical Issues in Early Greek Lyric, With Special Reference to Mimnermus*, Amsterdam.

Smyth, H. W. (1920) *A Greek Grammar for Colleges*, New York.

Snell, B. (1953) *The Discovery of the Mind*, Oxford.

Snell, B. and Maehler, H. (1987–1989)[8] *Pindari carmina cum fragmentis*, 2 vols, Leipzig.

Snowden, F. M. (1970) *Blacks in Antiquity: Ethiopians in the Greco-Roman Experience*, Cambridge, MA.

Sommerstein, A. H. (2010) 'Textual and Other Notes on Aeschylus (Part 2)', *Prometheus* 36, 97–122.

Sourvinou-Inwood, C. (1995) *'Reading' Greek Death to the End of the Classical Period*, Oxford.

Spalinger, A. J. (1978) 'The Date of the Death of Gyges and Its Historical Implications', *JAOS* 98, 400–409.

Spanoudakis, K. (2001) 'Poets and Telchines in Callimachus' *Aetia*-Prologue', *Mnemosyne* 54, 425–41.

Spanoudakis, K. (2002) *Philitas of Cos*, Leiden.

Steffen, V. (1955) *Quaestiones lyricae*, vol. 1, Poznań.

Stégen, G. (1969) 'Questions et réponses', *Otia: Association des classiques del' Université de Liège* 17, 51–52.

Steinmetz, P. (1969) 'Das Erwachen des geschichtlichen Bewußtseins in der Polis', in P. Steinmetz (ed.) *Politeia und Res publica*, Wiesbaden, 52–78.

Stieber, M. (2004) *The Poetics of Appearance in the Attic Korai*, Austin, TX.

Suárez de la Torre, E. (1985) 'El viaje nocturno del sol y la Nanno de Mimnermo', *EClás* 89, 5–20.

Svenbro, J. (1993) *Phrasikleia: An Anthropology of Reading in Ancient Greece*, New York.

Swift, L. (2015) 'Lyric Visions of Epic Combat: The Spectacle of War in Archaic Personal Song', in A. Bakogianni and V. Hope (eds) *War as Spectacle*, London, 93–109.

Swift, L. (2019) *Archilochus: The Poems*, Oxford.

Swift, L. (ed.) (2022) *A Companion to Greek Lyric*, Oxford.

Swift, L. and Carey, C. (eds) (2016) *Iambus and Elegy: New Approaches*, Oxford.

Szádeczky-Kardoss, S. (1942) 'Wenn lebte Mimnermos?', *Egyetemes Philologiai Közlöny* 66, 76–80.

Szádeczky-Kardoss, S. (1959) *Testimonia de Mimnermi vita et carminibus*, Szeged.

Szádeczky-Kardoss, S. (1968) 'Mimnermos', in *Paulys Realencyclopädie der classischen Altertumswissenschaft*, Suppl. 11, 935–51.

Theunissen, M. (2000) *Pindar: Menschenlos und Wende der Zeit*, Munich.

Thomas, R. F. (1999) *Reading Virgil and His Texts: Studies in Intertextuality*, Ann Arbor.

Thumiger, C. (2021) 'The Ophthalmology of Lovesickness: Poetry, Philosophy, Medicine', in D. Kanellakis (ed.) *Pathologies of Love in Classical Literature*, Berlin/Boston, 23–46.

Töchterle, K. (1980) 'Die μεγάλη γυνή des Mimnermos bei Kallimachos', *RhM* 123, 225–34.

Torraca, L. (1969) *Il prologo dei Telchini e l'inizio degli Aitia di Callimaco*, Naples.

Treu, M. (1968) 'Von Pentameterdiharesen', *QUCC* 6, 101–13.

Trincavelius, V. (ed.) (1536) *Ἰωάννου τοῦ Στοβαίου ἐκλογαὶ ἀποφθεγμάτων*, Venice.

Tsagarakis, O. (1977) *Self-Expression in Early Greek Lyric*, Wiesbaden.

Tsetskhladze, G. R. (1998) 'Greek Colonization of the Black Sea Area: Stages, Models, and Native Population', in *idem* (ed.) *The Greek Colonization of the Black Sea Area*, Stuttgart, 9–68.

Tsetskhladze, G. R. (2006) 'Introduction: Revisiting Ancient Greek Colonisation', in *idem* (ed.) *Greek Colonisation*, vol. 1, Leiden, xxiii–lxxxiii.

Turnebus, A. (ed.) (1553) *Sententiosa poetarum vetustissimorum quae supersunt opera: Theognidis [...] Mimnermi [...]*, Paris.

Ulf, C. (2009) 'The World of Homer and Hesiod', in Raaflaub and Wees 2009: 81–99.

Vance, N. (1985) *The Sinews of the Spirit: The Ideal of Christian Manliness in Victorian Literature and Religious Thought*, Cambridge.

Verdenius, W. J. (1953) 'Mimnermus 1.6', *Mnemosyne* 6, 197.

Vetta, M. (1984) 'Identificazione di un caso di catena simposiale nel corpus teognideo', in B. Gentili *et al.* (eds) *Lirica greca da Archiloco a Elitis*, Padova, 113–26.

Vojatzi, M. (1982) *Frühe Argonautenbilder*, Würzburg.

Wachter, R. (2001) *Non-Attic Greek Vase Inscriptions*, Oxford.

Wachter, R. (2021) 'The Genesis of the Local Alphabets of Archaic Greece', in R. Parker and P. Steele (eds) *The Early Greek Alphabets: Origin, Diffusion, Uses*, Oxford, 21–31.

Walker, H. (1910) *The Literature of the Victorian Era*, New York.

Wees, H. van (1994) 'The Homeric Way of War: The *Iliad* and The Hoplite Phalanx (I)', *G&R* 41, 1–18.

West, M. L. (1967) 'The Berlin Tyrtaeus', *ZPE* 1, 173–82.
West, M. L. (1974) *Studies in Greek Elegy and Iambus*, Berlin.
West, M. L. (1981) 'Early Greek Elegy', *CR* 31, 1–2.
West, M. L. (1987) *Introduction to Greek Metre*, Oxford.
West, M. L. (1989–1992)[2] *Iambi et elegi graeci*, 2 vols, Oxford.
West, M. L. (1992) *Ancient Greek Music*, Oxford.
West, M. L. (1993) 'Simonides Redivivus', *ZPE* 98, 1–14.
West, M. L. (1997) *The East Face of Helicon: West Asiatic Elements in Greek Poetry and Myth*, Oxford.
West, M. L. (2005a) 'The New Sappho', *ZPE* 151, 1–9.
West, M. L. (2005b) '*Odyssey* and *Argonautica*', *CQ* 55, 39–64.
West, M. L. (2011) *The Making of the Iliad*, Oxford.
Wet, B. X. de (1988) 'Plutarch's Use of the Poets', *AClass* 31, 13–25.
Wilamowitz-Moellendorff, U. von (1913) *Sappho und Simonides*, Berlin.
Wilkinson, L. P. (1956) 'Greek Influence on the Poetry of Ovid', in *Fondation Hardt II: L'influence grecque sur la poésie latine de Catulle à Ovide*, Geneve, 223–43.
Wilson, J. P. (2009) 'Literacy', in Raaflaub and Wees 2009: 542–63.
Wimmel, W. (1960) *Kallimachos in Rom. Die Nachfolge seines apologetischen Dichtens in der Augusteerzeit*, Wiesbaden.
Winkler, J. J. (1990) 'The Ephebes' Song: Tragoidia and Polis', in J. J. Winkler and F. I. Zeitlin (eds) *Nothing to Do with Dionysos? Athenian Drama in Its Social Context*, Princeton, 20–62.
Woodward, G. R. (1924) *Greek Anthology: 133 Love-Epigrams in English Verse*, London.

INDEX

The entries for authors (e.g. 'Aristotle', 'Homer') do *not* index individual passages of them, unless those passages receive some comment in the book, other than mere citation or quotation.

www.ingramcontent.com/pod-product-compliance
Lightning Source LLC
Chambersburg PA
CBHW070346040426
42428CB00041B/2697

* 9 7 8 1 8 3 5 5 3 7 6 5 7 *